NEW VOICES

Geoff Smith is a composer who studied music at Nottingham University, The Queen's College, Oxford, and for a PhD at Huddersfield University with Gavin Bryars. Nicola Walker Smith studied music at Keele and Birmingham Universities and studied singing with Linda Hirst. Together, they have recorded two albums on Kitchenware Records (*The Garden* and *Gas. Food. Lodging.*) and have recently recorded their first album for Sony Classical, *fifteen wild decembers*.

# NEW VOICES

## American Composers
## Talk About Their Music

GEOFF SMITH AND
NICOLA WALKER SMITH

AMADEUS PRESS

Reinhard G. Pauly, *General Editor*

PORTLAND, OREGON

Published in the United Kingdom under the title
*American Originals: Interviews with 25 Contemporary Composers*

Copyright © by Geoff Smith and Nicola Walker Smith

The copyright in the photographs remains with the
individual photographers listed on p. vi.

First published in North America in 1995 by
Amadeus Press (an imprint of Timber Press, Inc.)
The Haseltine Building
133 S.W. Second Avenue, Suite 450
Portland, Oregon 97204, U.S.A.

ISBN 0–931340–85–3

Printed in the United Kingdom

# CONTENTS

# ACKNOWLEDGEMENTS

The authors would like to acknowledge the generous support of the Winston Churchill Memorial Trust, the British Academy, The Queen's College (Oxford), the University of Oxford and the University of Huddersfield. We would also like to thank Jane Feaver of Faber and Faber for her enthusiasm and efficiency, Charles Amirkhanian for his assistance, and James Fulkerson for giving us John Cage's phone number.

*Photograph acknowledgements*

John Adams, by Deborah O'Grady
Charles Amirkhanian, by Esther Kutnick
Laurie Anderson, by Annie Leibowitz/Contact Press Images
Robert Ashley, by Patrice Binet
Glenn Branca, by After Art/Joachim Riedl
Harold Budd, by David Perry
John Cage, by Susan Schwartzenberg
Philip Corner, by Rachel Corner
George Crumb, by William R. Crumb
Paul Dresher, by Cristiana Ceppas
James Fulkerson, by Benno Voorham
Philip Glass, by Tom Caravaglia
Lou Harrison, by David Harsany
Alison Knowles, by Melanie Hedlund
Daniel Lentz, by Medelghnia Lentz
Alvin Lucier, by Babette Mangolte
Ingram Marshall, by Collette Valli
Meredith Monk, by Walter Kranl
Robert Moran, by Thomas Osmon
Pauline Oliveros, by Paula Cort
Steve Reich, by Andrew Pothecary
Terry Riley, by Betty Freeman
Michael Torke, by Marcel Prins
Christian Wolff, by Rebecca Begiun
La Monte Young, by Ulrich Wagner

# INTRODUCTION

This book, five years in the making, began with John Cage, the subject of our postgraduate theses and whom I first telephoned as a nervous student from an Oxford phonebox in early 1988. Having raised enough money for our fares, we made our first visit to New York and, encouraged by his warm reception, spent the remainder of our trip talking to other composers whose work also interested us. Six months later, the idea of a collection dawned and we returned to Manhattan to continue what we had begun. The project snowballed and the more talking we did, the more we realized there was to be done.

In a sense, New York is a culture unto itself and therefore by no means wholly representative of new American music. This realization led us eventually to cover several thousands of miles of east and west coast highway in search of the wider picture. We never intended to paint the *entire* picture, however, as our interests led us only to those composers whose music was in some way essentially American and not derived from or inspired by European models. Whether tagged as 'experimental' or 'minimal', the composers in this book, for all their diversity of approach, are linked by a fundamental desire to rediscover the essentials of shared musical experience with little or no reference to European traditions. From Cage's belief that one should hear music as sound rather than language, through Lucier's refusal to complicate his processes with 'composerly intent', to Riley's reassertion of music's fundamentals or Harrison's 'not being afraid to make something pretty', all seek to reaffirm the primacy of sound over metaphor.

It is interesting to note that almost all of the composers we spoke to expressed some debt to Cage, not as an originator of compositional techniques that they might develop but as a 'permission giver', an inspirational catalyst who disarmed the system that might have stifled them. As one young downtown composer told us, the question is no longer 'Can we do it?', but 'What shall we do?' The result of this shift is an overwhelming plurality of styles and, though the spirit that motivates them may be a common one, many of the composers in this collection, from Budd to Branca, from Monk to Moran, are stylistically worlds apart. Nor are there any 'schools of thought', only individuals, and the more individuals we spoke to, the more ludicrous the 'isms' became. Hence the title, *American Originals*.

Finally, our thanks are due to all of the composers who, without exception, showed genuine warmth and openness, and who gave us some memorable experiences, from the sanctuary of Terry Riley's 'Moonshine Ranch' in the foothills of the Sierra Nevadas to an afternoon sipping iced-tea with John Cage, a composer whom many consider to have been one of the great spiritual men of our time.

Geoff Smith

# AMERICAN ORIGINALS

*For Harry Jack
and Joseph Samuel*

# JOHN ADAMS

*b. Massachusetts 1947*

After graduating from Harvard University in 1971, John Adams moved to California where he taught and conducted at the San Francisco Conservatory of Music for ten years. He worked for a while as contemporary music adviser to the San Francisco Symphony and from 1979 to 1985 as the orchestra's composer-in-residence, during which time his reputation became established with the success of such works as *Harmonium* and *Harmonielehre*. Other large-scale works include *Fearful Symmetries* (1988) for orchestra and *The Wound Dresser* (1989) for baritone and orchestra, but it is his operas *Nixon in China* (1987) and *The Death of Klinghoffer* (1991) for which he is perhaps best known. In 1991 an American Symphony Orchestra League survey found him to be the most frequently-performed living American composer.

Having absorbed the surface, if not the doctrines, of minimalism, Adams's music is the product of an eclectic range of influences covering a variety of historical and vernacular traditions. Rather than relying on any preconceived compositional systems or processes, Adams prefers to work intuitively and develop his often large-scale structures by 'feel', like an architect 'building on an empty site without a blueprint'.

*How would you say that your music relates to the so-called 'Fathers of Minimalism' like La Monte Young and Terry Riley?*

I don't have much of a response to parentage or lineage or stuff like that. I can tell you what my own personal influences were, but I always find it interesting that questions so often start with minimalism because it's only a fraction of my musical life. In America that's really not much of an issue any more. But in Europe they're much more interested, maybe because people feel that minimalism is specifically an American invention.

*Do you think it was?*

It depends on how you define it. I think of it as a musical technique that has three very salient features – repetition of small cells, tonal harmony with generally slow harmonic rhythm, and more or less regular pulsation. I view it as a technique rather than a way of life. I think it was a very important breakthrough when it came, because it was an alternative to an approach towards composition that had become very sporadic, very self-referential and obscure. This was an utterly stripped-down re-evaluation of extremely primal, fundamental musical concepts – pulsation, tonality, repetition. It's interesting that all three of these elements are virtually *verboten* in what we might now refer to as 'classical' European avant-garde music. It's funny that we're now at the point of calling it classical, but I'm speaking of Webern onwards – post-war serialist. It also exists very prevalently in university music in this country.

*So your music uses those three primary elements but you don't 'live' the way of life of minimalism?*

Well, I found it a tremendously liberating point of view for technique. It also fits my compositional psyche, you might say. I've always been attracted to music that had large architecture and was tonal. I have never at any point in my life been a non-tonal composer. Being a child of two parents who were amateur jazz musicians and having grown up in the 1960s, I am a person who is very fond of pulsation. That's certainly a very American feature in my music. I feel very convinced that these elements are really fundamental. I don't think that it's a retroactive attitude. In a hundred years or more, people will look back on the period of serialism, atonality and aperiodicity as being more of a little pocket in music history that happened and then had its closure. I don't agree with the polemics that say that this is the future, the kind of hotly-debated polemics that you find at Darmstadt or that you can read about in Boulez's books and even in Schoenberg.

*Do you think Western contemporary art music has gone off the rails?*

No, I don't think it has gone off the rails. I think that, starting with Schoenberg, it was an experiment basically in atomization of the elements to see if music could be organized by other principles than it had been since recorded history began. I think some really important and interesting pieces were written, but I don't see that these organizational principles developed by Schoenberg, Cage and Babbitt etc. are really the beginning of a huge new millennium in music. I see them more as a specialized, individual thing. There's a very interesting book by an American theorist, Fred Leodol, called *Toward a Generative Grammar of Tonal Music*. That had a lot of influence on me. It's a study of tonal music and why tonality has a kind of unified meaning for people. His point is that tonality and periodicity and those types of fundamental organizational principles are like a grammar that everyone understands, just like we understand each other when we speak a language – we all share the grammar, we share the organizational principles of it. He's very much influenced by linguistic philosophers like Noam Chomsky. I was interested when I read it because I felt that, in a certain way, it reaffirmed some of my thoughts. My thoughts were purely intuitive. But what's fundamentally important is that composers write the music that means something to themselves, and that they don't try to tell other people what's right and what's wrong.

*Does it annoy you when people call your music minimalist?*

Well, it doesn't annoy me if somebody says it's minimalist or that it has minimalist elements, I think it's simply erroneous. I think minimalist is a perfectly useful term. I use it all the time to describe many of the procedures in my music, but to ask me to describe my music is a difficult question because if I could describe it I probably wouldn't bother to write. I said on the BBC recently that I thought minimalism was the only really important development in Western art music since World War Two, which was really throwing the gauntlet down. But I do think it's been a watershed. I'm inclined to think that stylistic evolution has reached a point now where it's going to relax for a while, like it did in Brahms's or Bach's day and that composers are just going to feed like cattle in a great big pasture, which is the way I work. In *Klinghoffer*, for example, there's all sorts of stuff. I'm feeding on not just minimalism but Berg, Stravinsky, rock 'n' roll, doo-wop music, Arabic music and Jewish music. It makes it really fun to compose now, if you don't let those theoreticians get you down.

*How much do you rely on intuition when you're writing?*

I rely a great deal on intuition. But I don't really put it like that – as 'relying' on it. I define it as a mixture of conscious and subconscious activity that is both feeling and thinking. I know where your question comes from, and I would say that a lot of Western art music – European and American – in the past fifty years or so has placed itself very much in the domain of rationalist principles. I think this happens in the history of art. If you look back through the history of music alone, you will see periods of rationalist activity and then other periods of very intuitive and very emotional expressive activity. It just happens, the pendulum swings back and forth. I think that we're in a period now where we are moving away from the domain of rationalism toward, hopefully, a more balanced mode of creation.

*How do you actually go about writing a large-scale work? Do you have a vision of the entire thing?*

No, I don't. The material you start working on is like the 'gene pool' for the piece, and it takes time to get to know what the genetic structure, the personality of the piece is. It's like a human foetus. I can't impose an arbitrary, imagined shape or personality on to material that I really don't know myself very well. I think that's a very Germanic point of view – this business of the composer controlling the whole image. I've read this in Schoenberg and Hindemith and other German composers, this feeling of the necessity for total control over the shape. But I think there is a passive aspect to composing as well as an aggressive one. The passive one is very interesting. What I mean by passive is that I play the music back, I listen to it a lot and I sort of 'go with it'. A good day of composing is a wonderful mixture of wilful activity and following one's sense of . . . It's like a dog following a track in the woods, you're kind of scenting where the material is going to lead you but you're not really sure. So it's largely a voyage of discovery and that's what makes composing interesting for me. It's why I want to do it every day. I never have a day when I wake up and say, 'Oh, God, I don't feel like composing'. I always want to do it and there's always something interesting out there.

*How would you say that you relate to Western European art music?*

I'm not very interested in Western art music right now. I don't listen to any contemporary music. I find it unbelievably boring, though that doesn't mean I feel that what other composers are doing is not important. It just doesn't interest me. What I listen to almost all the time now is music from other cultures. I'm very interested in Arabic, African and Indian music and lots of different musics from the Americas. I've always been that way. I grew up in a family where there was lots of music in the house – recorded music, performed music, chamber music. I played in a band with my father, my mother sang musicals and I used to sing with her. The nice thing about the family was that there was never a distinction made between what was important music and what wasn't important music – it was just music. After years of college and sophistication, I'm trying to rediscover that sense of innocence I had as a child where, as long as something had an intensity of feeling and a thoroughness of execution, it didn't matter where it was from or for whom it was written. I'm a great believer in the influence of what I call, for want of a better term, the vernacular on high art. I've learned from reading about Goethe, for example, that Faust is not only the greatest poem of the German language but also an enormous compendium of different types of verse from children's rhymes, peasants and street workers to very lofty and sophisticated prosody. I think this is almost always the case with great art, that the writer, composer or painter is very close to the vernacular of his time.

*So you don't particularly feel that you are continuing any Western classical tradition?*

Well, I write for orchestra, so that puts me in a problematic situation right away. I write for orchestra partly because I've done it all my life: I had my first orchestral experience at a very young age, I began composing for orchestra when I was fifteen, I conducted an orchestra for the first time when I was about fifteen, and I played clarinet in orchestras from the age of ten until I was in my thirties. So it's a natural way of thinking for me. But it's also a problem, because I'm always aware that I'm writing for a convention that I really think is an artefact of the past. That's why I very much admire composers who develop their own ensemble to embody their own sound image. To me that's a thrilling thing. My way of veering towards it is not by developing my own ensemble but by doing more and more electronic music. I just finished an album that I did entirely in my studio with synthesizers and samplers, and I love it. I love the sound of it. I've been working with synthesizers since the late 1960s.

That to me is unquestionably the future. Stylistic things can come and go but technology is here to stay. I've always thought that technology precedes artistic invention, that the electric guitar was invented before rock 'n' roll. Someone couldn't come along and say, 'Gee, I want to make rock 'n' roll, so go out and invent me an electric guitar.' It doesn't work that way, it works the other way. The tape recorder suggested lots of the compositional routines that minimalists and various other composers thought up. No one would have thought of creating musical structures by tight repetition of the same material, had it not been for the tape recorder.

*What kind of equipment do you use?*

I use synthesizers and samplers. I don't use them with anyway near the technical sophistication that a lot of other composers do. They spend enormous amounts of time putting a sample into a digital software programme then massaging it and changing it. I've reached a kind of Buddhist Middle Path where technology and creation are concerned, because I think it's very easy to get seduced down the path of technology. I find it very sad when I go to university music departments and talk to young composers and they're so gone on the technical aspects that they've hardly written a piece, or the pieces are bad because their minds are not essentially attuned to their creative selves. They're too involved in the technology. I let someone else do the inventing for me, and I think of myself as a composer.

*How do you feel that the technology integrates with the orchestral instruments in, say,* The Death of Klinghoffer?

I think I'm paddling away on a sinking ship with this orchestral thing. The orchestra is a very beautiful medium, but it is also an extremely arbitrary one; there's very little wiggle room economically. If I decide I don't want to write for each of the winds and so many strings and I want to write a piece that has thirty violas and fifteen trumpets, then the piece will get done maybe once at a special music festival but never again, because the economic situation forbids any kind of varying from the package you're presented with. It's something you have to accept. So either you're lucky enough to continue thinking of imaginative ways to exploit this strangely arbitrary grouping of instruments, or you just get out of it altogether.

*Are we likely to see the 'John Adams Band' arising in the future then?*

I don't think so. I think I'm too old and too feeble to go out and put together that kind of band, though I know that a lot of composers have done it. What you're more likely to see is just more use of electronics. But I'll probably, till the end of my days, write for one or another forms of orchestra or mixes of conventional instruments. But I acknowledge that in a hundred years, people will not write for violins, clarinets and oboes at all.

*What's your position as regards opera, which is also a very classical form?*

Well, it doesn't have to be. Opera can be anything, as its name implies. There is institutionalized opera, which I suppose I work upon the margins of, and there are composers who are wildly radical in their approach to the form and that's an exciting development.

*What are the attractions of writing opera?*

For me, music has a potential for great moral force. Now, great music doesn't necessarily have to have that. There's pure music and there's whatever the other is – let's hope it's not 'impure' – but let's call it music that is about human values and issues. That's the kind of music that interests me. That's one of the reasons why I find Benjamin Britten an interesting composer because he felt moral issues very deeply, as many theatrical composers do. I think Mozart did. Opera is a great territory to work in if you're interested in human dynamics. Opera seems to be an art form better suited than any other to deal with what I call the Big Issues – national identity, national destiny or great confrontations between huge groups of people, whether they be nations or races or whatever.

*Your operas make use of recent historical events for their themes . . .*

Yes, why not? I'm always amazed when people ask me that question. Not that you're asking it in a perplexed way, but people often put that question as if there was something unusual about it. If I were a film-maker, a novelist or a playwright, it would be assumed that I would write about subjects from contemporary life. But somehow, doing that in the realm of opera is slightly shocking. I just can't imagine doing any other.

*Why do you think it shocks?*

I guess it just shows up the fact that, in most people's minds,

opera is an archaic form. That's a bad sign. It's a sign that opera
is not growing and moving along with the tide in the way other
art forms are.

*How do you feel about the reactions you got to some of the
performances of* Klinghoffer?

Well, *Klinghoffer* played many performances in Europe before it
came to the United States, and there was very little comment
about any perceived improprieties in our approach. But when it
got to Brooklyn, New York, it was a whole different kettle of fish.
A lot of people felt that the opera turned the Palestinian terrorists
into noble savages at the expense of making fun of the Jewish
passengers on the ship. I was of course very upset about it and so
were my collaborators, because we felt that we had written a
serious work that did great honour to the memory of Leon
Klinghoffer and his wife, and which attempted to tackle an issue
that is not particularly popular in this country – the destiny or
rights of the Palestinian people. It's an issue that's rarely discussed
in the media, and when it is there's always a demand for equal time
for the other side, although that doesn't work both ways
unfortunately. I guess I knew that this was going to happen, but
when it did I was much more upset than I imagined I would be.

*Did the Glass operas have any influence on you when you set out
on* Nixon?

I only know one Glass opera, which is *Satyagraha*. I have heard
some of the music to *Einstein on the Beach* but I haven't seen it,
and I haven't seen any of his later operas. I liked *Satyagraha* very
much. It was a very moving piece, and the musical technique
expressed the subject-matter of passive resistance in a wonderful
way. I think I was probably very much influenced by it. I certainly
know that in the first year of *Nixon* being around, I had to sit and
listen over and over again about how *Nixon* had borrowed so
much from Glass. After a while, however, you get tired of hearing
that and begin to resent it.

In the past, in many schools of thought or periods of style, such
as Cubism or Elizabethan drama or the Mannheim symphony,
many composers, writers or artists were absolutely struck by an
idea and they were all working on it at the same time. Maybe one

person was the first to get there, but we can be very grateful that the other people didn't shy away from that idea simply because someone else had thought of it first. If you think about Mozart, Haydn and early Beethoven, they're all basically hoeing this one very fertile field. So I think that a lot of the ideas, the procedures, the moods and the ambiences that you can find in something like *Satyagraha* or my operas are embodiments of a *zeitgeist*, a spirit of the time. And there's something very thrilling about that, because in a way the composers or writers can feed each other. Philip probably knows a lot of my music and I know a lot of his music, and it's the same with many other composers. None of us likes to open up the newspaper and find that we're 'ripping someone else off'. But the fact is, what's really important is whether major works of art are created. I think this is a very normal kind of thing, this kind of symbiosis. But what people come after me with is rarely minimalism any more, it's the much more hostile question about accessibility or 'having a public', like it's some kind of slightly indecent behaviour. I get a lot of this flak when I go to London, from the Establishment. It's very funny because London has a big classical music audience, so on the other hand I have a very satisfying sense of recognition and appreciation in London. I mean, three times coming into Heathrow, the guy that stamped my passport has known who I was! That makes you feel wonderful and it would never happen in this country, never, not on your life. But then the British press comes after me with scalpels and blowtorches and they just find this music beneath contempt.

*Why do you think that is?*

The British classical music establishment bought the post-war modernist, Boulezian ideology whole cloth and digested it, but I think they're gagging on it now. It must be very hard to be a young composer there. But it's interesting to see a new generation of people who are handling it by being Angry Young Men – the Steve Martland types who remind me of Francis Bacon and that generation of British artists and playwrights who dealt with the rigor mortis of British artistic life by having a kind of 'fuck you' attitude. But some of them are also very sophisticated and very clever about how they manipulate their image.

*How do you view the musical climate in the United States?*

It's hard to say. Somebody asked Ligeti that when he was here at Stanford back in the 1970s, and he said, 'You simply can't make a judgement. The distances are so huge in this country'.

*Do you come up against the same criticism of being too 'accessible'?*

Oh, I get it from some critics. But I think that, very slowly, people have begun to understand that whether you like what I do or not, I'm basically an honest composer. I'm doing what I want to do and I'm not doing it just to get an audience. I think that slowly people have begun at least to grudge me that. But the climate of support is not very healthy in this country. For all my problems with the British music establishment, I find Britain a wonderful place because there's a lot of opportunity and support, and there are lots of intelligent people who care deeply about music. In this country, the first problem is that music education is so wretched. The state of California voted in 1979 essentially to remove music education from the public schools. So if you don't educate your own kid yourself, there's no music. Even among young serious composers in this country, those that haven't become academics, there's a strange, hectic romance with pop music, and I think that part of its feverish quality has to do with the fact that young composers are afraid they're not going to get recognized or appreciated, that they'll have no audience or money, so they've embraced popular music with a fierce, almost angry zeal. It's possible that this may produce a new generation of composers, people that will be as fresh and as outrageous as someone like Copland was when he was in his twenties. The stuff he wrote in the 1920s was really *outré* – jazzy, dissonant and very provocative.

*Are you talking about people like Glenn Branca?*

Yes, Branca's a very interesting case. I was profoundly affected by a concert he gave here a few years ago. It was one of the most shockingly new ideas I'd ever heard. But he, like a lot of composers who live and work in that area, has a real problem with lack of technical range. They're just not well enough educated musically. They become slaves to their own limited technique and can only do one thing. Composers like Harry Partch, Conlon Nancarrow and more recent figures have had brilliant ideas, but have only been able to work within a limited expressive or intellectual mode because they're musically rather limited. That's a common thing in this country. Steve Reich is an interesting case of somebody whose actual music education is not as thorough as many other university or conservatory-trained composers, but his life as a composer has been a sort of triumph. He's triumphed over his technical weaknesses and he's found a way to get around it through the force of his personality. By using instruments to help him along, whether they be tape recorders and synthesizers or whatever, he's managed to avoid becoming marginalized. Unfortunately, many important voices in this country end up marginalizing themselves because of their lack of musical command.

*Can you tell us something about the ideas in* El Dorado?

*El Dorado* is a very strange piece. I knew when I was writing it that it was a statement, unlike some of my other pieces which are born more out of musical necessity. This piece came out of the expression of a deeply-disturbed frame of mind that I was in – and probably still am in – which has to do with the world around me and particularly with living where I do – the United States in the 1980s and early 1990s – and wanting to find a musical metaphor for what appeared to me a philosophy of absolutely unconscious, untrammelled growth and ultimate destruction of where we live. So *El Dorado* was a metaphor. I chose a title that was almost banal – it's the name of a Cadillac. It's also the name of California. There was something very ironic about the choice of that title. I think of it as a landscape in two parts, but I suppose you could think of it as a symphony. People are disturbed by this piece, particularly by the first movement, which is not entirely pretty.

*What do you think gives West Coast music its 'West Coast-ness'?*

I don't want to quote Lou Harrison, who said a thing that was cute but not entirely true, something like 'West Coast composers are not afraid to be pretty'. You can just hear Lou Harrison saying that – I guess he found that it struck gold, so he said it many times. But there is a modicum of truth in it. For example, I've always written tonal music, and composers that I've known like Daniel Lentz, Ingram Marshall, Lou himself and Harold Budd have always written tonal music, and it's been attractive music. We've been bashed for that and told it's a little on the lightweight side, that we're not very deep because our music is pretty, just like California culture – bronze bodies, blonde hair. Those kind of analogies are made, but I think they're all rather superficial. I don't find much connection with that sensibility, but I find a great deal of inspiration and identification with things that happened in California twenty, thirty or forty years ago. For example, the great Californian photographers that belonged to what was called the F/64 group, people like Edward Weston and Eugene Cunningham. These were people who lived in California when it was really the frontier, when you had to drive for ten days to get here – you couldn't hop on a plane. They were very close to the landscape before it became over-populated and they made wonderful documents. California does not have much of a history of great painting, but its photography tradition is wonderful and unique. There's nothing like it anywhere in the world. I think that in a piece of mine like *El Dorado* or even *Harmonium* – some of my big landscape pieces – there is a sense of the vastness one gets from living here that you just don't get from living in New England or New York, or Europe for that matter. You can come around the corner here and there's eighty miles of nothing. That affects you as an artist.

# CHARLES AMIRKHANIAN

*b. California 1945*

Since 1965 Charles Amirkhanian has used speech as a primary element in his music. Using the recording studio as a compositional tool, he began to experiment with ambient sound recordings, tape loops, delays and multi-tracking to produce enigmatic wordscapes characterized by intense rhythmic activity and the resultant transformation of words into sound objects.

Influenced by the prose and poetry of Gertrude Stein and the non-syntactical extensions of her ideas in the work of Clark Coolidge, Amirkhanian developed a style of 'restless minimalism' in which repeated figures were sustained for only relatively short periods before giving way to further, expansive variations.

More recently he has been working with the Synclavier Digital Synthesizer to sample and modify ambient sound, and this has led to a series of pieces that explore the field between abstract (or musical) and ambient (or representational) sounds to produce a dream-like, non-linguistic surrealism. For example, his 28-minute tribute to Percy Grainger, *Walking Tune* (1987), mixes fragments of solo violin and other conventional musical sources with a variety of field recordings including humming birds, ducks, hot springs and rusty gates.

*You've been described as one of the leading exponents of text-sound composition in the USA. How did you come to start working in text-sound?*

I was a percussionist and had been studying the music of Lou Harrison and Cage. I was composing, completely self-taught, a lot of different pieces that primarily used rhythm. I began to think about speech as a non-pitched sound the way that a bass drum is thought of as a non-pitched sound. So, having also been interested in poetry and writing for a long time, I began to combine those interests, and when I heard the *Geographical Fugue* of Ernst Toch and some other early material I was reinforced in the idea that I would like to make some speech pieces myself. I began to make some pieces on my typewriter for speakers, speaking in relative time-frames and sometimes in unison. Often these people would have percussion beaters or pieces of metal or something to emphasize various parts of the text. That was the beginning of that interest. Later I discovered that there was a long history of this kind of writing in Europe going back to the beginning of the century, and that it wasn't exclusively by musicians. It was Futurists and Dadaists and people in the visual arts and other fields, and that extended my interest as well.

*What kind of texts did you use? Did you make your own?*

Yes, they were 'stream of consciousness' things. I had also been influenced by reading Clark Coolidge's poetry and Gertrude Stein. As a young person at university I began to realize (I was an English major, not a Music major) that the poetry which interested me most was that of Charles Olsen and Pound, also the writings of Jack Kerouac, which were very musical. When I moved to San Francisco I discovered the experimental writers who formed what is now called the Language School of Poetry, and Clark Coolidge, who is still probably the most interesting of that group for me, became a friend. He walked into the record store where I was working and asked to buy a Gertrude Stein record. I knew of the record already – it had played a large part in my development – so I began to talk to him. I realized that this was the guy who was putting out the little magazines that I'd been buying down at City Lights Bookstore. When I took my position at KPFA Radio I immediately invited Coolidge to do some programmes on the radio.

*You've been music director at KPFA since 1969 – what does that entail?*

Well, the first duty is to have lots of volunteer programmers who are experts in different fields. They present music at various hours of the day to fill our schedule and also to present unusual kinds of music that aren't heard elsewhere on American radio. I also do my own programmes. For instance, when John Cage died I did an obituary for him on the news – a seven-minute piece that interspersed music with his voice and other comments. The next day I did a two-hour programme with phone-ins from some of his ex-colleagues and a survey of his music. So we respond to immediate situations. We also have guest composers who do things for our Yamaha Disclavier piano. They send us floppies and we play them. We also have live musicians coming in to the studios to perform. In general, I'm a kind of advocate from that position for contemporary composers. Since 1949, when KPFA went on the air, all the people who've worked in that position have been either composers or music critics.

*Modesty aside, how would you assess your influence on the development of West Coast new music?*

Well, primarily I'd say that the only influence I've had has been through KPFA. Anybody who has worked at KPFA has had a large influence on the way things go here. First of all, there's no other regular contemporary music broadcast on a station with that much transmission power, so people can hear us quite far away. In my college days I lived 208 miles away in Fresno, but in the evenings I could go to a particular house that had a large antenna in the back yard and we could hear KPFA. I could hear Pauline Oliveros and Ramon Sender at the Tape Centre performing live. This got me very excited because I realized I had a connection to the Bay Area that way. Quite a lot of people have had their only exposure to contemporary music through KPFA, and by pure accident – they'll just be tuning over, they listen and get hooked. And because the station provides access for composers, a tremendous number of people have been seduced into listening more carefully. One of my goals in being on the radio there was to personalize contemporary music, so that by interviewing people and demystifying the process of composing and playing the music, I hope to have reached more people with it.

*How would you say that your position at KPFA has influenced your own music and compositions?*

Well, being around all those tape recorders has certainly had a lot to do with it. And not having so much time to rehearse and work with musicians directly, I've had to spend much of my time writing pieces that exist on tape. In the early days I created most of my pieces in the studio. From 1969 to 1972 I was working quite a bit with the multiple tape recorders that we had in one room. I could go in and layer things just by running lots of tapes at once and trying things out, without having to worry about paying an exorbitant rate per hour to do it. But using my voice in a microphone also influenced me, speaking close to a mike and changing the quality of my voice that way. Being around radio microphones and lots of recording equipment has certainly played a major role in how I work.

*Have you always performed your text-sound pieces, or did that begin when you started working with KPFA radio?*

No, when I was living in Fresno I did some speech pieces for four speakers. What I liked about working in a multi-track situation was that I could replicate my own voice four times, and therefore the mixture of the words became quite a different matter. If you have four recognizably different voices speaking, you don't hear the overlaps of words in the same way. When I began to overlap my own voice, there was a blending of the words which made combination words – that's something I learned from Coolidge when he was doing experiments with a tape loop machine at Mills College. It was an eight-loop machine that somebody had devised. Clark went out there one day and put loops of words on this machine. There would be one word on this loop, two words on that loop and three words on this one, and he just let them play for thirty minutes so that this kind of process piece arose. He had heard *Come Out* by Steve Reich and decided that this would be his treatment of that idea. My treatment of it was to use a loop idea of Coolidge and Reich, but to have the words and sections changing more frequently. So it was a kind of restless minimalism. I think I was among the first people who really used this idea of hearing the same phrase over and over again, or different permutations of the same phrase, and actually changing the loops more frequently to make it move through time more quickly – an idea which later lots of minimalists found attractive. John Adams uses that as well, the idea of moving through many phrases more quickly – it's something that developed about ten years later.

*Were you ever interested in working with pitched sound and conventional instruments?*

I spent my first ten years as a musician studying the piano and playing, without much formal compositional training. So I was a bit wary of harmony and counterpoint and what to do with pitches. I looked around and saw that so many people were doing so well with those things that I decided to investigate this other area, which was speech. At the time, you have to understand, there was no consciousness about speech – there was a bit of interest in Schoenberg's *sprechstimme*, there was a passing acquaintance with Kurt Schwitters' *Ursonate*, which we only knew from books. But not many people gave credence to Dada in the 1960s – it was passé and out of favour. What I was doing was to point out that there was a lot more to be done with the idea of sound poetry, which I thought had just been tapped superficially by the Dada poets, who didn't have any musical background at all. I thought I was bringing a musical intelligence to it. If I had been trained more conventionally, I probably would have done something quite different.

*How did you go about making those early pieces?*

I made lists of words in books. Usually the lists had to do with how the rhythms and the sounds jangled against each other. I would read these into a microphone, record them on a loop, and then have seven or eight loops that I would start in various orders. I would then record those from a single stereo or mono tape deck to a multi-track machine. Then I tried to compose by building up layers. In 1972 when I worked at Swedish Radio I had to have nine machines going to one two-track because there was no four-track machine there. So a piece like *Just*, which uses the words 'rainbow chug bandit bomb', required three engineers just to start all the loops at one time. It was really quite amusing because they had never had that many mono tape recorders in one room at a time. It was a very small studio packed with engineers and machines all over the place, and they considered that quite extravagant. Of course, on an eight-track it would have been so simple, but one of the shocking things about *Just* when it was heard at that period was that it had so many layers and was so cleanly done. Many people who tried these experiments in those days would dub from one machine to another to build up layers, and you couldn't possibly get a nice sound that way. The tape loop pieces were made by beginning with various sketches, poems, groups or clusters of words and then building up a multi-track continuum, in some cases making it sound as if you went from beginning to end without ever starting or stopping the final machine. In fact, this was not true – we had to splice to change things. It did shock people that things changed so frequently, but it was through very careful editing that we were able to create the illusion of people being able to switch samples, as it were.

*How do you present your tape music? Is there also a visual element?*

In some cases there are slide projections that my wife Carol Law has done. She's a visual artist who likes to work with scale the way that I work with scale. That is to say, in the sonic aspect of the pieces you'll hear very close-miked sounds, voice, ambient sounds, people walking and so forth. Carol will take a very close-up shot of an object so that you don't quite recognize it at first. Then gradually all of it is revealed by successive layers of slides that dissolve from one to the other. So I'm dissolving from one sound to another and she's dissolving from one image to another. I did that after five or six years of playing tape pieces just on tape and realizing that in some situations I would have liked more. So sometimes we have this other, visual element. Sometimes I also add a layer of live speaking over the tape along with the music.

*You've said that you haven't had a normal compositional training. But who would you say your musical influences have been?*

Well, early on I was very influenced by Hovhaness and Cage. My parents accidently gave me some records of Hovhaness when I was five years old, thinking it was Armenian folk music because there was an Armenian rug on the cover. So I began from an early age hearing these pieces by Hovhaness in which raga-like patterns would suddenly cease at the end of a lot of continuous eighth-note activity. That image of the two pitches of drums pounding along and then suddenly stopping without a cadence was very influential. I used it a lot in the speech pieces I composed later. Cage had an influence because he opened up my ideas about what was permitted. Harrison and Cowell and the others who wrote percussion music influenced me a lot. Steve Reich also had a huge influence on me. I was listening to an LP at my home in San Francisco when I'd just moved here in 1967. It was a Richard Maxfield piece that had lots of insect-like sounds. I went to sleep on my bed and I woke up with a start when *Come Out*, the next item on the disc, appeared. I thought someone was in the room and was about to attack me – I'd never heard anything like that on a record before. That had a profound influence, the discovery of this phasing system was very important.

*Would you still call yourself a minimalist?*

I'm not sure. I still work in the same way but I'm using samples now, and sometimes the samples go on for minutes at a time, sometimes for ten seconds. For instance, in a piece called *Walking Tune*, there is a continuum for twenty-eight minutes during which you hear a lot of footsteps and melodic patterns on violins, then imitations of those patterns in a recording from a J. C. Bach cantata which has been sampled and treated. The piece is segmented like a Rondo, so you keep coming back to this violin pattern, but in between lots of other diversions happen. These pieces are more episodic, like a journey where you start in one place and explore it for a bit and then you somehow find yourself merging into another place. So you go from A to Z rather than from A to B and back to A again.

*Is there ever some sort of rationale behind where you go to and how long you spend there and whether you come back or not? Or do you just work through it intuitively in the studio?*

It's much more intuitive because I'm working with the actual sound itself. I don't map everything out on a score before I go into the studio. What I do is to collect lots of samples and try them out on the Synclavier, manipulating them to see which things work well in different cases. I've often found that something I think will make an excellent tone-cluster turns out not to work well that way. But it might work well in a pattern in which you walk around the keyboard in thirds, for example. I've developed a number of ways to work with samples to disguise the fact that they are samples. For instance, I'll have one texture that will play along for, let's say, three minutes and it will be recorded in a particular environment. At the same time, I have samples of, let's say, fifteen seconds of that three-minute environment repeating themselves. So you get a kind of ambiguity that I like, because it masks both the fact that you've got a continuous recording and the fact that you've got a repeated recording. So the mind begins to play games to try to discover what is going on.

*So you compose as you go along? You don't know what you're going to come out with?*

No, not exactly. The plan doesn't really develop until I'm working in the studio and I'm moulding the sound as I'm going. It's like an improvisational process. I sometimes find that various samples will 'take' in different ways to different treatments, but that's not possible to determine in advance.

*How did you put together the* Pas de Voix? *You must have had quite a precise idea of the finished object, otherwise you wouldn't have gone and collected 'fart' and 'urination' samples. Did you know everything that you wanted to put in there, but just not quite how you wanted to put them together?*

No, that's not right. I collected lots of things in Paris and brought them back, and I had independently recorded the urination and other things. I began to create from this palette, which also included items related to the biography of Beckett I had just read. The fact that the bells of Notre Dame were recorded was really by chance; I happened to be up on the top of the cathedral one day with Erik Bauersfeld, my colleague from KPFA who was in Paris at the time. I wouldn't have thought to do that pertaining to Beckett, it seemed too religious somehow and not quite the right thing. But it turned out to be just right when I actually heard the recording, months later when I was working on the piece. So it wasn't exactly planned in that way. I didn't consciously go out to record those things first.

*So there's an element of chance, not quite knowing if something's going to work?*

Well, you don't really know. If you do pre-plan everything you'll be sorry, because there's no Rimsky-Korsakov book to help you solve these problems. That's the problem, you see; you don't know what any particular 'instrument' will do for you until you actually do with it what you're going to do.

*Do you have any rules at all?*

Good taste! I suppose there are certain things I tend to do. One of my rules is to do what a good photographer would do. If you have a negative that's thin, don't try to save it. Throw it out and rephotograph it. If I have a sample that is badly recorded and there are lots of extraneous sounds that I don't want, I throw it out and go and record it properly. I have a fetish about making the final product clean-sounding and focused on the sound I want the listener to hear. But no, I can't think of a lot of rules.

*How do you describe your music?*

Well, if I'm describing the pieces that I do now, I would say that I'm trying to explore the idea of representational sounds and non-representational sounds in combination. By that I mean that

I'm mixing purely musical pitch writing with referential sounds that you can identify as footsteps or the sounds of particular animals, waterfalls etc. These create pictures in the mind and relate very much to the sounds going on in film and our perception of the cinema. When you put together these combinations of elements, you can take people on a journey that is very personal, because most people have their own references to the sounds and these will conjure up particular things for an individual. That's a nice possibility. I also like the variety of responses I'll get to one piece. Even with the voice pieces where the words are four nouns repeated over and over again that don't have a syntax, there will be people who will say, 'Oh, that piece is about OD-ing on drugs because a "rainbow" is what people get from heroin, and "chug" is drinking beer and "bandit" etc . . .' They make up the most amazing things. Therefore you have an oblique, referential response which is fascinating. It's like the interpretation of dreams, and involves the subconscious. Because I work in radio where nobody can see me, there's that reference as well – conjuring up something and not letting people know exactly how you did it. I'm always fascinated when someone does that to me on the radio, when I don't quite know how they achieve something. Occasionally you'll hear some real stroke of genius on the radio by somebody who's just starting out in the medium and doesn't have preconceived notions of what to do with it. When that happens, you know that you're on to somebody to watch.

*Regarding* Chululu, *a one-minute collage piece with many samples of different musics from traditional cultures, you've said that's a direction you're thinking of going in even more – the 60-second burst of chaos!*

Well, I would like to make a longer piece using that technique, which is to take a sample of something prerecorded and add lots of different ones that move from one to the other quickly. There's a kind of vertigo effect from having all those things succeed one another so rapidly. I would be very interested to know how long that could be sustained without being too abrasive or silly. It shocked me that I was able to get so many different bits of music into that fifty or so seconds. If I could do that in fifty seconds, I wonder what I could do in fifteen or twenty minutes? John Cage heard a particular piece called *Politics as Usual*. There are a lot of individual sounds where you hear a metallic percussion instrument being bowed, so you hear a kind of pitch-change and you just focus on that one sound, which goes around for fifteen seconds. Cage came up to me afterwards and said, 'Wouldn't it be lovely if you put all those sounds together in five minutes and just layered them so that there was a lot of density.' That's one thing that I've avoided because there's a muddiness that you can achieve if you're not careful. With digital recording there is a possibility of doing that in an interesting way. I also did a piece recently called *Im Frühling*, which is a kind of reverse tone-poem. Instead of taking orchestral instruments and having them imitate nature, I took lots of sounds from nature and had them imitate orchestral textures. The piece uses a segment where twelve different bird-calls are layered over themselves. Because it's in such a high frequency range you can distinctly hear each bird, all twelve of them, at the same time. Cage's comment inspired the experiment.

*Could you ever see a situation where that might come more to the fore, not necessarily using conventional instruments but doing, say, a pitched Synclavier piece?*

Sure, I've already done a piece for chamber orchestra with tape called *His Anxious Hours*. It was a commission by three ensembles in the US, and was for a large group of instrumentalists dressed in mens' pyjamas. They were evoking a particular evening in the life of Johannes Brahms, the night before he composed a particular piano piece, and what might have been going on in his mind. So you hear snippets of the piano piece played on a Synclavier, but slowed down. The instrumentalists pick up parts of that line, amplify it and perform it around. And it accumulates into this big climax. It's performed by candlelight, of course. So I'm not averse to pitch, I just don't write string quartets.

*What is 'West Coast-ness'? Does it still exist?*

Why, of course. It's not a myth. I think it has to do with Charles Seeger teaching Henry Cowell that folk music was OK. Seeger taught a respect for non-European cultures to Henry Cowell when he was an extremely young man here at the University of California in Berkeley. Cowell then came into contact with Cage and Harrison who, because of their 'West Coast-ness', had been close to Chinese, Indonesian and Japanese music, and had realized that there was genuine stimulation to be derived from going to Chinese opera, for example. Lou Harrison went more frequently to Chinese opera than to the San Francisco opera, which did conventional Rossini and Verdi. After his conventional training, it was, for him, the start of a new fascination with investigating other classical forms. He studied Korean music, Indonesian music of all types, and that legacy was passed down to us through the percussion music movement and through the Henry Cowell *New Music Edition* which circulated these ideas widely throughout the country. Henry Cowell put forth the idea that you could be interested in non-European music and still have the skill of a European composer. That had a very good influence, but an influence that was rejected by all the academics and by the Copland/Bernstein group. Nevertheless, it's endured and become the West Coast model for people like Daniel Lentz, Harold Budd and others. The idea first of all is that music can be consonant in just intonation, beautiful and influenced by Indonesia – none of those things came out of Princeton and Columbia.

*Is there still that great divide between East and West Coast, or are things more fluid now?*

Yes, there are people who go both ways. For example, the University of California has several faculty members who are quite prominent as composers yet don't subscribe to these feelings about world music, and there is a minority on the East Coast who do – it's just that they're marginalized. In New York, for example, you have a group of composers like Philip Corner and Daniel Goode who have tried to bring forth an interest in Indonesian music or other kinds of music that are overtly pretty, but it hasn't worked out so well for them career-wise. On the West Coast, these people continue to compose music – Lou Harrison has inspired Gamelan groups in various cities. There is a great deal of interest here in composers who write that kind of music, and it's been a good place for them to flourish. But they are not supported by the San Francisco Symphony and other organizations which have modern music series. We get George Benjamin imported to play his favourite composers, and that's where the big money goes. John Adams was the exception. John started the 'New and Unusual Music Series' with the Symphony Orchestra. That was profoundly influential for four years because he would have Milton Babbitt and Glenn Branca in the same series, which was quite a range. You could go and hear Meredith Monk one night and the next time you would hear somebody much more conventional writing a large ensemble piece. That kind of catholicity is very instructive. But since then we have had Charles Wuorinen and George Benjamin and things haven't been so interesting.

*Do you feel that what you do comes out of the Western classical tradition, or are you working in a different discipline?*

That's funny. I see myself as in the same discipline, but I get the feeling that many people who listen to what I do think I haven't any relationship to it, that I'm doing something that's more related to *hörspiel* or radio-drama or sound-art. I see myself as closely related to the kind of aesthetic that Cowell, Harrison and Cage were working with in the 1940s and 1950s. A lot of the pieces I've written are dedicated to Grainger, Slonimsky and others from the music world. I guess I see myself as a composer rather than a sound-artist. I wouldn't want to do this if I didn't think that it came out of some tradition and was leading somewhere. With the advent of digital technology, the kinds of collage tape pieces that were produced in the 1950s are now naturally changing into something else because we can do different things with ambient sounds. I think that's as legitimate a vehicle for musical exploration as the twelve pitches on a Western instrument.

There was a period when minimalist music wasn't accepted in Europe, just as it wasn't accepted in New York for a while. That was the most important transition in twentieth century music; moving away from pointillistic, dissonant, modern music into constant, repetitive, trance-oriented music has had a much greater influence than the Impressionism of Debussy and Ravel, a much greater influence than the revolt against Wagner by Les Six. It has pervaded popular music and jazz (Jarrett and Corea and all those composers). The influence of minimalism has been profound partly because it's such an organic part of the way we hear and the way we relate to physical experience. We're moving out of the purely cerebral aspects of composing. When I began to hear minimalist music on TV commercials, I knew it had penetrated the very depths of our psyche!

*Yet Europe still turns out countless composers who act as if it never happened.*

Well, that's OK because the fact is that there are fifty directions at once now. There's not a continuum any more, and there never will be again. You will have people doing experimental punk music who are perfectly happy to thrash for three seconds then stop. For them that's a great musical experience.

# LAURIE ANDERSON

*b. Florida 1955*

Laurie Anderson is widely regarded as one of America's most successful performance artists. At once intriguing, challenging and entertaining, her work has attracted huge popular and critical acclaim. After receiving her MFA in Sculpture from Columbia University in 1972, Anderson became active in New York's downtown avant-garde scene before recording *O Superman* in 1981, a 7-inch EP which rose to number two in the UK pop charts and was subsequently included on *Big Science*, the first of five albums for Warner Brothers.

Her primary interest is in the spoken word and in walking the lines between communication and alienation, between man and machine, between reality and fiction. Having recently returned from an ill-fated trek through Tibet, she is, at the time of writing, currently working on her sixth Warner Brothers album, with Brian Eno as producer. Together with Peter Gabriel, Eno is Anderson's co-conspirator in the long-term planning of *Real World*, a large amusement-cum-theme park to be located in Barcelona.

*What brought you to New York?*

I wanted to come here since I first saw television, which my parents didn't actually let us have – we saw it at friends. This was before videotape, so they'd say, 'Good evening, it's nine o'clock', and you'd look at the clock and it was eight o'clock, and you'd say, 'Whoa! New York City! It's so exciting. It's so much later and darker. Everything seems to come from there.' So I always wanted to move there because it seemed like a futuristic place. It doesn't seem like that to me now. It doesn't seem like everything comes from here at all. I've come full circle on that.

*Having started out more as a painter and art critic, how did you come to be principally involved with music?*

Through talking, I think, and the talking becoming more musical – and now it's becoming more like talking again. I suppose that that's the aspect of talking, as opposed to meandering, that I like the most. A true conversation, if it's on a roll like in the best jazz where you react to what someone just said, is the most fun. So a lot of the work I do comes out of situations like that, just talking to people.

*Would you say your work is autobiographical?*

It used to be maybe ten years ago. I'm not sure how it started, but lately there've been a lot more political things in the work, more so than autobiographical. But it's easy, understandably, to mix up autobiographical work with fiction because I use the words 'I' and 'you' though not meaning myself at all. Of course, like any fiction writer, you try and put yourself into that point of view while you're writing a certain story or song, but it doesn't necessarily mean that, once you stop writing, you actually had anything to do with that. It's an act of faith and imagination to be that particular 'I' jumping into somebody else's skin. It's just a device.

*Your earlier work was very experimental. How did you move from that into the more popular area you're working in now?*

Well, it seemed to me that the context and the press changed. In the 1970s I was written about by small avant-garde publications – they wrote in those terms and I was just doing what I did. I don't think I was doing different things – I was still playing the same old instrument, talking and telling stories, but I was doing them in different places. So a different kind of people reported on them, and said, 'Oh, it's a pop thing because lots of people are here – it's a popular event.' I mean, I don't want to pretend that performing for five thousand people is the same as performing for fifty because there are things you have to change; that kind of thing wasn't alluring to me, and was confusing too. But I don't think that I completely changed my work.

In fact, the avant-garde was much more consistent than I thought. It's hard to be an artist anywhere, even in the supposed art capital New York, so the avant-garde forms a protective little group around these people, writes about them and supports them, which is wonderful. But because it's so isolated from the rest of the culture, the avant-garde tends to go, '*We* know. Those people out there are slobs. They don't know.' They have to do that to survive. And I benefited from that attitude for years. But then I went out there, and the avant-garde had to be consistent. They couldn't suddenly say, 'Those people know.' They had to say, 'She left. She no longer knows.' Now, while there was a grain of truth in the fact that some things changed, for the most part it was not like that. It was more a question of a different press style. I was being considered by people who didn't know where I was coming from. They thought I'd invented this art form because they had no idea what the avant-garde had been doing for the last fifty years. They were saying, 'What's she from? This is so original!', just because it was in a different context. I suffered from media attack because they were all vying to say how different it was.

I think that a more interesting subject than the development of art in the United States is the development of media. I'm really fascinated by that. I wish someone would figure it out, because so much of the art world hinges on it. It's about media attacks on these poor eighteen-year-old painters who now have an artistic life-span of about two years, as opposed to the ten years you were allowed before – with the few exceptions of people like John Cage who just managed to pull through and consistently make interesting work, which is the main thing. But also, as soon as newspapers and money get involved, they affect the art world in a way that's really fascinating. I'd also love to see something written about the British press because that's a real art form – the rag trade. It's one of the reasons why Americans have such screwed-up ideas about you British. I mean, the oddest headlines like, 'Six-headed woman gives birth to nine-headed insect!' All those things have datelines Birmingham or Manchester or Liverpool because it's too far for us to check!

*Is this examination of the media one of the aspects of your piece* United States?

It was one of the interests but, in a lot of ways, I think that's always been a part of my work.

*It seems you're focusing on the media's alienation of people from their environment?*

Well, my interest in this takes different shapes. But part of it is certainly that so-called 'communication' is nothing to do with actual communication and much more to do with alienation under the guise of, 'Oh, you're part of the world, look what happened today!' That actually makes you less a part of the world.

*Is communication the basis of your work?*

Yes, to me the richer the image is, the better. By richer I mean clearer. It has no obstructions, it gets right across and people can understand it. I sometimes try to use myself as a judge of that, and I find that often I'm a better judge than I think – that the things that make me laugh or cry are actually the things that do that for other people too. Sometimes I forget that. So anyway, what I'm trying to do is to make images that are as vivid as I can and to get them across as well as I can. Otherwise, I could entertain myself pretty well by making a lot of things that only made *me* laugh, but then I'd just stay at home and laugh! But I've chosen to be an artist and half of that, at least, is in the communication of it. Half is also in the production of it. Obviously, you can't really tear those two things apart. But I think you could stay at home and make a painting, or better still you could be on the moon making a painting, by yourself and it could be the best painting that had ever been made, but it would miss the other half of what I think of as art – that nobody else received it.

*So you don't feel that your work is complete until it's been observed by the audience?*

No. And I feel that the work has really succeeded when somebody says, 'I saw or heard your piece and I got so many ideas from it'. Then they tell me what the ideas were, and they've nothing to do with what *I* was doing. That suggests to me that the piece was rich enough for them to take something from it and do what they wanted.

*Perhaps that's the measure of a good art work, when it makes you almost want it to finish so that you can go and do something yourself.*

Right! It makes you want to jump up and get out of there. I absolutely agree. That's a good definition. It doesn't push you down and make you say, 'Well, I should think about this. It probably means something but, you know, maybe in ten years I'll understand it.' Maybe there is some work like that that's ahead of its time, and it's wonderful to have some mystery too – I'm not saying that everything should be like a Coke ad! But I think that a lot of things slip by under the cloak of obscurity, wilful obscurity, with people saying things like, 'You're just too stupid to understand this. This is one of the best works of art that's ever been made!'

*How much control do you have over the different aspects of your work, the various media that you employ? Your film* Home of the Brave, *for example, seemed to involve about two hundred personnel.*

Well, that's an exception for me. Generally I work as a complete recluse, then I come out and do something. With the film, it had to be 'coming out and doing something' from the very beginning. I had to trust a lot of people. I would probably have preferred to have lit it myself, trucked it in myself and catered it myself, but I didn't have thirty-five years to spare so I decided to trust other people. So occasionally I had to say, 'Use your judgement and do the best you can' and that was very hard for me to say. I almost couldn't get it past my lips because, like most artists, I'm a control freak. If I have to take responsibility for it, I want to shape its final form.

So often when things jump into other media, whether into book form or review form, or are reinterpreted as a miniature version, it can be the opposite of what your intentions were. And besides, my interest is in the essential things rather than in the meaning – the colour of what that is, for instance, the very particular way that sounds – so those aren't details for me. For example, people have asked me to give a score to someone else and have them do the performances with other instruments. I decided that my music wasn't in that kind of reproducible form, probably because, for one thing, I use things like tape and samples, and those can't really be duplicated on a viola. You'd have to have all the same tape decks and electronics to do it. If I went to see something like that, it would just be creepy. Also, when I have done things that could be replicated, like orchestra pieces, I've found that, unless I'm somehow more specific, they're less successful. I mean, a whole orchestra just rehearses one night for all the works that are going to be presented the next day. So you go to the rehearsal for the very first time and you go, 'Oh, my God! The trombones should be doing what the 'cellos are doing and this is horrible! It's all upside down!' I'm a terrible orchestrator, so these are horrible shocks – and besides, you don't have any time to change it. And then they say, 'Well, thank you very much for coming to the rehearsal. We're going to be rehearsing the next work now,' and you say, 'You mean, that's it?!' Then you spend the whole of the concert with your head buried in your hands and it's just a nightmare. I'm used to mixing every single little thing, so when an orchestra plays it, it sounds like something out of control to me.

*With so much of your work being text-based, do you have to translate it for performances abroad?*

Yes, I work with translators a lot to get things just right, and the things that I can't do in those languages are subtitled. It's wonderful to find this key and turn it in the lock, to see the faces of people going, 'Oh, you're speaking our language. We get it.' But of course, you go out on to the street and you're foreign again – you've locked off.

*So you just memorize the translations of each piece?*

Yes. I do it phonetically, which led me into some problems when I tried to do it in Japanese! After the first concert, the promoter came and said, 'Excuse me, pardon me. You speak English rather well, but in Japanese you have, pardon me, a slight stutter.' And I realized that the guy who had made the cassette for me that I'd learned phonetically had a slight stutter, and that I'd learnt all of this stuff dead on. So I was noting that this word was 'tsutsuru' and this one was 'tsutsutsuru' – and it was very difficult to learn! And I could never just say 'tsuru' instead of 'tsutsuru' because it had become integrated into the music. It was scanning that way, and even if it was just spoken and not sung, it was part of the melody of the paragraph. It made me feel very machine-like not to be able to forget that, because I pride myself and other human beings on the fact that we are different from machines because we can forget! They can learn but they can't forget.

# ROBERT ASHLEY

*b. Michigan 1930*

Robert Ashley studied composition with Ross Lee Finney and Roberto Gerhard at the University of Michigan, and later with Wallingford Reigger at the Manhattan School of Music. During the 1960s he co-organized the legendary ONCE festivals and became director of the highly influential ONCE group, a music–theatre collaboration that toured the United States from 1965–9. In 1969 he became Director of the Center for Contemporary Music at Mills College in Oakland, California, and from 1966 to 1976 he toured extensively with the Sonic Arts Union, a composers' collective that included David Behrman, Alvin Lucier and Gordon Mumma.

During 1975–6 he produced his first television opera, *Music with Roots in the Aether*. In 1978 the Kitchen Center in New York City commissioned *Perfect Lives*, an opera for television produced in collaboration with Channel Four. He has also written extensively for dance (*Problems in the Flying Saucer*, 1988, for the Merce Cunningham Dance Company) and orchestra (*My Brother Called*, 1987, for solo voice and orchestra).

*How important was the experience of the ONCE Group for you?*

The ONCE Group was active in the 1960s and I think the last performance we gave was in 1971. There were about ten people in the basic group. Most of them were not professional musicians. They were architects, painters and writers who were all very good at musical ideas, but they didn't pretend to be violin players or anything like that. So we did almost exclusively vocal music, which was good for me.

*Did that involve mixed media?*

Well, not too much. Everything then was supposed to be mixed-media, but it was actually very crude compared to a typical rock concert now. Technically, it was something that would have to happen in America, because we didn't then (and don't yet) have a tradition of producing opera. What the ONCE Group was doing was essentially small-scale, avant-garde opera. Whatever mixed media we used was mainly incidental to the idea of telling a story. There were artists in the ONCE Group working on their own projects which were much more like mixed media, with light projection, live electronic music, film and that kind of thing. But the ONCE Group proper was a sort of portable, touring opera company that did mainly vocal pieces with very elaborate story-telling.

*Were they group compositions?*

They weren't group compositions in the sense, as I understand it, that theatre people use the term. Theatre people speak of technical exercises that are used to develop material. We never did that. I would write the piece, or somebody else would write the piece, and then the group would work on it together, but mainly on the technical question of how to produce it. One person took responsibility for the staging, another for the lighting, another for the electronics and so forth. Everybody would find their responsibilities within different pieces, depending on the circumstances.

*In what ways did this differ from your work with the Sonic Arts Union?*

Sonic Arts Union was totally different. We were four composers living in different parts of the country, and basically we got together for practical reasons – to give concerts and to tour. We were friends, and we were all getting opportunities to do concerts in the US and Europe. It was an administrative and technical arrangement. We were performers in each other's pieces, of course, but the idea was to combine our concert activities so that we had more possibilities to perform.

*I believe you and Gordon Mumma built your own electronic devices. Was that for financial reasons, or because you couldn't find what you wanted anywhere else at that time?*

That was the prehistoric era – there was nothing unless you made it yourself. Now, of course, things are totally different, but that change has only happened in the last couple of decades. Even fifteen years ago you couldn't buy electronic equipment that was portable. The so-called performance instruments, the Polymoog or the Fender Rhodes, you couldn't lift them.

*Are you still involved with electronics?*

I'm too old to be involved from the design point of view. I don't know why age has anything to do with it, but it seems to. I don't try to keep up with the catalogues and the grapevine, and you have to do that to be really involved. I was still designing when I went to California in 1969, and I designed the studios at the Mills College Center for Contemporary Music with Nick Bertoni, who was the engineer. But that was the end of my designing career – you stop because your eyesight starts to go. Of course, everyone uses electronic instruments now, but the idea of designing has really changed. Electronics circuit design has mainly gone back to engineering studios because the tools for designing are expensive and specialized.

*Do you think it's a disadvantage for musicians that they are less involved in designing the equipment that they use these days?*

Well, it's a trade-off. There is still a lot of unexplored sound territory, because most electronic instruments are made to satisfy some sort of consumer profile – an important part of which is that you don't want to scare anybody – and so commercially-available instruments all do more or less the same thing. If you're in a situation where you have to design the materials for the sounds you use – whether you are designing electronics or computer programmes or whatever – it makes your sounds more original, more unique. But it takes you longer to do it.

*More recently you've been working with recorded media – records, film and so on . . .*

For the last fifteen years I've been working on the idea of opera-for-television and I've finished production on two of these. One is called *Music with Roots in the Aether*; there are seven two-hour programmes, the main 'characters' are composers (David Behrman, Philip Glass, Alvin Lucier, Gordon Mumma, Pauline Oliveros, Terry Riley and myself), and the dramatic materials are the musicians and musical performances. It is a very 'avant-garde' opera form. And it came out very well. It has been shown in closed-circuit to many thousands of people, and recently it has started to be shown on television in the US. The other project is *Perfect Lives*, an opera in seven half-hour programmes that I produced with The Kitchen Center in New York in collaboration with Channel Four in Great Britain. It is the middle part (or middle group) of a trilogy of 'serial' operas for TV that will have a total duration of fourteen hours. I picked the middle group to begin with because it was the easiest to produce. The first part of the trilogy is a group of three programmes of ninety minutes each called *Atalanta (Acts of God)*. We have been performing these pieces on stage for about five years and now I'm trying to get them produced for television. The last part of the trilogy is a set of four operas of ninety minutes each called *Now Eleanor's Idea*. I've begun working on this group by producing audio recordings for commercial release before we take them to the stage (and before the television production), because of the complicated technical requirements of the productions. The trilogy is – this is preposterous to say – a kind of history of the consciousness Americans have of their 'origins' – something Americans think about a lot. The trilogy is a travelogue across the USA from the east coast to the west coast, and it's also a sort of historical travelogue from the time when Europeans first arrived until the future, when they all get to LA and just disappear.

*The telling of stories seems to be an important part of your work.*

I think that's what everybody's trying to do right now. I've always done it. We do it because we are interested in our 'origins'.

*That couldn't have been very fashionable in the 1950s . . .*

I'm afraid that I have not been very fashionable until the last few years. I'm glad everybody's starting to see it my way. Now everybody's telling stories, so that's great. If I tell better stories, it's because I've been at it longer.

*Where do you get the material for your stories?*

I use things that have happened to me and seem important because I haven't been able to forget them. I have a problem in that I think that what has happened to me is the only thing I can really understand. *Perfect Lives*, for instance, is mostly a collection of things people said to me or ideas I got specifically from things that were said in my presence. As many as possible of those sayings are verbatim in the text. It is a collection of dozens of short portraits of real people, all of whom are more or less 'impersonated' by the characters in the plot. The plot is a ficticious interpretation of a real event that I use to demonstrate a love story. The interpretation of the event is otherwise both sublime and corny. Everything in the plot happens in the period of a few days. That same interpretation of the real historical event is the basis for 'co-ordinating' what happens in *Atalanta (Acts of God)* and in *Now Eleanor's Idea*.

*Do you put yourself in any of your stories?*

Yes, but in spite of what I just said, autobiography is a different idea, and I can't do that. It's like trying to make sense out of your life. My life doesn't make any sense to me, so there's no point in trying to make sense of it for anybody else!

*Does your work with recorded media (TV and film) require a different approach to your work with ONCE and the indeterminate instrumental pieces?*

Well, the ONCE Group was a wonderful thing to do. The situation for composers here is probably no harder than in any place else, but it's hard for a different reason. In the US there is virtually no connection between composers and the Establishment. The Establishment would like to pretend there is, for whatever reasons, but it's not true. (I mean the Establishment in the sense of who's got the money to carry out big ideas.) When you're young, you think the reason everything is so hard is because of your age. But you get older and nothing changes. It's as if there are two cultures going on in parallel. Things may be a little better now than thirty years ago, but not much. One problem with this arrangement is that the young composer doesn't actually know what he or she is destined to do until it's very late – in many cases too late. American composers fool around with every idea under the sun in the process of finding out who they are. So the element of luck is very big. I was definitely lucky. It wouldn't have been possible for me to develop what I am apparently good at without working through something like the ONCE Group. You don't have relationships with orchestras or opera companies or radio studios or publishers or whatever. There's none of that. It doesn't exist. You start your own band, just like in popular music. If you are lucky in that, as I was lucky in having the ONCE Group, the experience forms your ideas. The problem is that the scale of your ambitions (for the music) has to remain only as large as what you can do by yourself, and that's frustrating enough to make many composers just give up when their energy or their self-esteem runs out. So working with the ONCE Group was wonderful for me; what we did amazed everybody and it was famous around the world, but finally it had to stop. We were operating on exactly the same scale of ambitions as, say, Wagner, but we had no money and there was no money in sight. When you get to the point where what you are doing is just trying to give people an idea about what *might* happen, you have to stop out of respect for the music. It is a very serious moment.

After the ONCE Group broke up I didn't do anything for four or five years, except teach to make a living. Then I thought I could possibly find some sort of support making music for television. And indeed I got more money and support for *Music with Roots in the Aether*, which is cheap by TV standards, than I had ever got for a stage piece. So it's good for me to think in terms of television, even if I can't work as a composer of opera 'in television'. Nothing much has changed as regards my chances of having a work developed by a major opera company.

*Is the attraction of television for you mainly financial, or also to do with the nature of the medium – the ability to reach a wider audience?*

It's financial. But also it has to do with the style of producing the work. Television is a form of 'real time', like music.

*When working with film, are you making a piece for posterity or do you think in terms of a once-only broadcast?*

The reason I haven't worked with opera for motion-pictures is mainly a technical one – but that technical reason is why movies are what they are. Motion-picture production stops every minute or so and repeats what has just been done in order to 'improve' it. The idea of movies is that there is really only one version and your job is to find it. The best television is real time captured, like music. The subject matter of television exists whether or not the camera is there, which is not true of movies. But which is true of music. The way I work on developing a new piece is exactly the way it's always been done in music. And when the piece is 'finished', it's ready for the camera. By the time I got *Perfect Lives* on tape we had performed it hundreds of times. There were thousands of hours of history in the piece, so the recorded version is only one version of the opera. It's not meant to be *the* version. The idea is to be able to feel that quality in hearing and seeing the television broadcast.

*You once said that you view all your work as inherently theatrical. Is theatre a necessary element for all your music?*

I think it is now. In our situation, in the way music exists in America and probably all over the media world now, there is no 'given' language, a language you can use without feeling self-conscious. There are too many styles and too many complicated ideas that the composer has to acknowledge, if only to himself. You can't tell a story without thinking of how you are doing it. Everybody is totally conscious of technique. When you are in that situation as a composer, you automatically associate every musical thought with a reason, and that reason makes the music theatrical. You can't help it. You can imagine a naïve approach to music in a culture where there is a uniform musical language. The stories you tell in that language, or the constructions you make, are ideas independent of the need to make a new language. This is probably a fiction in itself, but if for instance you live in a small town and you don't know that there is anything outside of that town, your work only has to do with where you are in the town, and where you are has a specific meaning. But today it doesn't matter much where you are in the town. You think of your work in terms of the whole world. You think, 'I'm going down to the grocery store in this little town on the sea-coast in England, and somewhere there is London and somewhere there is Paris and somewhere there is Beirut, where they are killing people right this minute.' So you're self-conscious. You are constructing your voyage to the grocery store in the context of South Africa, Israel, Russia.

*So you go to the deli in global terms?*

You go to the deli in a very complicated way, because you've got all this stuff going on. And that's the way you write music. You can't do it in any other way. You start to work and you think, 'They're killing people in Israel. What am I doing?'

*So your music is intended to be very self-reflective?*

You can't help it. There is no such thing as being innocent any more. Everything is theatrical. If it's not, you're a fool.

*Usually an audience just wants to be entertained, but you make them feel self-conscious. Do you think people view an Ashley concert as some kind of 'therapy'?*

Well, I don't know. I don't think my music is much different in the matter of self-consciousness from most other serious music. I have big audiences and they probably go to hear everything else they can. The question of what 'entertains' you is complicated. I mean, I don't know why anybody goes to anything. I know the reason I go, but I don't know about anybody else. I am perfectly happy listening to music even though I'm self-conscious. In fact, I think that's supposed to be the idea. Why else would we need music? When I go to a concert I don't forget about South Africa. I am listening to the music and thinking about that at the same time. In some way I am 'comparing' the musical experience to the thought. It's the civilized thing to do.

*So you've never regarded art as a kind of drug?*

No.

*Yet many composers would like their music to alter peoples' consciousness so that they lose themselves in the music and forget all external preoccupations.*

I don't think that's possible. It's not possible for me.

*You have a number of Cage's books on your shelves. How much of an influence has he been on you?*

John was an influence on everybody. He was one of the few people who tried to write about how you do it. Everybody has read John Cage's writings.

# GLENN BRANCA

*b. Pennsylvania 1948*

As a musician and composer, Glenn Branca is self-taught. With a background in dramatic arts, he moved to New York in 1976 and formed the experimental rock bands *Theoretical Girls* and *The Static*. 1979 saw the first fruits of his interest in acoustic phenomena, sound fields and tuning systems with *Instrumental (For Six Guitars)*, closely followed by *Dissonance, The Spectacular Commodity* and *Lesson No. 1 (For Electric Guitar)*.

The Glenn Branca Ensemble was formed in 1980 and is best known as the platform for his radical, concert-length symphonies, described by one critic as 'the most intense music you'll ever hear'. He developed a compositional system based on the intervals of the harmonic series, and his ensemble largely uses instruments of his own invention, such as various mallet guitars, the harmonics guitar and the motorized harmonic keyboard.

The Glenn Branca experience is an explosive one which has sent critics worldwide scurrying for superlatives and which led one writer to suggest that, had the composer lived three hundred years earlier, he would have been hanged for witchcraft.

*How did you first become interested in using different types of tuning systems?*

Well, I was trying a lot of different ideas early on with a variety of instruments, tape techniques, metal, plastic, whatever I could find. So it made sense when I started working with the guitar that I would try something different with that as well. For instance, I was getting ideas for changing the tunings, as well as ideas for using steel, copper and brass wire instead of actual guitar strings. It was all part of the same thing – experimenting with different ideas involving instruments. The first thing I did came about because I wanted to have a tuning that didn't require the musicians to change strings. It was just an open tuning in octaves, and when I heard how incredible it sounded I started working with more tunings. I was also trying compositional ideas that were developing along with the tunings. I tried a few different things, and hit upon something that really worked for me – a 'field' of sound. You didn't really hear changes happening in an overt way, but the change was happening within the whole field. I was also beginning to hear what I thought of as acoustic phenomena inside the field. I was hearing things that I clearly hadn't written, and I wanted to bring these phenomena more into the foreground. I saw that when I was using very close harmonies, I was getting more phenomena – so I was trying tunings that would give me this type of sound, and compositional ideas that would bring me closer to it. That was the first development.

The next step was to begin altering the instruments completely. That led to an instrument I called a mallet-guitar, which is basically a dulcimer played with sticks. One change involved the addition of a third bridge, which made for a much warmer sound than you would normally get. I wanted to work with open strings because that sound also seemed to contribute to the sound that I was looking for. Also, with the mallet-guitar, I was able to have a much greater variety of open strings. With the guitar I can only have up to six open strings. With the mallet-guitar I was able to have each person playing the equivalent of three or four guitars, so I didn't need as many musicians.

Around that time I started working with my harmonic series tuning system, which is related to the work of La Monte Young. The harmonic series system just came out of general experimentation with tuning, and I decided to use it as a simple tuning system. I had no particular interest in the harmonic series itself, or in any kind of theoretical ideas about it – it was just going to be another experiment. But when I started working with it, I discovered a lot more going on than I would have thought. I found that I could derive compositional ideas from the system, that the system itself had a kind of logical structure, that it seemed to have almost a kind of intelligence behind it – it was amazing to me. That was around the time of *Symphony No 3*. For this system, which can have as many as sixty-four intervals to the octave, I again needed new instruments, and this led to the harpsichord instruments, which I really thought of as 'keyed guitars'. I thought of them as the next step from the guitar, except that in this case each musician had access to as many as nine, ten, eleven, twelve guitars on the length of the keyboard. I also used my middle bridge idea on the harpsichord, which again gave it a much warmer sound. I became completely involved with the harmonic series, and it got to the point where I almost forgot about the music. I got involved with mathematics, which is something I never thought would happen to me. I never realized that mathematics was really an area of philosophy. I found myself working with ideas involving the series that were far too difficult to attempt to realize in music. But I still wanted to think about these things and work with them.

*You've said that you see your pieces almost like pit-stops on the way to something, or realizations of an ongoing process . . .*

Well, what it really comes down to is the kind of music I want to hear. It seems like I never get it right, which means that I just have to try again. It's as simple as that. I'd say there are four or five kinds of piece that I want to hear, none of which I've successfully written yet. At some point you actually have to stop, do a piece and take your shot at it again. As I go along, the situation gets more complex. When you start bringing the harmonic series into the picture, its potential starts raising a whole new set of issues. But I seem to keep coming back to these same few ideas. I have to be careful – it can become obsessive. There is a point at which you can't bring your dreams down into the real world – it just isn't going to happen, and you have to start being realistic, or at least extremely patient.

*Can you pinpoint more specifically what it is you're searching for?*

Well, on the vaguest possible level, it's trying to make some kind of music that I've never heard before, or indeed that anyone's ever heard before. This is where it gets messy, because you start to get into psychological things. It may not be physically possible for us even to hear this kind of music, because we have to filter everything back through what we've heard in the past. If we don't have a memory of something set into our system, how could we hear it? So that may not even be possible, but the next step is how to invent this kind of music. I've never heard it, so how can I sit down and write it? You have to try and write music that leaves a lot of room for something new to happen which you haven't written. Sometimes I set up a system, sometimes it's just a kind of process or structural idea. It's a way of determining a piece of music that will have a specific compositional content, but at the same time will have the potential to give you something you haven't written. I'm going for a field of sound, which I think of as a kind of non-linear music. But within this amorphous structure I try to create some kind of development, because something has to happen musically, even if it doesn't seem like it's happening, otherwise it is going to be just a lot of noise.

John Cage's music, for instance, becomes completely undifferentiated. Nothing ever happens, it's always the same thing – at least that's the way it sounds to me. It's not that I dislike John Cage, but some of his music is probably the most difficult to listen to I've ever heard. 'Boring' is the word normally used, I think. I'm not interested in writing boring music that is strictly theoretical. I have succeeded in doing that, but I prefer not to. I really want to find some way of dealing with this field compositionally. It's a hard process because if you put too much of yourself into it, too much composition, then you ruin it and it becomes just another piece of music again. And if you go too far on the other level, you just get a lot of noise that's completely undifferentiated and worthless.

*Didn't John Cage describe your work as fascist?*

He happened to see a piece of mine at a New Music America festival, and said that it sounded evil to him. He thought it was dangerous, and that if this music were to continue it could bring on the Apocalypse. I was in a complete state of shock. I have thought about it quite a lot since then, because it just doesn't make very much sense. I've always respected Cage; his writings are extremely interesting and, I think, important as far as twentieth-century music goes – it's just his music that I don't like. But I can't really say why he felt like that. He just freaked out!

*Why do you call these pieces 'symphonies'?*

Well, it seemed as though, as far as musical form goes, this was the one that described the kind of piece I wanted to make. I've never had much interest in titles anyway. To me, the title means nothing. So to call it a symphony was a nice way of avoiding that.

*How do you see your position within the experimental scene? Are your bridging the gap between experimental music and rock?*

Well, I'm certainly not bridging the gap between experimental and commercial music. I just want to do what I want to do, it's as simple as that. And there happens to be no place for that. People in the rock world think that my place is in the 'serious' music world, and the people over there think that I belong in the rock world – progressive or experimental rock, or whatever you want to call it. Neither of them really wants to have anything to do with me. Of course, this is an absurd generalization. I wouldn't exist if people weren't interested in my work – but if you're going to try to make music that no-one's ever heard before, how can you fit into anything? I remember in the mid-1970s, when I was thinking about where I would go with music, I realized that if someone got to a point where they didn't want to make conventional rock any more and wanted to do something a little more extreme – where did they go? In those days, a lot of people would work their way towards the jazz world. Unless you had gone through that whole system, you just couldn't enter the classical field. But if you didn't want to do straight rock and you didn't want to do jazz, what were you to do? Nowadays it seems obvious, but then it was not.

# HAROLD BUDD

*b. California 1936*

A principal figure in the Californian avant-garde of the 1960s, Harold Budd's earliest minimalist works – including *Cirio*, a 24-hour piece for solo gong – sought to explore the outer limits of perception and tolerance. As a teacher at the California Institute of the Arts from 1970–6, Budd influenced a generation of composers. After Lou Harrison, he is widely regarded as an originator of the Californian sound in new music; that is, a musical language based on prettiness and surface decoration.

In the early 1980s Budd began to use the recording studio as his primary compositional tool, and his seven albums from that decade include collaborations with Brian Eno (*The Pearl*) and The Cocteau Twins (*The Moon and the Melodies*). *By the Dawn's Early Light* (1991) and *Music for Three Pianos* (1992, co-written with Ruben Garcia and Daniel Lentz) signal a departure from studio-produced albums and a return to more formal modes of composition.

*Can you tell us something about your early compositional environment and how it shaped your work?*

I was raised in a family that wasn't particularly musical or artistic, save for my mother who played harmonium in Christmas carols, Protestant hymns and sentimental Victorian songs. They were my earliest memories of hearing anything that moved me in any way.

This is not at all astonishing, but I used to love to go to parades and listen to the Scots drummers as they marched in cadence. I thought that was an absolute thrill. But every kid loves that – I was just pole-axed by this wonderful, ritualized thing.

*How did you come to new music?*

Well, when I was a teenager I discovered be-bop. Me and my friends were such snobs that we wouldn't even acknowledge any other kind of music, especially the people who liked Elvis Presley or things like that. We were totally committed to Lennie Tristano, Charlie Parker and Thelonius Monk. I learned early on how to get interested in something that was, to say the least, highly abstract, and moving from there into new music wasn't much of a leap. It was just a matter of discovery, being told, being shown.

I didn't start my formal education until relatively late – I was 22 years old. I really started it because I didn't want to get a job. There's nothing unusual about that, since I'd worked for four or five years in maintainence jobs. I was looking for an escape, a way to break out of the role I was forced into. I had one good harmony and counterpoint teacher at my local city college who turned me on to everything – he wouldn't take no for an answer. I was encouraged. I also saw it as a way out of poverty. I thought that even if I couldn't make my living as a composer, I could certainly make my living doing something if I just stuck it out and got a degree.

Most of my friends were film-makers and painters, proto-architects, that sort of thing. That kind of world looked infinitely more glamorous to me than composing music for a symphony orchestra, for example. I very nearly wanted to be a painter – that looked like a really exciting life. But I wasn't quite the Bohemian. I wanted a more staid world.

*When did composing become a serious option for you?*

Right away. The minute I found out which direction the stems went, I started crudely putting things together and seeing what they would do. I had no skill as a musician, and still don't. I mean, I'm not an athlete, I can't play anything very well. So it was all imagination. I think being forced into an unorthodox method of doing things was a benefit in my case.

*Would your music necessarily be different if you were a musical athlete?*

I think I would take advantage of that kind of skill. But since it isn't a skill that I'm ever going to have, it doesn't pose a threat to me. If you could hear me play, you'd see there would be absolutely no threat.

*What sort of music did you compose initially?*

Well, in those first couple of years the free jazz movement started, and I thought that was going to turn everything around. I heard Don Cherry and those guys for the first time, and I was even a little bit embarrassed about being in school. But then I heard other aspects of the movement. For example, Paul Bley – a more, shall we say, intellectual approach to free jazz, more structured, more thought-through, more disciplined. That seemed enormously attractive to me, and I thought I could continue analysing Stravinsky and Milhaud without any conflict. But I was a complete babe in the woods – I didn't know anything. I knew a bit about the masters of twentieth-century music, and I also became very fond of minor masters like Delius, who I still hold in great reverence; I think he was a wonderful artist. And Americans of that same persuasion, like Hovhaness and Roy Harris. I still have a great fondness for that kind of music, and I picked it all up in my first two years of formal education.

*When did you start to shape your own musical voice?*

I went into the army for two years. Everything was put on the back burner for a long time, although it was a very good learning experience; I was in the army band and almost everyone there was a professional musician, whereas I was a complete novice. Once a week the band used to have a radio programme in Monterey, California, and I was the only one willing to conduct. That's when I seriously started to get skilful at score-reading because it wasn't very difficult music. So I got on well with a lot of these really good players, and learned a tremendous amount from them – what they could do and how they'd stretch their imaginations.

When I got out of the army I went to a local university here, largely because of the head of the music department, Gerald Strang, who had designed this school. I knew him from one album I had heard years earlier with the umbrella title of 'The California Percussion School': Harry Partch, John Cage, Lou Harrison, Henry Cowell, Gerald Strang. I thought this was exactly what I sought. Maybe I wouldn't have to listen to Brahms very much. The first semester I was there he brought John Cage in for a lecture with David Tudor. So I had the chance of actually seeing Cage, hearing what he had to say, hearing what he did, and all this coinciding with the publication of his first book, *Silence*; this was 1961. When I think of it now, I realize he was 'on the road' promoting this book. Isn't that funny? Instead of doing the TV talk shows with those dreadful people, Cage is going round universities! Anyway, this poor guy Dr Strang was fired for having brought in this person. I was so angry that I just gave up. I stayed on and got my degree as quickly as I could, without any commitment to the school, but that had sealed my fate in so far as new music was concerned. I wasn't going to be a Cageian all my life, but I could see that that influence, plus my interests in the visual arts – especially the more gestural artists – would form into something I would be responsible for. I was positive of it from that moment on.

*So out went the hopes for a sensible day job?*

Precisely.

*Can you describe the music you were writing at this stage?*

Experimental. Somebody had told me that Morton Feldman did graph pieces. I thought, 'No kidding? Where can you see these things?' The school I was at certainly didn't carry any Morton Feldman scores. I mean, they fired the guy that brought John Cage – they'd have a book-burning! So I thought, 'Well, hell, I'll do it myself.' So I made up my own graph and used coloured pencils. I gave it to this guy [Peter Hewitt] who first turned me on to Cage. He sat down and sight-read it at the piano, or at least a version that I thought was pretty good. I just thought, 'This is great, man! You don't have to write notes.' So I started at that time heavily influenced by Cage and Feldman.

*Was that very much an East Coast influence that spread across the country, or was there a 'West Coast-ness' to it even then?*

There was a 'West Coast-ness' to it because it was indigenous there, and then it moved away because there was no support for it. There was enormous support for Cage on the East Coast.

*How would you describe 'West Coast-ness'?*

I think it probably has something to do with the fact that people on the West Coast are a very long way from Europe. When Americans that live on the East Coast say 'colonial', they mean English colonial. But 'colonial' in the west means Spanish. I think its roots are there, plus the tremendous influence of people from Asia and the Asian philosophy. A kind of Bohemian, Zen thinking is typical of California, Oregon and Washington.

*Lou Harrison described 'West Coast-ness' as 'not being afraid to do something pretty'.*

Well, I can't say it better. I'm going to remember that and use it the next time I'm asked this question, and I'll try my best to cite my source. It's just perfect, absolutely correct.

*Are there any other particular features apart from being immediately pretty?*

Being immediately pretty is the most important component, probably so important that it overrides all other concerns of structure, environment and so on. Now, whether or not it's profound and deep are legitimate questions, but not ones that I choose to deal with because it seems pointless. If you've already made your point by being even superficially pretty, or by making highly-polished, well-finished little gems of something, that seems adequate to me. I'll have fulfilled my role and my promise to myself.

*You yourself are largely responsible for the way West Coast music has developed, in that many young composers here cite you as a major influence. Would you accept that?*

I can't. That's very flattering, but it's a double-edged sword. It's also my 'fault', you know; 'all that Harold Budd stuff'!

*How would you describe your music? Is it a branch of minimalism?*

Well, it does come from minimalism, there's no question of that – from that sensibility, but certainly not the kind that Steve Reich has been responsible for. I'm at the other end of the same family. But 'minimalism' was a word used to describe four composers a long time ago. To me, minimalism was an art term that I associated with West Coast painters. I likened my work to that world more than to the musical world. I had already known the painters at Los Angeles, the so-called 'Finish-Fetish' school of artists. I knew their work intimately, far better than Steve Reich's. In fact, I didn't hear Reich's music until Jon Gibson played some for me, and by that time I was already a fairly well-formed, mature composer. So I didn't hear much of the classic minimalists of the East Coast at all. Pauline Oliveros is the one that really got me interested in exploring all the ramifications of drone music. It didn't come from La Monte Young at all.

*How did you, and do you, relate to the European avant-garde?*

I was crucially aware of almost everything that was going on. I don't even have to mention the names. I found Stockhausen to be a particularly intriguing mind, whereas I didn't find Boulez an intriguing mind or language at all. It was kind of scattershot. I thought Luigi Nono's music was sublimely wonderful, and still do. He was a great composer. But, by and large, it seemed there was an awful lot of pressure from your professors to 'get with it'. I resented that a little bit. Cage was the solution here – it just threw the avant-garde totally out of sync, it just ruined it, which was the best thing that could have happened. Having said that, I still consider Cage and Feldman as the avant-garde, but they're not the kind that belong in school! It's a very different thing altogether. As for the ones that did belong in school, Boulez and whatnot, it was a point of honour to consider them the enemy. And I still do to a large extent.

*Does much of your inspiration still come from painting and painters?*

Yes, it does. I'm influenced by things I admire a lot. But it doesn't mean there's some philosophy or hidden 'vibe' that I'm trying to make a one-to-one relationship with – it's nothing remotely like that. Actually, I'm very jealous of painters because they can do their work and then it's done, it's there, they have a product you can actually touch. I really like that.

*Don't you also have that in your albums?*

I almost do have that. I used to be accused of laziness when I wouldn't write things out very well, or would just sketch something. Or if I got upset with the way things were going, I'd say, 'Well, never mind that. Can't you just sort of do this instead? I'll take care of it later.' I still like working that way, it works out best for me.

*Do you play live? Tour the album?*

Sure, but many of my things are solo keyboard, and that makes for a very dry concert. When I have an audience that's just 'so-so', I often say to myself when I'm out there performing, 'This is absolutely the last time. Never am I going to put myself through this nonsense again.' But sometimes when I'm really with the audience or I just know they're 'there', I have a wonderful time. But that isn't my strong suit. As a performer, I am the first one to admit that I am there just to meet those people. I'm really curious about who it is that likes what this is. I really want to know, because we must share something fundamental. But I'm not there selling a product or putting on a show the same way that a really skilled musician could. I make no bones about that, and I happily tell everyone beforehand that this is not going to be your usual concert!

*Can you tell us how you make your pieces?*

No, I can't, because it's a complete mystery to me. I try to be as prepared as possible, simply because it costs so much to work in a studio. In the last album I did I pretty much had the concept together, as it's the first time in ages that I actually worked with an ensemble. I couldn't very well expect these nice people who were doing their best to make it all happen just to 'wing it'. I owed them more than that; I owed the concept that I came up with, rather than just messing around in the studio. So there's very little, if any 'studio technique' – you know the usual tricks. It's acoustic music. It goes directly through microphones. You can hear the traffic outside, the bus pull up, the motorcycle pull away. If you listen really carefully, it's all there. But we all decided to keep the spirit of the thing. When it was a good performance, it didn't make any difference that there were slight ambient interruptions. I always think that way anyway, but sometimes the musicians are a little picky about it, or you get an engineer who's not as interested in music as he is in engineering. And you have these continual waits while some really fractional problem is solved, when all this time you could be getting right to the heart of the thing, and then everyone's going to forgive you – except audiophile maniacs, and they're not interesting people anyway.

I'm putting out a CD of old out-takes. I call it the *Orange Ranch Archives*. These were all done in a shed on an orange ranch in Fillmore, California, from 1981 to 1983 – my friend Gene Bowen lived there. The recording quality is low-tech, they're real garage recordings, but there is something there that is absolutely magical. I don't think we could have gotten some of these sketches down if we had ever thought that this was the final product, or that everyone was going to hear this some day. We're just 'winging it', trying things out, and I couldn't be more thrilled.

*I would have expected you to be hyper-critical about detail in the products that you make, especially in the age of the CD, but it's refreshing to see that you're not.*

Good! Absolutely.

*What sort of equipment do you use?*

I work very much in the way an assemblage artist works. I treat what's in the studio like a found object. I think on the last album I used an Indian tom-tom that was hanging around. There was one of those real inexpensive autoharps that teachers use to stroke the harmonies when the children are singing. This studio had an electric autoharp, and if you press the button where it says C sharp minor a chord comes out. They cost $40 and they're made to help grammar-school teachers have the children do their sing-a-long during the day. I used it all the time. It's just a great sound. It's hidden in there but it's there.

*Do you process those sounds?*

No. I have done all the process bit – everyone does – but it's almost a cliché. I look back on some things and think, 'Thank God it says when this album was made, so people can see it was at least a decade before everyone else'.

*You say you can't reveal the mystery of how you actually make your music – but what do you go to the studio with? A piano idea or . . .*

When I did the *White Arcades* album, I went to the studio with a list of titles and that's all. I was talking to some friends in England [The Cocteau Twins] and they told me about this really wonderful, laid-back studio in Edinburgh, Scotland. They came in and said, 'Well, we've booked you two weeks in the studio starting next Monday. You're going to love it'. They described the dinners that are made there, how great it is at tea-time, only one pub in the village. So I went up there and, sure enough, these people were the salt of the earth.

My philosophy is that, if you are with wonderful people who like what you do and know what you do, and you still can't make an album under those circumstances, then you're certainly in the wrong profession. And you use whatever's necessary – it's always a discovery.

I started out on one thing recording a sort of piano loop. It sounds like a loop but in fact it isn't, it's just straight-ahead piano. But since I can't play the piano very well, I had to back up and play the second bit on another channel along with it. Well, in the process of doing that, I discovered that just by knocking out a certain portion of it, I came up with a pattern that was really interesting and which I could never have dreamed up myself or written down.

*Your titles are extremely evocative. Do they come first?*

Very frequently. I carry them around like baggage sometimes. I often can't wait to find a piece so I can get rid of this title that's been haunting me for so long.

*Can't you offload the title until you find the right piece?*

No, it's just got to work.

*And you just know which is the right one?*

Yes.

*What do you get from collaborating?*

I do it because I want to see what happens and I like the work of the person I'm collaborating with. The idea is to come up with something that neither side would have come up with on their own. I've never worked with musicians who know how to read music. That's always swell for me, because it means I'm locked into people who have a hell of a lot of experience of being open-minded about the art world generally. I like audiences like that and I like people like that.

*How did the Cocteau Twins collaboration come about?*

That came about in a kind of a circle. They were going to cover one of the pieces that Brian [Eno] and I did ages ago. Simon [Raymonde] called me up, wanting some helpful hints on the piano part, and I assured him there was absolutely nothing to it. All he had to do was go into the studio and do it his own way, and that would be perfectly OK. Then suddenly Robin [Guthrie] called and asked if I had any free time, and whether I'd like to come over and see if we could do something together. That's exactly how it was. I was a little bit – I won't say hesitant – but I didn't quite know what was going to happen because I didn't know their music very well. I subsequently did; I went and got a mixture of their things, and I liked it a lot. Of course the first thing you hear is Elizabeth's voice, but I didn't know exactly what I was going to do. And I guess the end result, for me, is a little bit problematic. But so what? There it is. No-one's fainted or lost their job because of it. It has some nice things, and it has some things that are very puzzling. But trying to do art without risk doesn't seem worth the time.

*It seems that you've always had a foot in both camps – popular music and art music. Is that true? Did it just happen that way?*

Yes, it did just happen that way. But I think that, in fact, I'm not in pop music very much at all. I'm only there as a kind of voyeur. I take advantage of that occasionally, but I don't belong there very comfortably. But this is my own opinion. I'm not responsible for what anyone else's opinion is . . . fortunately! But that's the drawback of making records – it's not yours any more. People will tell you what you are, and you have to accept it and say, 'Well, all right!'

*You're also unusual for an art composer in that you're writing for a relatively large audience. Through your albums you reach a much larger audience than most.*

I like finding out who those people are. I've been working with Bill Nelson, for example. He is typical of most intelligent artists (in his case he's a musician) in that you can carry on an extremely informed discussion about all facets of art music, art itself, sculpture, literature, arcane literature and pop literature. Since I fancy myself as one of those people who is attracted to large varieties of serious art work – it doesn't make any difference what camp it comes from – I gravitate towards and work best with people who have like interests. That makes for a sure-fire combination that often enough pays off somehow; I don't mean in a commercial way, but in an aesthetically satisfying way.

# JOHN CAGE

*b. Los Angeles 1912*

After early studies with Cowell and Schoenberg, John Cage embarked on a long and varied career based on continual questioning of all musical, social and philosophical assumptions. The son of an inventor, his pioneering work with live electronics, the prepared piano, indeterminacy is well documented. Inspired by the tenets of Zen Buddhism, he aimed to free sound from its use as communication, to free the composer from his 'self', music from all notions of theory and history, and the mind from all intellectual limitations.

Whilst in later life he came to be regarded as the elder statesman of the avant-garde, he never lost his childlike alertness, questioning and openness. As early as 1974 he felt that 'strictly musical questions [were] no longer serious questions'. Of course he never abandoned music; it was his way of reintroducing us 'to the very life we're living'. This integration of art and life, which developed from an earlier discovery of the unity of sound and silence, led to wider concerns for him, not least the matching of human needs and resources.

Finally, it is interesting to note that there are very few interviewees in this collection who, for all their diversity, do not express some debt to Cage as a liberating influence. He died suddenly in New York in 1992.

*You've held many positions at various universities, most recently a post at Harvard held by Buckminster Fuller in 1962, the Charles Elliot Norton Professor of Poetry. You once said that universities were on the side of government, so I wondered how and why you sometimes work in that environment?*

Well, my position has always been somewhat aside from the institution itself. I once asked David Tudor how he thought I should behave in going to universities, and he said, 'As a hit-and-run driver.'

*Do you feel your string of university posts has lent your work increased 'credibility' and helped you to be taken more seriously in certain circles?*

I'm afraid I don't think of whether I'm being taken seriously or not. I take myself seriously and I do as well as I can, and if other people do or don't take me seriously that's their business, their action, rather than mine. I always had opposition from the beginning, so I'm used to it. I noticed that opposition of people to ideas and actions when I was a child, with my father's experience as an inventor.

*How have you managed to cope with the amount of opposition that you've experienced?*

Well, you can measure, if you wish, or get a kind of description of what you're doing, by the reactions of other people. If there isn't opposition, I have the feeling that I'm not going in a radical enough direction. Not that I want to shock or offend people, but it's very good, it's like a thermometer.

*You must have had some high readings! Some people think that you don't 'suffer' enough for your art, that you enjoy it too much.*

Well, there are two ways of looking at the work of an artist. I think that most music is thought of as some form of talking or some form of communication, or if you wish, the expression of ideas and feelings. The path of my work has been more and more *not* to do that. Instead of saying something, I'm *doing* something, and I'm doing it so that the sounds, if there's any talking or speaking, are doing it themselves. I'm doing less and less. In my recent work it seems almost absurd that I should even be involved, but then I see that if I weren't involved, it wouldn't be done.

*Is there a danger, though, that you've come to be known as the famous composer who circumvented his ego?*

Well, that wouldn't be a danger. I don't think it's a circumvention but an opening. Sometimes in Christian talk the word 'conversion' is used, but that means 'a turning around' – I don't think that is the case. I'm thinking more of the image that Suzuki gave, of letting the things that are not you flow through you so that there's no real 'turning'. Or you could put it another way: one could go in any direction.

*Do you feel that your ideas are now being confirmed by contemporary science? Is there a sense of gratification that you, who championed process all along, were 'right'?*

One of the books that most influenced me at the beginning was *The Huang Po Doctrine of Universal Mind*, published in London by The Buddhist Society. In the introduction there was a defence of Buddhism on the grounds of modern physics. That gave me, I wouldn't say 'gratification', but a sense of corroboration. Once in the early 1950s when I was working with the *I Ching*, my door opened and it was an old friend from California. She had married a physicist who was working on Long Island, and she asked me what I was doing. When I told her, she said that was what her husband was doing!

*Many of your works have been categorized as 'happenings' – a term coined by Allan Kaprow from his work* 18 Happenings in 6 Parts (*of which you have expressed disapproval because of its intention and police-like situation in compelling one to move from one room to the next). Do you regard your works as 'happenings'?*

Sometimes. When they're theatrical. But I would try to fix it so that people were free in space, both those who were performing and those who were attending. I had a similar experience to the Kaprow one recently when I went to Russia. I ran into a group called Pop Mechanics. They're artists and musicians and I haven't seen one of their performances, but I'm told that they can be very large and very interesting, that they involve, say, one hundred and fifty people. They begin by making a few sounds, then start to build a structure in the space and all kinds of things happen, so that it's an active use of 'happening'. When I visited them, they wanted me to engage in what you might call a 'Chamber Music Happening' in the studio. They said that we could have some 'wet' music and they wanted me to perform it. I said at first that I wanted to be a listener, but they insisted that I performed. Then they proceeded to tell me what to do: 'Now pour from this to that' and so on. I tried to tell them all along that what I wanted was a 'happening' in which people didn't tell each other what to do, but they had been so affected by their bureaucracy and government that the only way they could conceive of was to continue that sort of thing independently. I don't think they know or even imagine a world in which people don't tell other people what to do.

Four of them had come to the concert where my music was played and said they wanted to talk to me. It turned out that they felt my work, and all the work they had heard that morning, was academic. They wanted something less academic. What they were hearing was my recent work *Music For* —, which has no conductor. They apparently didn't notice there was no conductor. The mere fact that there were pitches, instead of just noises, made them think it was academic. In other words, they were at the point of cutting off a great deal that can be sensed through the ears, simply because it has something to do with another body of material. I'm working nowadays, as you probably know, more and more with conventional sound sources like voice, violin and piano.

*Why is that?*

It seems to me that it's useful to show that the old, conventional sources are still capable of action.

*Do you feel that in some cases your ideas have been interpreted too simplistically, say to the exclusion of conventional instruments?*

Well, we don't really know what, if any, effect our work has on others. We get that instruction from the game where you whisper in somebody's ear . . .

*. . . Chinese Whispers.*

. . . and so I don't really trust the fact. Someone said recently that I have no influence whatsoever, which I don't think is true either. I think we all influence one another a great deal. I tried to show that in my text called *Themes and Variations*, where I just started with fifteen people, but I could have gone to sixty – any number of people who've influenced me.

*Such movements as Dada, Futurism, Surrealism and the theories of Artaud can be seen as precursors of many of your ideas. Could you say to what extent these influenced you?*

The most was Artaud, through his book *The Theatre and its Double*. The idea I had from reading his book was that all the elements of theatre can be viewed independently one from the other, with none being subordinate to a narrative thread that goes through everything. I went to a performance recently that involved dancing, music and moving pictures. The unfortunate thing was that there was a narrative that continued through the whole thing, making it all make, so to speak, sense, making it understandable, whereas everything else was not doing that. My feeling was that it was spoilt. I really think it's important to be in a situation, both in art and in life, where you don't understand what's going on.

*To be bewildered . . .*

Yes, where you are bewildered. I think it's absolutely essential. I think this is the nature of the koan. If you're not in such a situation, you find yourself dealing, so to speak, with dust for which you have no use.

*New York can certainly be bewildering . . .*

Yes, it's an amazing city. Many of us love it, but it can be shocking too and very threatening. Jasper Johns says he always feels it can't last ten more minutes this way. But it does. I have a friend who's living in a house where the people are otherwise black and where, in the hallways, cocaine and other drugs are given in exchange for money. The whole neighbourhood is full of it. But that's part of this war that's going on. The people who have nothing have to have something to make life bearable. I've never taken drugs other than tea and alcohol – I've given up smoking and sometimes I give up drinking alcohol. These could be on a par with the others. I was told that the effect of cocaine is to make one feel that one's walking off the ground, that one is elevated. And you can see, if someone's terribly poor and doesn't know how he's going to pay the rent and so forth, that it would be an advantage to have a little cocaine to take your mind off the problems.

*That sounds like Zen, where 'men are once again men but their feet are a little way off the ground'.*

Yes. I don't think we can blame anyone for the things they do.

*How do you view the work of composers who continue the Western classical tradition?*

I would group most music as talking, saying something, and I for one am not interested in being spoken to by music. I'm not even really willing to be spoken to with words. I want also to be bewildered by words. I still enjoy Joyce and I enjoy non-sense in general, and I don't like clear messages – they're too intentional. The moment you enter the world of non-sense, you don't know what's being said and so you're free to hear whatever you wish.

*And to structure it for yourself?*

Yes, or structure yourself differently in relation to it. I don't see any need for theory or laws or government in music or in life. I think we can perfectly well get along with intelligence, in the use of materials and in social relations. By 'intelligence' I mean recognizing the problems and solving them. The problems seem to be such things as having something to eat, some place to live, air to breathe – all of these things, the utilities.

*How do you view the presentation of electronic music? You once said that it wasn't enough just to turn out the lights – so do you feel that there should be some live element in electronic music in order to give a sense of theatre?*

I think so. In so far as we can make things theatrical, I think we should. Which is to say that we should involve seeing. If you go to the Museum of Modern Art and walk slowly through the gallery on the second floor, you come to the Duchamp room. You soon realize that you've come to something that is not like what preceded it. It's entirely different, and that difference changes our way of seeing, so that the things in the room that are not art have become as aesthetically interesting as the artwork.

*You once said, 'If you want to write music, go study Duchamp.' Yet there appears to be a large contradiction in your ideas. Duchamp said that he wanted to put painting once again at the service of the mind, whereas you say we should hear a sound suddenly, before our thinking has got in the way of it.*

Yes, I know. They seem almost to be saying the opposite. Morton Feldman was aware of this contradiction and he said that I had nothing to do with Duchamp. Very often people think that the arts are doing the same thing, but I think that music is doing one thing and painting is doing something else. What was being done in music had to take a different shape to what it was in painting. You can see that the background of painting was, say, a field with a horse. It wasn't a fugue. Whereas the background of music is a fugue. So what had to be done in music was to get the ears to work, and what had to be done in painting was to get the mind to work.

*There was a great deal of cross-fertilization in the arts in New York during the 1950s. What were the musicians learning from the painters and poets?*

Well, so much had happened in modern painting since the early part of the century.

*Did you learn more from painters than musicians?*

Well, I studied with musicians. But musicians continually refused to accept what I was doing as music. As late as 1941 or 1942 I applied for a job as a musician to the WPA [Works Project Administration]. It was an arm of the government that gave artists jobs for doing their work, and didn't tell them what to do. So I applied to the Music Branch in San Francisco, and they said, 'But you're not a musician'. I said, 'But I work with sound, where should I go?' and they said, 'Try the Recreation Department', which I did.

*You've always placed great emphasis on making music socially useful. Is it possible to do this without making a point, without 'saying something', as perhaps Cardew did?*

Well, he was not averse to politics. Whereas I am opposed to politics. So I have to find some way to do it without telling people.

*So how might you convince the man in the street to drop hierarchical forms and thought patterns?*

The man in the street is not apt to need music, let alone modern music.

*Can't music help him?*

I don't know. I think that he has to find out whether he needs it. Don't you think so?

*Do you think that anyone really needs music?*

I need it. I always have loved sound, and I continue to love it.

*But then, as there's sound all around us, why bother to make music?*

Well, why not? You know that there are many answers to that, but I think one could say 'why not?' to the question 'why?'.

*Can you tell us about some of your recent work and ideas?*

I find I have perhaps two ideas. One is multiplicity and the other . . . I guess the best word is 'non-intention'. I keep this image of traffic sound and environmental sound in mind, and I want my work to have the same purposelessness and – I was about to say constant and unpredictable change, but lately I've been getting interested in constant sounds, such as this hum from the fan on the one hand and the humidifier on the other. I like both sounds, the unpredictable one and the constant one. I'm really in a very pleasant situation. I haven't yet heard anything that I don't enjoy, except when it's full of intention and is directed in a way to hurt someone.

*You have been careful in your work to avoid the creation of fixed objects . . .*

Yes. A wall, for example, receives so many things, like dust and shadows and so on. Or look at this movement of air, what it's doing to the plants. In other words, anything that produces change will be useful. So what you want is something that will introduce change in what affects the seeing, and something that would affect the hearing wouldn't be bad either. I've always been attracted to having something very slightly disturbing coming from another room.

*I believe you keep even your earliest serial works. Are you conscious of a development?*

I'm not sure that it's a development, but it's a wandering or an adventure, a series of changes. I felt obliged to keep those changes, in so far as I can, 'studyable' or noticeable.

*Is that for us or for you?*

For other people. It would be better for me, for my reputation, to get rid of some of the bad works!

*I believe there's a story in Walden where Thoreau tells of some Indians who, every fifty-two years, have ritual burnings of the contents of their homes as a means of purification to rid themselves of their past accumulations.*

That would be nice. I don't do that. I'm a funny kind of keeper – I don't want them myself but I want to keep things. I think they can be used. I met a historian who told me that the ephemera, the things that come to us in the mail that we generally throw away, the advertisements and so on, describe a period in history better than anything else. So I save every little bit that comes to me and send it off to the universities.

*Could you tell us something about your use of the* I Ching?

Well, my use of it is to open . . . to free me from likes and dislikes. You know that image that Suzuki gave me?

*Absolute, Ego and Relative?*

Yes. So you see, I was looking for something to open my mind. And I've never felt that it didn't work, and I've never felt that it was working poorly.

*Do you ever use it as an oracle?*

Sometimes. Quite rarely. I began going to an astrologer about twelve years ago. I went to her first because I was becoming so well-known and didn't quite know how to behave in the circumstances. She made my horoscope and said, 'Well, it's going to get worse, so you'd just better adapt yourself to it'.

*Can we talk about your changing relationship with Zen? You've said that no one can naïvely believe in Zen in the twentieth century, or take it too seriously. Feldman said that you talked less and less about Zen until eventually you only gave it an affectionate pat on the shoulder. Do you like to mention the word now? Is it still relevant to you?*

Oh, I love Suzuki as much as ever. What I like about Zen – and maybe I misinterpret it – is its humour, its good nature and its practicality, its recognition of how things are and its uncompromising character, its willingness to go to extremes. It's also very dry and unemotional, but full of humour. I think the drawings associated with Zen are very striking when you go to the Museum of Oriental Art – *Man Laughing at the Moon* or something like that.

*I recently saw an article by Suzuki in which he linked Basho and Thoreau . . .*

Yes. I think this is the great difference between Thoreau and Emerson. Emerson thought that Thoreau's ideas were his ideas, and that Thoreau simply gave them a better 'dress' (he used that word). Whereas Thoreau felt that his roots were in the Orient, that Emerson's roots were in Greece, and that there's a great difference. Emerson finally recognizes that. It may be this thing about 'practicality', knowing how things are, that makes Thoreau give an instance of something, so that there's an immediate illustration, whereas Emerson would stay in the world of generalities. He knew this, and he knew that his work was without excitement, at least in comparison to Thoreau's.

*Zen is often criticized for being apolitical in its acceptance of the way things are. It seems that this attitude can be easily abused. Let's take starvation as an example. According to Zen, is that just an unhappy situation that we have to accept, or should we do something about it?*

Oh, I think we should do something about it. But we should be careful to do something that works rather than something that doesn't work. I don't think we should do something about it in order to be good. I don't think that by changing the nature of my music I would be doing the right thing to help starvation in some part of the world. If we could get a situation that was not political, but was, as I keep saying, *intelligent*, then the problems could be solved no matter what they were, whether they were starvation or drug addiction as they are here, where we're all in danger of being mugged in our own homes. But we're in the midst of a war between the rich and the poor. In Russia they have other problems. They don't have any mugging as far as I can tell, because everybody has almost nothing, but they don't have anything they know they might have if they were out of Russia. They know that the problem is not with people but with governments. No matter which government, they're all wrong because they're unintelligent. They're thinking of different ways of amusing us rather than helping us.

*You've said many times that practicality is of the essence, knowing how things are and accepting that in one's work and plans.*

That's true. I had some students at one time and one of the first things I taught was that you shouldn't do something that wasn't going to be performed. Or, if you wanted to do it, you should take the consequences and not be glum over the fact that it wasn't being performed.

*Do you think perhaps that a work is never completed until it is performed?*

Right. I would say so, but at the same time I would like to say that they have nothing to do with one another. That they are really different things.

*Are you still working as much as you always have done?*

I'm incredibly active. I don't know why I do so much, and sometimes (I'm in such a period right now) I don't seem to be doing anything, so I turn to my correspondence and try to get rid of it. But there's always a lot to do, there's always the plants to water and cooking to be done. My astrologer says that, now things are getting really complicated for me, I must use cooking and taking care of the plants to remain unaffected and undisturbed by the complexity.

*Every few years you seem to be asked for your Top Ten book list, so I feel a responsibility to ask you for an update.*

Well, you ask me that at a time when I'm so to speak changing or leaving the doors open to change about what the books would be. That's why I've been reading Emerson lately. But I'm not convinced I'm going to take Emerson to heart. That's my present problem, discovering whether or not Emerson is involved. I've also been reading Wittgenstein without understanding it, and enjoying it. I find it very mysterious and elating. If you put me in a corner and have me read Wittgenstein to myself, not understanding it, when you get me out of the corner four hours later you'll see that I'm quite light-headed.

*Another kind of drug?*

I think so. Don't you think that art in general is a kind of drug? Have you noticed that when you are sitting at a concert, say, and then go outdoors, the sounds seem to be outside too? In other words, you've been led to listen in a particular way to whatever you hear.

*It's difficult to say 'That piece changed my life' without sounding sickly . . .*

But if you say 'changed the way I hear', it might not be so.

*Do you still read the books that were important to you earlier, like Coomaraswamy?*

I haven't read Coomaraswamy for ages, but I would read *The Huang Po Doctrine* and I'm very fond of *Not This, Not That* by L. C. Beckett – it's almost my biography. It's a very beautiful book. It starts off with the remark of Christ on the cross, 'Why hast thou forsaken me?', and attempts to answer it by saying that, at that point, Jesus was at the point of nothingness from which all things come. Then he answers that question in many different ways, making the point that the universe didn't start at any time, neither will it stop, but is continually being born and being destroyed at every moment. Isn't that marvellous? Don't you think that theoretical physics is coming more and more to that point of view?

*Yes, it all seems to be coming together, theoretical physics, Oriental philosophy and your ideas . . . are you suspicious that it's all beginning to make sense?*

I don't think so. Most of science has been to show that things are organized, but a group of scientists have begun thinking, as Buddhists do, that everything causes everything else – it's called the Butterfly Effect. Apparently some butterfly in China waves its wings and causes something else, and they're now studying chaos in that sense, which is another way of saying the interrelationship or . . . finally knowing you can't just think of one thing and . . . come out with the good.

# PHILIP CORNER

*b. New York 1933*

A major figure in New York's experimental music scene, Philip Corner studied at Columbia University with Luening and Cowell and attended Messiaen's classes at the Paris Conservatoire. Whilst serving in Korea with the United States Army he became interested in oriental calligraphy, music and thought, which have had a profound influence on his work.

Often minimalist in the extreme, his output includes a series of pieces entitled *One Note Once*, in which he aims to convey an entire compositional statement in a single moment of sound, and *Elementals*, an indeterminate work calling for unvaried repetition of any sound, at any tempo, for any duration. A 1977 performance of the latter lasted for 123 hours and involved the C sharp above middle C played at a tempo of 60 notes per minute by a team of singers, pianists, guitarists and wind players.

An early member of the Fluxus group and the Judson Dance Theater, Corner has also been involved with the American gamelan Son of Lion for many years and has taught at Rutgers University since 1972.

*You studied at the Paris Conservatoire. What do you feel you gained from that experience?*

Well, in the first place I discovered Messiaen. His music really turned me on, and that was at a time when he was by no means as famous or well thought-of as he is now. So studying with him was an excuse to study all of his music. I think he was one of the greatest composers ever. Take this question of so-called 'minimalism', for instance. I really hate anything to do with 'isms' or self-conscious ideology, but I guess the word does mean something in terms of a movement towards simplicity and repetition. Since people call *me* a minimalist, I've got to defend myself in a way. But when I'm asked where I got it from, I always mention Messiaen. You can see him as a minimalist in spite of this tremendous richness, complexity and lushness. There's still that sense of repetition, timelessness, non-developmental aspects, a long sense of patience and time. To me, that's the essence of minimalism, and I certainly got that from him.

*As an experimental composer, how would you characterize your relationship to the Western classical tradition?*

Well, firstly there's the whole question of what's experimental. I don't know exactly what the definition is.

*Let's take Cage's definition . . .*

. . . where you don't know the results of your action? Well, I mean, Cage was great – but some of the things he said! There's also Varèse, who said that he did his experimentation in the laboratory and by the time it came out it was a success. I think what they both have in common is their confrontation with the unknown. I wouldn't like to think of it as progress. In a strange sense, this whole linear idea of progress, which I associate with twelve-tone thinking, is not 'experimental' (though a lot of my colleagues would disagree with me). I remember being shocked (I guess it was through the writings of Boulez that I first saw this attitude) that newness in the arts was supposed to be a kind of linear vector from the past, where you don't just search for the new or keep yourself open to possibilities – you've got to go in a straight line from what the past has done and make the next step. So you get locked into a competition between who can run the fastest in a predetermined direction. You already see where the great tradition of Western culture is supposed to go; who's the genius who will get there first? I detest that attitude. In both Cage and Varèse, whether the music was experimental before or during the concert, there is a sense of openness and unpredictability rather than a predetermined idea of where you're going to go. So, in that sense, I identify with that.

However, there's always a difference between what you do and what you say. I think many people have been misled by following what Cage said, or at least what they *thought* he said. He certainly didn't feel bound by it himself! I remember him saying with glee before a performance of one of his multi-orchestra pieces, 'You know, I don't know ahead of time what it's going to sound like.' But does that really mean he had no idea of what the music might sound like? From that point of view, it's obviously not true. But if you think about the most carefully written-out piece, or take a compulsively ordered mind like Boulez or any of the great classicists for example, did they know what it was going to sound like? Did they really comprehend fully the nature of the sound beforehand? I remember Cage said at a panel discussion that he never rewrote or revised. When asked why, he said, 'Because I know what I'm doing.' Now that seems somehow at odds with not knowing the results of your actions. Of course, you could say that he does know what he's doing, but that's not the same as knowing what the result of the action is going to be, but that's a little coy because you can't possibly know what you're doing without having *some* idea of what it's going to be like. He could well have said, 'I don't revise because I accept everything I get', but he didn't say that. It may be true that he would not tamper with his system, but if he didn't like the results, he'd change the system and do it over again. There's a strange dialectic between the two poles of unpredictability and of knowing what you're doing. Maybe they're not incompatible.

*You've mentioned Cage's system. What about your own use of chance techniques?*

Well, I remember saying to Cage in the early 1960s, with a certain amount of trepidation, 'You know, I realize that, with all my respect for you and all that I've learnt from you, I've never really done what you're doing. I've never used systematic chance.' He said, 'Well, maybe you didn't need to.' My way of using chance was a little bit more like action – throwing rice or peas down on a piece of paper and circling them. I would make some action-like gesture rather than throw dice and go through an intellectual procedure. Then I did a lot of indeterminacy; in a way that's different, because you can set up something which could be generated not by chance, and then you allow it to be indeterminate in performance. I always saw indeterminacy as an aspect of improvisation, and I wasn't ever willing to fix it in the kind of rigid way where you can't respond to each other.

In the same way, I never use a system in composing, because I feel that what the system does is to open up a set of possibilities which you then hear and comprehend. So once you comprehend the system, why do you need a system in order to generate it? You could say that, in a way, Cage either opened up these possibilities as something you could hear and understand, or else he just opened up your mind so that you could say you comprehended the system of possibilities. But I think you can do that mentally without necessarily casting dice. If you look at the way Cage worked, it was very much like the European people, even total serialism, which he seems to be a reaction against (this is not to minimize the very great differences) – but in both cases it's a system. Whatever the system is, it generates automatic results, and then you're bound by it. Somehow that seems to contradict the search for freedom that all these methods imply. I think that if you don't have individual choice to do what you want, then you don't really have freedom – even if doing what you want is in fact not freedom either, because it's limited consciousness. So you can get to a point where the possible results of something like chance which generates things you wouldn't ordinarily choose can infuse your mind and your understanding. Then you can accept them and be free to improvise on them.

I also think that in both composing and performing there's a certain irrationality which is beyond any kind of systematization (remember that even formulating chance is a form of system). From the compositional point of view, there's what used to be called 'inspiration', which opens up an infinite number of possibilities, always something that's surprising and unexpected and visionary. When I write, a very clear sense of what I want to do comes into my mind. In a sense, this is compatible with Cage's definition of what is 'experimental': there's a 'system' of possibilities, and there may be a hundred thousand different manifestations of it. And that image of the set of possibilities has always been so clear for me that I never felt it was necessary to throw dice or consult the *I Ching* for the formulation of the pieces.

*The influence of Eastern thought and music has also had an important impact on your work . . .*

Yes. The first thing that struck me was the quality of sound. I was in the army from 1959 to 1961 and was sent to Korea. I had already done some scores which had a small amount of graphic design, because my music, even from the late 1950s, was concerned with the quality of sound and evolution of timbre. When I went to Korea, I found that they went very far in that direction. Western notation is too primitive to deal with the kinds of sounds that are used in oriental music, but I wanted to use those sounds for my own music. So what came out of that was a whole series of calligraphic pieces where I used a brush or a pen very freely, always thinking about the way it would be translated into sound. A stroke of the pen would wobble and go from dark to soft, and that would suggest all the modulation and intonation and timbre.

After that, I started to make the graphic pieces. These are in a way an attempt to make a visual corollary of a sound, but I always do it with some indeterminacy. The most extreme one I did was for a Korean flutist, and was called *Sprouting*. I made these small lines and squiggles suggesting a very calligraphic, free type of movement, then I cut them up into little pieces. You would look at the forms as you threw them down on to a piece of paper. So there's the original action, then the action in the course of the performance, and finally the action by the performer of having to realize where it lands by chance. There is still a sense of being able to play around with the durations, stretch the time a little bit, and enter into it with a complete vision of the possibility, rather than being calculating and analysing it. So that was a way of combining all these elements I've been talking about and trying to be precise, yet suggestive of something that was open.

*Can we talk about your use of meditation as a means of increasing musical awareness and perception? It seems akin to the way that Pauline Oliveros uses it, as a means of involving listeners rather than as a personal way of focusing the self.*

This is in a way a continuation of the question you asked about the Orient, because I think that this whole increase in attention span is 'oriental'. Although many of the minimalists, particularly the famous ones, are doing things that seem like a return to traditional Western practices and seem to have little experimental or direct oriental influence, the very fact that there's a sense of focused consciousness on a repetitive thing that endures for a long time – even if it is a couple of Western triads in arpeggio – has ultimately to be traced to oriental influence. But I guess it's more conscious with me, because I've done it with the intent of expressing a kind of focused consciousness through the music.

I remember going to a meditation session – one of the many forms of spiritual self-help groups on eclectic orientalism that were going around – and it seemed to me there was a hell of a lot of talk for a meditation session. There was a discussion of 'transverbal consciousness' and raising consciousness, but it was just a lot of talk. They ended by singing *om* three times, and I remember thinking that this was where you could get beyond words and enter into this one note, this one syllable. This could be an avenue to the kind of consciousness they were talking about. That made me want to use 'musicianship' as something that would serve 'spirituality'. So I started two things. One was singing; not being a singer, this meant going into something where I had to renounce professional competence. Secondly, and by extension, I wanted to make music in a way that did not mean it could only be done 'professionally', on the basis of high skill.

These are discoveries of something that's more universal, and I've tried to keep that alive in my work. It's manifested itself through the years in different ways, but always going more and more into simplicity. The ultimate simplicity is of course just a single tone, just a totally unmodulated single tone. That opens up a lot of questions about patience, duration, interest, everything.

*Another important influence for you has been the gamelan orchestra. How have you approached writing for this medium?*

My scores for the gamelan are mostly written on graph paper, and they're all combinations of graphic and verbal descriptions of a process which then has to be realized in the same way. Some of the pieces are very minimalistic, very repetitive, some have a system, some are more irrational in that the evolution comes from intuition rather than the working-out of a system, and some of them actually bend all the way back to my early music – I did so many things that were repetitive, hypnotic, mystic, and had some kind of relationship to oriental music, even using some of the modes. Then, because of Lou Harrison, I was lured closer to direct imitation of Javanese music than I ever thought I would permit myself. But I saw it as studying Javanese music, and I thought maybe I could take something from this and enrich what I was doing.

I see my work going round in cycles, as if it's all aspects of the same thing. If there's any progress in my work, it has to do with broadening – possibilities I didn't see before are coming in and deepening it. So it just keeps spiralling and coming back, hopefully, on a higher cycle. But there's definitely a cyclical process and a sense of connection with my own past. Obviously there's also a connection with the whole of the past, not just with Western culture but with world culture because – without falling into this Boulezian thing I described earlier, where you have to move your culture forward and the next step is given – whatever you do *is* based on what was given in the past. But if you put yourself into an appreciative relationship with the past, it should hopefully be liberating.

# GEORGE CRUMB

*b. West Virginia 1929*

George Crumb studied at the University of Illinois, received his doctorate from the University of Michigan, and currently teaches at the University of Pennsylvania as Annenberg Professor of Music.

Drawing on elements of ritual and a vast sense of eclecticism, Crumb's music seeks to 'mirror the innermost recesses of the soul'. In this search, Crumb uses every tool and technique at his disposal, combining and juxtaposing harmonic systems, colouristic effects, direct musical quotations, and conventional instruments with children's toys. His *Black Angels* (1970) for electric string quartet, subtitled 'Thirteen Images from the Dark Land' and to be amplified 'to the threshold of pain', inspired the formation of the Kronos Quartet. Another work composed in 1970 and based on the poetry of Lorca (a lifelong interest of Crumb's), *Ancient Voices of Children*, combines soprano, boy soprano and small ensemble with a toy piano, Tibetan prayer stones, Japanese temple bells, musical saw and harmonica.

*Can you tell us about your early influences and education, and how they helped shape your career?*

Well, I didn't really find my own voice until I was in my thirties. I had a rather classical background – my parents were both classical musicians, and I had the normal university instruction. I had an excellent teacher in Ann Arbor, Ross Lee Finney, who was very good for technical work. But I hadn't found my own way of writing music at that time.

*What were you writing?*

I was writing *à la* Bartók. This would have been the early 1950s; the Bartók style was at that time very strong in the States, and next to that Webern. I must say that, even today, I feel so much rapport with Bartók. I believe in connections of all kinds. I think that, as a musician, all the musical worlds there have been up to now are still very much a part of me. Psychologically, there's no way we can divorce ourselves from that. We have memories, we have all our early years and influences, and that is a vibrant thing. So I've always believed that music doesn't compartmentalize, but rather it's one stream that just goes on.

*You've mentioned Bartók as an early influence. Were there any Americans that also influenced you?*

Well no, except that in my thirties I got to know Charles Ives pretty well. I must say that the impact was quite strong. But American music before Ives was of course just European music rewritten and there wasn't anything essentially American in it. I mean, I love European music but I've often wondered what it has to do with the situation here.

*What about other European models? Who else were you listening to?*

Well, mostly turn-of-the-century or early twentieth-century composers like Bartók, Mahler and Ives. Those were the composers that interested me because they were facing the very problems that we face today – that is, how to pull a variety of musics into one music. Most of the music of the middle of this century was, it seems to me, a more purist kind of music. That was the influence of the twelve-tone style, and led to what I would now call academic American music (which I don't think is relevant today). I think that the last turn of the century was in a crazy way very much like the approaching turn of the century, which is only a few years away. Those resonances from the earlier time relate to our present situation.

*I'd like to ask a little more about what you think of serialism and post-serialism.*

I think this music took a wrong path altogether. I've always said that you can't improvise in the twelve-tone style, and improvisation was the life-blood of the earlier music. One can improvise sonatas and rondos and variations – you can do it on the spot. But I've never met a composer who can improvise in a twelve-tone style and be consistent.

*So what do you think was essentially wrong with serialism?*

It was a movement which took just one percent of Beethoven's output – certain third-period pieces like the *Grosse Fuge* – and constructed an aesthetic on it. But Beethoven was a flesh-and-blood human being, who wrote ingratiating rondos and other, more emotionally-direct pieces. So I regard serial music as an aberration.

*What would you say your music is for? Why do you create it?*

Well, I have to write it, and I hope that it reaches the listener. I just have to do it. The idea that composers should be disdainful of the audience is not a very good one.

*You mean the 'Who cares if you listen?' aesthetic?*

Yes. The greatest constructors of music, the two greatest architects that music has ever known, were probably J. S. Bach and Ludwig van Beethoven. Beethoven always said that he had a picture in his mind when he was writing his music, whether it was a play by Shakespeare or some other reference. Bach was also involved with all kinds of visual and extramusical allusions in his music.

*Can you tell us a little about how you actually go about composing?*

Well, it's a very slow process for me!

*Do you have a routine?*

I do, but the last two years have been especially slow. I have no rational system at all. I work entirely by ear.

*Through intuition?*

Yes. I've always had the feeling that no super-rational system would deliver the right notes, that these can only resonate in the inner ear.

*How much do you rely on intuition? How far do you let that go before you let the opposite come in?*

There's always a balance between the technical and the intuitive aspects. With all the early composers, all the composers we love, there was always this balance between the two things. But for a time there have been composers who are either dilettantes or university composers. They somehow don't agree that both elements should coexist in a composition, which amazes me because, as I see it, that's what all music reflects. We're a civilization that seems to deal only with extremes.

*When did you finally feel you'd found your own voice? Was it* Five Pieces for Piano?

Partially, yes. There was a good bit of my own voice in that work.

*Did that realization come suddenly, or was it a gradual process?*

It came suddenly. At the age of thirty-three or whatever I was at that time, it struck me that, before then, I had just been rewriting other composers' music, which is a normal thing to do. But everybody's development seems to be belated in our times, maybe because we live longer. If I were Mozart, I would have been dead already for twenty years or more!

*What was it about that piece that made you realize it was the start of your own voice?*

Actually, it had something to do with John Cage. I was teaching at the University of Colorado and Cage came through to do one of his 'events'. I was taken with his totally refreshing way of challenging the basic things in music we had never questioned. He was a liberating influence for all kinds of composers through-out the world, even composers that one would not associate with his own very personal style. I think he was quite important as a musical philosopher.

*What does it mean to you to be a composer?*

Well, I don't think it's such a big deal. You're just doing your own thing, writing music. If you can write five or ten pieces in your life that are pretty good, that makes composing worthwhile. But there are no heroic figures like Mozart now. I'm not a big producer of music, and my works would only be counted in the low thirties over my whole life. But at least ten of these would be my very best.

*David Harrington of the Kronos Quartet has said that* Black Angels *single-handedly got the Kronos going.*

Yes, I've heard the story that the quartet was formed to play works like *Black Angels*. That's certainly my weirdest piece!

*Many of your pieces seem to have an almost apocalyptic element.*

I think that has to do with a sense of the approaching millen-nium. These thoughts would come to any artist these days – I mean, good Lord, it's not just the century but the millennium that's coming!

*Is it a feeling that this could be the last time we all turn this corner?*

I think so, yes. Everything will change.

*Do you have any view of what the future of music is going to be?*

It'll renew itself at every point, and young composers will come along and re-invent it to suit the times, that's for sure. But who knows what music could become? I suspect, though, that it will go back to being more visceral. No more 'university music' – that will have to go!

*You've set a great deal of Lorca's poetry. What was the attraction?*

I hit on his poetry as a student, and thought I could use it musically. Almost nobody else at that time was using it. I liked it, but it took me about five years before I could really deal with it. It was not until 1963 that I actually set my first Lorca – two poems in *Night Music 1*. In all, there are nine works that involve settings of Lorca. I think any composer will latch on to that poet whose language will evoke musical images for him.

*You mentioned it about other composers – Bach and Beethoven – but do your own pieces also tend to start from an extra-musical image or idea?*

It may seem a contradiction, but I think music essentially expresses itself, it comes out of itself. Even with the Beethoven sonatas, each one is a symbolic tone poem. You play them through and each one is a complete poem, not in the Lisztian sense but in a musical sense. I believe that music is an internal language in its own right. It expresses itself fully whether you call it a sonata, a prelude or *La Mer*. Maybe I'm naïve, but I think music can have integrity and yet still pull in images from the outside world.

*Is that related to the way you've used theatrical elements in your work?*

Yes. But those works can also be performed as ordinary chamber pieces.

*What do the other elements add? What were you trying to achieve?*

It's just an intensification of what composers have always required. A cellist who hums and grunts along with his playing is going beyond the actual playing of the notes. That element is always in music – with a good quartet or chamber group, there's always a 'choreography' involved.

*You've been described as essentially a 'colourist', and I wondered if your interest in timbre and colour has come from Debussy and that era?*

Yes, I think that's true. It comes from Debussy, whose *Prelude to the Afternoon of a Faun* is quite as revolutionary as *The Rite of Spring*, not only in colour but also in time-suspension. It's as revolutionary but probably not nearly as 'astonishing' a work for the audience.

*Do you think of the various elements of music separately, and if so, is timbre the most important one for you?*

All elements are important, but sound or timbre is exalted in my music, and is equal to rhythm or melody or harmony. It's because of our heightened sense of timbre that we even hear Mozart differently now than the listener did in earlier times. Our ears have also been totally turned around by the electronic experience.

*You've never worked in that medium yourself. Is that because it takes years to learn the technology, or because of aesthetic reasons?*

It's just that my music seems to demand human sounds, and more than that the 'danger element' involved in performance, where the music depends on a *tour de force* accomplished by the performer. Excitement and suspense are generated by a beautiful performance of any difficult music. Electronic music is too 'safe'. Only Bach could write a page of music that's loaded with purely compositional bravura, and that's why Bach's music is the most beautifully transcribable for electronic sound.

*How do you describe your musical language?*

Milton Babbitt once said, 'Never try to analyse a work of George Crumb.' I think he meant that my music is un-analysable, and I'm sure it is. I don't know whether Milton meant it as a compliment, but I took it as one because I myself have difficulty in analysing some of the great traditional works. Mozart's music is magic, but I can't account for the dynamic of the work, what drives this music. It looks so simple and inconsequential on paper.

*You've been linked to the minimalists because of your use of drones and sense of stasis. Do you see any connection yourself?*

I've never sensed much of a connection there. I would say that all good music is a little bit minimalist. I'm not coming down hard on the minimalists, but I wish they had a few more chords in there. What they gain from the 'hypnotic trance' element is sacrificed by the paucity of harmonic interest.

*What do you mean by 'all good music is a little bit minimalist'?*

All the music everybody loves strips away the redundancies. The principle of economy in the Beethoven sonatas for instance is incredible, but it still remains a rich music. But it's a question of how skeletal music can be and still be music. But I suppose that 'reduction to the absurd' is one process in art.

*Would you agree that there is a tremendous eclecticism in your music?*

Yes. It goes back to the turn of the century. Composers like Debussy were eclectic, and music was pulling in things that Brahms would never have thought of just a few years earlier. It was their mission at that time, and it is our mission now.

*Perhaps you'd call yourself more a 'maximalist'?*

I'm a minimalist in the sense that I use as few notes as possible, but a maximalist in the cultural sense. I really do think that, say, Indian music is as impressive in its own right as the late Beethoven quartets. I see all music as basically one. The world is getting smaller and we suspect that the universe is teeming with life, so what is going to happen when we confront all those extra-terrestrial musics?! That's not going to have anything to do with European music or world music.

*The use of musical quotations seems to have been an important part of your work. What inspired that idea?*

I can't account for why I do it. I think it's a statement that I don't divide music into compartments. Nowadays, philosophically, we're contemporaneous with all earlier music. As we're approaching the millennium we're pulling all the threads together, and quotation is a way of juxtaposing somebody else's ideas with something of your own, if you think there is some relationship between the two. For example, I use a quotation from the *Hammerklavier Sonata* in *Makrokosmos III*. The Beethoven work was a metaphysical music that seemed compatible with what I was thinking about when I was writing *Makrokosmos*.

*Your notations are often very visually striking . . .*

Notation is the composer's choice. But you're referring to my 'symbolic notations' – the circles etc. It's just a way of making graphic the fact that the music is circular in sound. It seemed the right way to notate it.

*Is there a particular work that you'd still like to write?*

I would one day like to write a piece that completely satisfies me – I haven't been able to do that yet!

# PAUL DRESHER

*b. California 1951*

Paul Dresher graduated from the University of California at Berkeley in 1977 and received his MA in Composition from the University of California at San Diego in 1979. His output comprises chamber and orchestral pieces, taped scores for dance, video and film, live instrumental works that utilize the latest in music technology, as well as experimental opera and music theatre.

It is this last category of work for which he is perhaps best known, particularly his trilogy of pieces examining diverse issues in contemporary American culture. The first of these, *Slow Fire* (1988), explores the alienating psychosis of contemporary urban living through its protagonist Bob, an American dreamer who, crushed by reminiscences of his father's idealized wisdom, transforms everyday objects (such as flashlights) into mystical totems and can only sleep with the light on.

Recent commissions have come from the Saint Paul Chamber Orchestra, the Kronos Quartet and the San Francisco Symphony.

*Let's start with your early musical background.*

Well, I was raised in a house where there was always a lot of music. My mother and my sister played instruments, my father played the record-player all the time, and we were always going to concerts, opera and theatre. It was an environment where doing music was a natural thing. I started piano lessons when I was about eight and I hated it, so I quit around twelve or thirteen. Then I immediately took up the guitar and started playing rock 'n' roll. I got very interested in rhythm and blues and more roots-oriented American music, and at the same time I was interested in rock 'n' roll and people like Jimmy Hendrix and Cream. So my guitar style started to emulate that, and I started working with feedback and electronics as soon as I could. I went to college at Berkeley and I wanted to do ethnomusicology because I was interested in world music, but Berkeley had no ethnomusicology programme so I just started studying out in the community. There were a lot of musicians from other parts of the world teaching here. I started studying North Indian classical music, West African drumming and Indonesian music. At a certain point I realized that I had to go back to school to get a basic training. I felt that although I was literate in terms of notation and understanding harmonic structure, there was so much about music history and basic musicianship that I didn't know. So I went back to school and got an undergraduate degree at Berkeley. Then I went to UC San Diego and got a graduate degree in composition; I studied with Bernard Rands, Robert Erickson, Pauline Oliveros and Roger Reynolds – a very diverse set of teachers. It was a wonderful programme, a really excellent place to study.

*One of the interesting things about your music is the way you manage to combine elements of classical and rock music in a very natural way.*

A lot of crossovers between art music and jazz or rock 'n' roll
have been so stilted and ineffectual in terms of understanding
what was at the core of each of those musics, what was powerful.
I won't claim that I've succeeded, but it's true that I grew up in
two really parallel worlds. One was classical music and the other
was rock 'n' roll. I made an arbitrary distinction when I was
around seventeen or eighteen that rock 'n' roll was a lesser form
than serious music, but when I finished graduate school I realized
that was no longer true. I realized I had to find a way to bring the
two together – that was the natural thing for me to do. The
division was more a result of intellectual snobbery than of
anything inherently distinctive about the two worlds. But there
are problems and there are some real limitations. Sometimes I
just step out of those limitations and address one approach in a
given piece. I might say, 'This piece has nothing to do with rock
'n' roll' and just explore the more formal manipulations, without
the visceral quality that I think is inherent in rock 'n' roll.

*You said it was you who really separated those two elements.
Wasn't there also outside pressure to do so?*

Well, when I was a student at Berkeley, the department was so
conservative I couldn't even show my serious contemporary
music there. When you were an undergraduate there, you were
not really a human being who might have worthy musical ideas.
It was like boot camp, which is basic training for the military.
There was no thought that a person who didn't have an
undergraduate degree might have any kind of developed musical
sensibility; they were there only for training. So I just went there
and took what they had to give – great courses in music history,
theory, counterpoint, and musicianship – but I did all my music
out in the community. When I got to San Diego, there was no
constraint. People were willing to listen and argue about anything you could intellectually or musically defend.

*You've described yourself as a 'pre-maximalist'. What do you
mean by that?*

That was a term I coined a long time ago, principally because I
was being called a post-minimalist composer, which is true. I was
second-generation minimalist. The people who had clearly

inspired my work were Steve Reich and Terry Riley. Now there's me, John Adams, Ingram Marshall, Daniel Lentz. We had been influenced by these composers, but we all wanted to expand the vocabulary and not be quite as limited as the pristine sonic palette that had characterized the music of Phil Glass, Steve Reich and Terry Riley. I felt that rather than look to the past, I'd rather look to the future, which to me meant an opening-up to possibilities from all kinds of worlds of sound. I felt that was going towards something more maximal, as opposed to minimal. I didn't define what maximal was, I just felt I was going in a direction that was about expanding and opening up. It's a term I wanted more to use as part of a critical dialogue, to get something going with people who find it necessary to create a term they can pigeonhole you into.

*Why do you choose to work in so many different contexts?*

Well, underlying all those different contexts I have a belief in the unity of all those different styles. An important goal in my life is to try to find some element deep inside each of those styles that really is linked to all music. For me, there has to be an emotional or intuitive response to a particular music to draw me to it, and I'll find something in that music I feel is universal. With all those pieces, the surface may sound different, but there is some kind of linkage between all my styles at core level. There are different ways of working, though. When I work in theatre and opera it's an extraordinarily collaborative process, but I find that after I've done a long theatre project I really want to be private, just to go away and explore sound for its own sake and not worry about the visual, dramatic and literary elements. There is a kind of renewal in moving between different styles. It's like moving between different procedures for working, and in the end each one informs the other. I have often found that some of my better orchestral ideas resulted from some notion I had developed in a more electronic music context, a procedure for manipulating sound, and wondered how I might turn it into something performed by orchestral instruments. While sometimes it fails miserably, often enough I'll find something that works magically and I'll find the right way to orchestrate it. For instance, I often used to work with tape loops and feedback loops; I would put a sound into the system, and each time it was rerecorded from the loop, it would go through some very small graphic equalizer that would filter it slowly. The sound was being gradually trans-formed by a filter process and I wondered how I could do that orchestrally. If you have a good enough orchestra and the right instruments, you can create wonderful things like that. Or if you can compose the effect of reverberation in an orchestra, it's a wonderful thing.

*Those are technical or procedural connections. Are there any more conceptual, musical connections, things that unify all your different approaches? Or is there no difference between them?*

Oh yes, there is a difference. One is technique. The success of the piece is based on your ability to orchestrate, which is more technical. You will find certain things that are consistent across all my music. There's obviously an interest in repetition, in permutation and slow development, where some element of the variation or permutation is clearly heard, where the listener is expected to engage with and follow the evolution of the sound, not as radical, sharp changes but as a procedure that's going on. That notion is at the core of the things that Steve Reich often said about his music, that the procedure is audible, that it's not obscured. You choose the material and the procedure in such a way that the listener can follow the evolution of your idea. I may have changed the rate speed or set multiple processes in motion.

*One thing that seems to run through your work is the accessibility. Is that intentional, or is it just a natural by-product?*

I think it's natural. I always felt that if the formal procedures are intellectually important to the justification of the piece, why should they be obscured? Why shouldn't they be heard? Why should you choose a musical language where you couldn't understand what the composer was manipulating? I always felt that serialism got itself into serious trouble when the listener couldn't apprehend what was going on. I don't think that was true in Webern. When you listen to some of those palindromic pieces, you can hear the structure. You can actually follow it, because the gestures and the material are clear enough for you to comprehend those pieces on the terms that the composer was actually involved in. To make a piece comprehensible is a strength, not a compromise. Accessibility comes naturally to me because of my interest in popular music. One of my goals is to see how I can take things that are apparently simple, like song forms or the material that usually goes with song form, and manipulate it in completely different ways. *Slow Fire* has good examples of that. There are arias and sections of that piece that sound like verse structures, but they're not repeating verses. The harmonies don't always return to where they started, each verse is not the same, and the verses are not verses in terms of poetic structure – they don't have the same length or the same sort of poetic forms in each one. So the surface of it is very accessible. You accept the notion of the structure of the piece, but underneath it's not conforming to the simple song structure you're expecting to hear.

*Your collaborations with the singer Rinde Eckert have been very important. He has a very distinctive style of presentation.*

Rinde is very physically athletic. He's almost like a dancer on stage. He has a special combination of skills that are hard to match – the physicality, the powerful tenor voice, a kind of speaking and declaiming that is really unique. There are few performers who can even come close to that style of declamation, which is so musical and can project so directly. He's also inherently a superb actor.

*Do you approach each project or each medium in a similar way?*

I think each is different. I try to set up each piece with different kinds of challenges, and the goals of the pieces are in different domains. Sometimes it's specific to the medium that it's to be performed in – whether that's musicians reading notation, a piece for electronic tape, or my own ensemble, which is much more like a rock 'n' roll band. I present them with a score with an outline of varying degrees of specificity and then we work on it together. Each of these requires a different procedure of composition, and as a result you approach the compositional possibilities differently in each one. There are certain overriding aspects which are probably part of my musical personality. I might set a very general goal; in the case of *Slow Fire*, I had just finished doing a very large-scale music theatre piece that was consistently slow and beautiful. I felt that I then wanted to do a piece that was a lot more aggressive. So in *Slow Fire* there is no slow-motion activity, it's all dynamic and the music is relatively loud and aggressive. For me, deciding that I wanted this piece to be principally aggressive was the overriding aesthetic that defined the work. When I write a vocal piece, I inevitably have to deal with the relationship between melody and accompaniment. For a long time I had a hard time accepting this. *Channels Passing*, for instance, is a quintessential example of a piece that has equal-voice polyphony. No instrument is accompaniment to another instrument's lead line. It's a latticework of seven instruments that have an equal role pretty much throughout the piece. When I started working with opera singers, it was very hard for me to accept the notion that one part was a lead line and the rest was an accompaniment. Now I've come to adore what singers can do and the quality they can bring. I just accept that this is a vocal piece, and thus the melodic line is going to be in the foreground and the other instruments are going to play a more supportive role.

*What's the essential motivation for your work?*

Well, generally I'm just interested in what sound can do. I love working in the studio, creating the sound and feeling it viscerally, and I love being on stage with a group of people. I'd always thought classical music performance often missed the power of a rock 'n' roll band. When I first came to play classical music, I kept feeling that the music was missing something really wonderful that happens in rock 'n' roll. It's just a completely unified feeling where the musicians are all listening to each other, as opposed to focusing all their musical skill and energy on a conductor. String quartets always play like a band. They have that unified sense of tuning, rhythm and phrasing. I love that feeling when I'm in a performing context, when you have that kind of energy.

*What motivated* American Trilogy?

When we started that work in 1985, I'd been doing a kind of music theatre that was devoid of any socio-political connection. It was a more abstract manipulation of perception, of sound and vision, and it was playing with our expectations of what theatre does. It also had no language. Its only use of language was to contradict the use of language for the purpose of conveying meaning. Rinde Eckert was also involved in this company, and we both felt that it was getting boring, that we were just repeating ourselves. I wanted to do a more politically-aware, language-engaged kind of theatre. That was the starting point. In each piece we looked at different facets of American culture. We had an idea for a character Bob (who's in *Slow Fire*), a kind of American Everyman, a survivalist, materialist, militarist, obsessed character, the kind of character who was a very prominent icon in the Reagan years – a person who represented the greed and nationalism we were seeing in the American economic and political scene of the mid-1980s. All this was distilled down to this one character. From that work we realized that we had all kinds of other facets to explore, and other ways that we could look at the things that were going on in our culture. Thus each piece looked at American culture in a different way.

*Is this essentially an American piece? There seem to be overtones of Arthur Miller's* Death of a Salesman.

Yes. Actually, some critic said that Bob is a cross between Willy Loman in *Death of a Salesman* and Rambo! I think those two elements are really well-integrated into the character.

*What are your aims in those pieces about contemporary culture? Are they just to reflect it, to suggest we do something about it, to try to transcend it, or show how bizarre it is?*

Just that, yes. It's to hold up mirrors to things that you accept in day-to-day life, but don't usually reflect on and don't usually get to see in a different context where you might find it shocking or disturbing. None of the pieces prescribes an appropriate course of behaviour, none of them say we should do this and we shouldn't do that. All of them have a sense that our culture is both engaging and entertaining, and can even be humorous, but at the same time can be dangerous and disturbing. *Pioneer* was one piece that threw that into the strongest relief. It's a very funny, angry and aggressive piece, a very profane piece. It excoriates all the myths of American history and the colonization of the Western hemisphere. We started with Columbus. It's a setting, mostly in traditional operatic singing, of texts from journals or letters by famous historical figures like Columbus, Cortez, President McKinley and Admiral Perry (the man who explored the North Pole). These are characters who are held up to us in our history classes as paragons of behaviour and as people to be emulated. In fact, what they said and did was not so wonderful. When you actually confront their own words, you realize how dangerous history is, how things we accept as high points of our history are in fact frequently quite despicable. Obviously, our political attitudes come through in the piece, but they don't say you should act this way and not that way. They just say, 'Look! This is what we're supposed to believe'.

*How has living on the West Coast influenced your music?*

Well, we are further from the cultural axis of Europe. Places like Princeton, Yale and Columbia still look to Europe for the principal justifications of how and why you make music. In California, where you're further from the cultural centre of Europe and quite close to Asia, there is a basic iconoclastic attitude. It's a raw, naïve, American kind of notion. It's the fact that you have more wilderness out here. Space is so different. I think this gives composers, if they choose to, the chance to operate more freely, away from European-oriented styles of composition. It started with Henry Cowell, and he influenced Cage and Harrison. Obviously, those are people who completely rejected – or just avoided – European intellectual models and developed their own. In the case of Lou Harrison, it was looking very much to Asia. In the case of Cage, it was philosophically looking to Asia but formally and intellectually it was very much European. I think the principal thing here is a kind of freedom. That freedom can take you in many different directions, into things that sound just like European music, or Asian music, or rock 'n' roll.

# JAMES FULKERSON

*b. Illinois 1945*

James Fulkerson has said of his formative experiences at the University of Illinois (MA 1968) that 'the most important thing was to examine our assumptions about art', and many of his textual, graphical and improvisational works from this period explore the theatrical and social implications of musical performance. Though his music has come to be less overtly conceptual, he has constantly maintained the idea of one's work being a result of the questions one poses.

Although influenced by the philosophies of John Cage, the clarity, sensuousness and wilful expressiveness of much of Fulkerson's work – *Elective Affinities III* (1987) or *The Archaeology of Silence* (1991), for example – owe more to the influence of Morton Feldman. A leading exponent of extended trombone techniques, Fulkerson has also been deeply involved with new dance, and has produced a huge variety of collaborative works with choreographers including Richard Olston, Rosemary Butcher and, most importantly, his wife Mary Fulkerson.

*Having worked in a variety of situations from Illinois to New York, from Melbourne to Amsterdam, how would you say your music has changed over the years?*

Well, I'm not so sure it has changed. Being in a foreign situation has been useful both to myself and Mary because we've been able to see what assumptions we make and what we bring with us, but it's also encouraged us to hang on to those things that interest us most about being Americans in an alien environment. In short, I don't think it's changed so much, although it has perhaps been clarified.

*You've said that 'music is an activity and* sometimes *sound results' . . .*

I said that at a time when I was doing things that were more conceptual than perhaps I am now. But I've consistently been interested in the theatrical situation of performing, and also in the social interaction of performing. I wouldn't necessarily say that we have to be making any sound together to be making music. It's actually the social interaction that I think is critical.

*What then do you see as your principal role as a composer?*

Well, I make things. In that sense, I'm typical of many people who have come after Cage. I moved into a situation where there was a very expanded sense of music or art, and I've often used the Dick Higgins phrase 'inter-media' for work which falls between classifications. To me, the classifications are not as important as the ideas.

*Many experimental composers seem to feel some debt to Cage. How would you characterize yours?*

Well, first of all, at the most personal level, he actually made my life easier. At times he quite literally supported me, saying, 'You should give this person a job' or 'You should play this person's music', so I was indebted to him for that. Also, when I was in graduate school and he was an artist in residence there, he gave me a great deal of personal encouragement at a time when things were rather heavy going for me. But I think he's actually been most important in the nature of what he's done. Even though I've experienced people yelling at me and trying to interrupt performances, that's more their problem than my problem, and I don't really choose to fight battles when they've been fought and won by someone else. So, in that respect I think many of us have a debt to Cage.

But I owe more to a composer like Morty Feldman for the sensuousness of the sound, and also for the kind of definitive action he became willing to make. In fact, many of my scores are quite un-Cage-like. In many cases I'm *composing* in a wilful sense, which is not usually considered to be what he was about. If I look at things like my choral piece *He was silent for a space . . .*, what is unusual is the fact that I was actually writing expressive music – and that was not an acceptable practice in 1978. The experimental people just weren't doing that. I now have quite an interest in what people either call the Neo-Romantic or the Post-Modern school, and my sense is that this music actually arose from young German composers. What they were doing was saying, 'Look, we're completely disenchanted with the music the Darmstadt people (their composition teachers) have given us.' I think it was both courageous and important that they turned their back on this nervous European stuff. It's interesting to see how there's still such aggression towards Neo-Romantic and Post-Modern music in England, because I think the whole education system encourages the English composer – as long as they go through the normal channels (the channels of elitism) – to repress feelings. They opt for the supposed profundity of thought in complex music. But I think it's actually the British way of ducking the important questions. There is a great deal of hostility towards both the new tonality and the simplicity of Americans, but I think that anything that enables feelings to arise in British classical music is ultimately unacceptable to the people in charge, like the BBC, Arts Council, ISCM, Sinfonietta et cetera.

*You often hear the argument that experimental music is a 'reaction' to European complexity . . .*

Yes, but the fact is we don't give a shit about European complexity. It's only a thing *they* say. We're quite clear about what we want to do, and our whole idea about freedom or experimentation is that anything is possible. If we want to pick up a bit of this, then great, we will. It's only American academics and the inflated egos of places like Britain that think we actually pay any attention to those problems. They aren't our problems. We're really a very different culture, and if I've learned something, it's about those differences. I can enjoy a lot of things over here, or obviously I wouldn't have stayed in Europe this long. On the other hand, I'm always at a distance from it. I can enjoy playing complex music, but what strikes me deep down as meaningful and important for my own work is something quite different. I came to tonality out of single-pitch work. Philip Corner and I were doing concerts that were two or three hours long using a single pitch. That's a single sound, but it's a very vast world. There is also the overtone structure of a sound. You can listen to a single pitch, listen to the overtones, and hear the entire history of music.

What really excites me at the moment is something Colin Wilson says in his book *The Strength to Dream*. He said that, at this point in time, it's neither fashionable nor possible to write an epic, but that there's nothing more important than the courage to try. That's where I stand as an artist. I have aspirations. I often play in situations where I know people are flabbergasted that I could be either so naïve or so straightforward as to attempt something like that. I think, 'Yeah, well, what can you do except what you know or what you're committed to?' If we can do those things, that's no small accomplishment. If we can actually realize what we're committed to doing or dreaming, that's a *great* accomplishment. That's what enables me to respect work that's quite different from what I do. I respect much of Elliott Carter's work and find it quite exciting, because I can understand what he's trying to do and I sense that at times he's successful in it. More and more I'm able to respond to that unity of vision and realization.

*I think what you're talking about is a particular characteristic of experimentalists – an openness of attitude which allows you to accept any type of music.*

Well, I find a lot of people in Europe who have similar attitudes, so I think it may be less about Europeans versus Americans and more about the kinds of vision that people have of the world. But you're right, I'm able to enjoy a great deal of music, and I think that's good. But I find the discussion of how we fit into traditions interesting, partly because of my academic background, partly because of the work that I do in academia, but also because I think that learning how to pose questions, which is a circular activity, is what really feeds us the material for our work. Many of us start by reacting to the environment around us, but if we don't learn how to ask questions, we're trapped by that method of working. We have nothing to do but react against things around us. I don't think you can live your life, always trying to work and grow, using that as the only way of going forward. At times you do have to rebel against things, but that's in a sense part of a 'teenage' period when you're trying to establish what you might be. I think we outgrow that rebellion, in the same way we outgrow it as people.

*You've been involved in many collaborations, but most significantly with dance. Why has dance been so important to you?*

Well, first of all, two of the most interesting artists I know are dancers – Yvonne Rainer and my wife, Mary O'Donnell Fulkerson. Both of them I find constantly stimulating as artists. For a long time dance has been a much more liberated art form than music, less concerned with boundaries. In the early 1970s, when it was absolutely taboo to look at meaning, Mary and Yvonne were working with films or text or both. I've worked with other dancers who are more formal, less concerned with pushing the edges, and I've also found that greatly satisfying because we make a thing which is much more concerned with an idea of beauty, with arriving at a sense of perfect form or elegance. Those are sensibilities that I have, or that I've developed, and I find it gratifying to work in a situation like that. I've always found dance to be a wide-open area for the imagination.

*How does your work with Mary differ from your other collaborations?*

Well, Mary's one of those people who, if she's done something, is not interested in doing it again. That can be frustrating, because of the time it takes you to make something. You think you're ready to tour it around, but she wants to do something else. She's always questing for the new, releasing the 'what-if' of the world!

*That's a typical experimental trait, never repeating yourself!*

Yes, but it's not always easy to live with! That is one of the things that's made working with Mary different. Her rate of change and the liveliness of her interest is very quick-paced.

*Your work with Mary seems to have focused to a large degree on the use of roles and texts . . .*

Yes. The interest with role grows out of two things. One is trying to look at meaning – how meaning/feeling walks this interesting line where you can push it over and it becomes sentimental and soft, or where it can be the real thing. When you're dealing with text, it's interesting to deal with an act that appears to be the person talking about their personal experiences. I find it interesting when it's difficult to determine whether that's only a role you are playing, or whether it's actually you speaking with commitment from your heart or your own experience. The work we do often has elements of both, so that you're shifting the perspective. Secondly, role-playing is interesting to the two of us because of the Jungian psychology which we've studied. Part of Jungian psychology is involved with the idea of there being many people within each of us. Self-actualization is to get to understand these other aspects of yourself and to integrate them in some way. Ultimately, that should make you a more conscious and stronger person. That's come out of the writing, but also out of my own experience of performing.

*How do you like to approach a dance collaboration?*

Well, that really depends upon who I'm working with. It seems like I've tried every approach. While I was doing the course work for a doctorate, I took a first-year architectural design course as one of my electives. That was a useful experience for me, because I began to see that in every commission or collaboration there are certain design configurations that are given to you. There invariably have to be some restrictions, so if a piece of music has to be twelve minutes then it has to be twelve minutes. I've never been bothered by the fact that there will be different design requirements with every collaboration, I just take that in my stride. For the same reasons, my notational systems have also been fairly varied. Again, I look back to my architectural experience and see that we're dealing with communications systems. In any score we have an incomplete situation. The composer has said, 'These are the things that I consider import-ant.' Arthur Weisburg said that even in a traditional score only thirty per cent of the information can be conveyed. Other research has shown that it may be as low as six per cent. My point is that performing is a re-creative act which involves the imagination of the performer. So I look at the whole thing of scoring as a question of efficiency – how can I carry the most important part of my ideas forward in the most efficient way?

*Is this why you've frequently made use of aural scores rather than written ones?*

Well, that grows out of the same interest, particularly if you're dealing with classical players who have worked from score formats as opposed to an aural tradition. These people have tended to learn to use their eyes, not their ears. As soon as you take the score away and the person has to use their ears instead of their eyes, then of course they play in a completely different way. Earlier you asked me about the social aspect of making music; well, I think the collaboration between composer and performer is one of the important exchanges. With people who are primarily classically-trained, it can be a great liberation to begin to use their ears. Notation is efficient and useful, but damning in its own way.

*Your work often makes use of electronics. How do you like to approach that medium?*

Well, if dance has been liberating for me, technology and electronics have been equally so. That is because they can also function as a camera. We're able to bring all these things in from the world, and they're really *there*. Therefore it's a very rich texture that you're making – that's always been interesting. Also, purely abstract sound has always been very exciting to me. The medium itself has been something that makes my pulse race. I've struggled in my life with the idea of playing the trombone. It's not intellectually respectable: 'What the hell can you do on a trombone?' I've tried to give it up at times, only to realize that playing the trombone is part of my life. If I play the trombone every day, I'm a more interesting person for the world than if I don't. On the other hand, as I imply in what I just said, playing the trombone is not enough in itself. So I have this other side of me which is trying to grow and be an artist. It's been a slow process to understand that my life is really about the physicality of playing, and that includes playing other people's music – but it's also about thinking and reflecting, being a composer.

*You've said, 'In all my work I feel the desire to split the focus of the audience's attention' . . .*

Yes. Another person who's been stimulating for me is Susan Sontag. (It's funny how, when I look at the people that are my models, they tend to be females rather than males – I haven't sorted through what that really means.) Anyway, Susan Sontag has been important as a source of thought. One of the things she talks about is the importance of art being a stimulus not only to the senses but also to the mind. The work that really interests me has that quality. It is intriguing or pulls us in at the level of sensuality, but at the same time it has to have an intellectual stimulus to be really captivating and truly gratifying. I think that's an interesting point, because people who are interested in the new complexity would look at my work and say there is no stimulus to the mind there at all. Where I differ from some of the 'new complexity' work is that the strands of information I present are I think all perceptible. In fact, I fault some of the 'new complexity' because it isn't complex: it doesn't stratify in a way that I can actually hear, so I don't hear the complexity they're supposed to be dealing with. I listened to a piece for percussion and trombone recently for which I didn't have the score. I knew the trombonist was counting like a little computer, but the fact is, all this poor man was doing was making absolutely banal, crude gestures of glissandi over an augmented fourth – and when I listened to what the drum was doing, it was basically a roll. And I thought, 'Where is the complexity in this thought?' Indeed, if you were improvising in this situation, you would immediately think, 'This is banal. I've got to do something more than this.' So I find it interesting that there's a level of 'complexity' which may not be complex at all, and that at the same time, just because we have nice, big, round, white notes on the page doesn't mean that we aren't dealing with complexity (to say nothing of significance).

One of the most interesting composers I'm listening to at the moment is the Polish composer Górecki. He's one that I would say has the 'strength to dream' and *is* writing epics. It's very interesting, because when you work with tonality or when you work with meaning or emotion, it can easily sour, or it can go the other way and be saccharine or sentimental. To me that's one of the interesting things – can you be moving but firm or tough? Is there a backbone there? When I say it's important that a man like Górecki is a religious man, I think it's that quality that is working there. He's not trying to manipulate your emotions, he's moving from a centre, from a point of strength, and that's important.

# PHILIP GLASS

*b. Baltimore 1937*

After studying philosophy and mathematics at the University of
Chicago, then composition at the Juilliard School of Music,
Philip Glass travelled to Paris to join the class of Nadia
Boulanger. It was whilst in Paris that he first encountered Ravi
Shankar and began to find inspiration in the forms and structures
of Indian music.

Returning to New York in 1967, he worked as a cab driver and
plumber to support his composing habit, founding the Philip
Glass Ensemble in 1969. A series of studies in extreme harmonic
and structural minimalism culminated in the four-hour *Music in
Twelve Parts*, released by Virgin Records in 1974.

In 1976 Glass received both popular and critical acclaim for
his opera collaboration with Robert Wilson, *Einstein on the
Beach*, and almost all of his subsequent work has been for the
theatre. A compulsive collaborator, he has worked with Doris
Lessing on *The Making of the Representative for Planet 8*, and
with Laurie Anderson, David Byrne, Paul Simon and Suzanne
Vega on *Songs from Liquid Days*, as well as several film and
dance scores. An extremely prolific composer, his recent projects
have included a recording of his *Low* symphony (based on the
early David Bowie album of the same name), and *The Voyage*, a
Metropolitan Opera commission to celebrate the 500th anniversary of the discovery of America.

*When did your interest in music begin?*

I began studying the violin when I was six, but I didn't really start properly until I was eight, when I began studying flute and percussion at the Peabody Conservatory in Baltimore. I began writing when I was fifteen, and went to Juilliard when I was nineteen.

*What kind of music were you writing then?*

I wrote what was then considered 'contemporary' music – twelve-tone music.

*Did that continue when you got to Juilliard?*

By then I was through with it. I began by studying Webern and Schoenberg. You have to remember that in 1952 we thought that *was* contemporary music.

*What changed your mind about it?*

I just got older, heard more music, and began to see it in a historical perspective. I think at some point I also began to realize that it was the music my grandfather would have written. It was OK, but it was the music of several generations before. It took me a long time before I realized that – I was about nineteen or twenty.

*And then what?*

Well, then I just wrote music like my teachers. I didn't do anything interesting for a good few years. I wrote like all my teachers did, but that's not a bad way to learn music. It's the way that artists learn to paint – you just copy.

*You learnt technique?*

Yes, basically technique. I learned technique by studying analysis, counterpoint, harmony and by copying music – literally copying out scores of Mahler or something – by imitating the music of other people. I did that until I was almost twenty-eight.

*When were you with Boulanger?*

I was with her for several years. It was a nightmare! A complete nightmare! But I loved it. How can you say two things like that? I got up at five or six in the morning – which is what I do now actually – and I worked at counterpoint, harmony and analysis all day long until it got dark. It was dark when I started, it was dark at the end of the day, and all I can remember was that I got blurry-eyed from doing it. What she did – you have to remember that, when I went to see her, I was twenty-seven and had a master's degree in music already – was basically start me over again. She said, 'Let's start from the beginning.' At twenty-five or twenty-six I did it much quicker than when I was fifteen. It was wonderful in a way, but it was also a kind of nightmare, especially at the age I was. I mean, I had friends who were younger and were off teaching school somewhere, but I thought it was the technique I needed.

*How did you develop and find your own musical voice?*

Well, it was about 1965. I was twenty-eight and living in Paris, and I just got sick of all that other music. You have to remember that, by then, I had been writing for almost twelve years. So I wasn't really a beginner, although in some ways I still was. I had not found my own voice, but had written in the styles of a lot of other people. But I just got tired of it. I was really lucky at that time to meet Ravi Shankar, and I became his assistant on a project. Through him, I began to take an interest in non-Western music. I went to India and North Africa, and I began to hear that there were other traditions in music worth thinking about besides the Western tradition. I came back to New York in 1966 or 1967 and studied with Ali Rahka, who was teaching at the City College of New York for a semester. I got very interested in the rhythmic structure of non-Western music, and that really gave me the clue for where to start. I had pieces from 1965 and 1966 that were based on repetitive structures, but I really began developing a technique of my own around 1967.

*Was your interest in exploring other musics an idea of your own,
or was it in the air?*

It's hard to say. When I was in Paris I was out of touch with what
other people were doing in America. Certainly no-one else in
Paris was doing it – they were all very much enthralled with the
second Viennese school. No-one paid any attention to world
music in Europe at that time. I was hired by Ravi because a friend
of mine was doing the photography for a film and they needed
someone to translate, notate and do a little conducting. It was a
complete coincidence I was there. Then I saw right away that the
ideas involved in non-Western music, when looked at from a
Western point of view, seemed a very fresh way of looking at
things. They changed all the rules: you didn't have to count from
one to twelve, you could count from one to eight. There's not
much difference there, but the whole tyranny of history, the
historical imperative of contemporary music, was demystified
entirely for me. It simply didn't matter any more. If you took one
step outside those institutions, it didn't matter any more. Of
course, that's what Cage was very good at. He was one of the
people I was reading at the time, and I would say he was then the
only Western composer who hinted at that. Most of us are
studying the traditions we're brought up in, because it's very
hard to break out of them.

*How do you feel you relate to that European tradition now?*

Well, you have to remember that I had a solid training in it. It
took me years to get over it, and then it took me years to
reintegrate it.

*Are you back on speaking terms with it now?*

You can hear it in the music – it's very clear. But the good thing is
that I had the technique to begin with. For example, I just wrote a
symphony based on *Low*, the record by David Bowie. When I
have to write a symphony, I have the technique to do it. I've come
across composers who, for example, only studied electronic
music, and then, when they decided they really wanted to write
counterpoint, they didn't know how to do it. They had never had
any training in it, so in their mid-thirties they have to go back and

learn basic music theory. It's tough to do that. It was good having that training to begin with – it was good leaving it and it was good coming back to it. I think the whole thing has worked out all right.

*What attracted you to opera?*

From 1965 to 1975, I was the music director of a theatre company. I was married to one of the people in the theatre, and my life was in the theatre. Actually, there were *two* parts to my life – there was the ensemble I wrote for, and there was the theatre. When I did *Einstein on the Beach* I put them together. It turned out that the opera house was the place where I could put all the things I knew about together into one form, working with dancers, writers, designers, choreographers, lighting people. That turns out to be a description of opera. We started with *Einstein*, and then there was *Satyagraha* in 1979. It's escalated since then. The hardest thing for me was to learn about singing – that's taken a good fifteen years to figure out.

*What motivates your music? What is it that really makes you sit down and write?*

Well, different things at different times. Motivation is a difficult word. I think I'm inspired by other people's ideas and by the talents of the people I work with. Working in the theatre as I did, I became a collaborator very early on, and the pieces are really a result of working with other people. My inspiration comes from material that is outside of music. It's interesting, though, that of all the people of our generation in this book, almost nobody, apart from Bob Moran, was a theatre composer.

*Now everybody's doing it. Was that down to you?*

Well, I'm happy to say I had a lot to do with it. *Einstein on the Beach* played to sold-out houses all over Europe and the United States. Before that, people thought it simply wasn't done. They used to say opera was dead, but they don't say it any more. I hardly know a composer today who isn't writing an opera. But the point is that there are two kinds of composer: theatre composers and composers of concert music. They're actually very different. I mean, there's probably a very good reason why

Verdi didn't write any symphonies and Brahms didn't write any operas. It's what the French call a different *métier*. It's a different way of working. For theatre composers, the source of the piece is very often some non-musical material, a story, an image or a dance. When you work with concert music, you're dealing with the language of music itself. For a lot of people that's been a problem. It's one of those unconscious hierarchies we make: we say that concert music is pure music, more important than theatre music, forgetting of course that the great innovations in music have come from the theatre – Monteverdi, Mozart, Wagner, Berg, Stravinsky – and not the concert hall.

*What about your own concert music?*

I hardly ever do it now. I write an odd piece here and there, but almost everything is theatre music and has been since 1975. Between 1965 and 1975, half was theatre and half was the ensemble. But theatre is a whole different way of working, and it comes back to the question of inspiration. The opera *Satyagraha* was inspired by the life of Gandhi; the idea of social change through non-violence was something I was keen on turning into a musical exposition of some kind. Similarly, *The Representative for Planet 8*, the opera I did with Doris Lessing, is a book whose ideas were attractive to me. Almost every theatre piece is involved with literary, historical or social ideas that are interesting to me. I work outside of the theatre with great difficulty and a certain awkwardness. I need a place to start from. For example, with the *Low* symphony I started from another man's work. In almost all of the non-theatrical works, if you examine them, you'll find there's actually a subtext which is theatrical. Theatre music is often criticized in Anglo-American culture, basically because our puritanism doesn't allow us to take seriously things that are apparently entertainment. But you can define opera as the place where art and entertainment come together. The French and Anglo-American traditions are suspicious of things which are 'near' entertainment: 'God help us that we should go to the theatre and be entertained!' For a long while in contemporary music, theatre was simply overlooked.

*What do you feel is the underlying theme of your operas?*

Well, I made it all up as I went along, but actually it's very clear. The operas are portraits of people who change the world through the power of ideas rather than through the force of arms. One is about modern science, one about religion and one about politics – the three big social themes. They're all quite different: I think of *Einstein* as an apocalyptic opera, *Satyagraha* as a very lyrical opera, and *Akhnaten* as a dramatic opera.

*How do you actually go about composing?*

I get up around five. It's a little hard to work in New York, so I often go to another city and just rent an apartment. I do that to get away from the phone. I went to South America for a while, and I have a house up in Canada. The ideal is to not be disturbed. Ideally, I will work from around seven to twelve and around two to six, about ten hours. I go to sleep early, about ten o'clock – I recommend it, especially if you like writing music. People think I write fast, but I just spend a lot of time writing. It only seems fast because I spend three times as many hours in the day writing than most other people do.

*How do you write? What's the process?*

Well, it depends on where I am with a piece. I'm usually working from a libretto or a text of some kind.

*So from that you have an overview of the whole thing?*

I try to do a lot of work before I even get to that point. I spent almost a year with the librettist and director of *The Voyage*, laying out the piece in terms of the formal structure, the dramatic structure, and the musical forces involved. I try to get the designer to deliver the designs before I begin writing. My goal is to have everything done before I begin the music – I seem to work well when I have a lot of help. In my studio I have the designs on the wall, I create an environment that is about the piece, and then the music is not so hard to do. I don't write a note until all those preliminaries are taken care of. With a large opera that can take two years, and then I spend the third year writing.

*Do you start at the beginning and just work through?*

Yes. Now that I've gotten older I find that I rewrite more.

*Satyagraha* and *Einstein* were virtually unchanged from the first drafts, but by the time I got into the other works, I began to start doing revisions, and now I rewrite whole scenes.

*How do the ideas work? Do you generally just set the text, or is it mainly harmonic ideas?*

It can be a number of things. Generally there's a musical argument to a piece, and you have to know what that is. With *The Making of . . .*, for example, it was the resolution of a particular cadence that took three hours to work in the music. With *Einstein* it was combining a rhythmic process I had evolved with a harmonic process; I was trying to discover a functional harmony that didn't depend on classical structure but on rhythmic structure. There is a musical argument or subtext to the music which is about the language of music, and that has to be there for me – it's usually what I'm happy to be thinking about at that moment of my life. But the subtext has changed over the years: in the early music I was mostly thinking about the structure, and now I'm thinking about tonal relationships – which sounds suspiciously like what twelve-tone music talks about. In fact, I think we've come to a stage at the end of the twentieth century where the crisis of tonality has reappeared in a new form. It arrived at the end of the nineteenth century, and we spent most of the twentieth century trying to resolve it. At the end of the twentieth century we're right back almost to where we were, except that we've learnt quite a lot about tonality along the way.

*What do you think we've learned? That what's happened since then is just one more technique that's available to composers rather than a way of being?*

No, I think it's more subtle than that. The experiments of the twelve-tone school have been crucial in changing how we listen to music, although the methodology has, I think, turned out to be not so helpful. That school didn't determine the future of music, as it had thought. It didn't even develop useful techniques for other composers. But if you go to the movies now, the harmonic language of the music is much denser. People listen to my music and think they're hearing triadic music, but they aren't – they just don't know the name for it. It's more complicated than they think because now they're hearing differently. We all do music in a much more complex way than we used to. What's happening now is that we're going back over some of the ground we've been over before, but I hope in a more sophisticated and less didactic way than before.

*What do you think inspired the minimalist movement?*

It was a very useful time, and for five or ten years there was a certain liveliness to that group of composers. But it was a very diverse group: everyone from Phil Niblock and John Gibson to Terry Riley and Meredith Monk, even some English composers like Gavin Bryars, and a few Europeans. That generation was telling the older generation that it had gone too far in the direction of polemical music. As a result, almost nobody talked about minimalist music from a theoretical point of view. Reich wrote one piece called *Music as a Gradual Process*, but I can hardly think of any other composers who wrote about what they were doing. Part of the reason was that the generation older than us had done so much writing and talking that we were sick to death of it. That was the generation which said that the music was better than it sounded! People actually believed that stuff. Our generation got back to a fundamental value in music which has to do with clarity and expressivity, yet is not without complexity. Clarity and expressivity do not deny complexity, although the older composers always felt this was so. Ours was a very threatening view at the time, and I've heard older composers characterize Terry's music by pounding a C major chord on the piano for twenty minutes as if that was all he did. There was a suspicion that this younger group was on to something and weren't going to be following neatly behind the teachers, in the way that *they* had evidently done. As I've said, one of the problems was that, for a long while, few people were talking about the new music because of the deluge of polemics. It still goes on: I have volumes of *Perspectives of New Music*, and you still see that kind of stuff. It created the idea that minimalism was an intellectual movement, which wasn't the case at all – it was simply a generation that wasn't going to fall into the trap of talking more than doing.

*Was it just that – a generation?*

That's how I think of it, as a generation rather than a category. I mean, I like Phil Niblock's music a lot but I don't know what to call it. The same would be true of Terry Jennings or Meredith Monk or Robert Ashley – it's not important. What has Robert Ashley's music got to do with mine? Not very much, but in fact we know each other quite well, we've been influenced by the same people, and we've worked with many of the same people. Stylistic identity is not the issue, not in America it isn't. But we have to remember that Americans tend to be less didactic than our European colleagues. Stylistic identity is taken much more seriously in Europe than it is here. I'm not quite sure why that is, but I think one of the reasons has to do with economics. There's very little money in the arts in America, but because of that you're much freer. You can do what you want. Also, there's a much more entrepreneurial spirit here: people start ensembles, record companies, music co-ops and all kinds of things. There's more independence – the fear of not getting historical or critical approval is simply not important. I find that Louis Andriessen, for example, is much more conscious of himself as a European composer in the tradition of Stravinsky. I go to Holland quite a lot, and I remember that at one point I was accused of betraying the minimalist movement. I never thought there was a movement to begin with, but my European colleagues felt that a betrayal had taken place.

*We spoke to John Adams about 'minimalism'. He said it's three things: pulsation, a return to tonality, and repetition of small motivic cells. Do you agree?*

I used to say something similar. There was a period in my music that was identified by tonality, repetitive structures and a constant steady beat.

*Yet La Monte Young or Terry Riley don't have all of those characteristics.*

La Monte doesn't, but Terry does. I don't know what La Monte is – he's a kind of inferno, a conceptual composer in a way. It wasn't intended to be that way, but our music turned out to be the opposite of what, say, Berio or Boulez did. Their music never repeated, ours repeated all the time; their rhythms were non-predictable, ours were extremely steady and predictable; their music was atonal, ours was tonal. They turn out to be polar opposites.

*So it just happened to turn out that way?*

Well, I don't think that one morning I said, 'I think I'll do the opposite.' It wasn't like that. What happened was that I got involved with Ravi Shankar, who introduced me to a whole other element of music. Those ideas could fit easily into another coherent musical language. I didn't really have to invent one. I borrowed a lot from Ravi and non-Western music to get started. One *could* have invented it by a construction of opposites, but in my case it didn't really happen that way. But people did it in different ways. The other important thing about Ravi for me was that he was a composer/performer. When I came back to New York I discovered that other people were doing that: Terry Riley, La Monte Young, and Steve Reich. There were good reasons to do that – no one else would play the music. Basically the avenues for presenting new music were closed to us.

*So you were forced to create your own network?*

Yes, a network without any institutional basis at all. It took a good ten years, and was quite tough at first – I played everywhere from parks to cafeterias. I never refused a concert anywhere, for any amount of money, at least for the first ten or fifteen years. It was also a way of getting around the fact that contemporary music had become, from our point of view, over-institutional-ized. You more or less needed permission to write music. The only one who gave you permission to write the music you wanted to was John Cage, who was also a performing composer. I saw him frequently – he and Merce Cunningham and Jasper Johns lived near me. I would have lunch with them from time to time and we talked about things. These weren't remote figures. One advantage (and there are not that many) of being in New York is that nothing is very remote. An important aspect of that generation is that we didn't have the institutional support, either financially or academically, and so we were a generation that evolved new places to play.

*Do you think that sense of artistic community still exists in New York?*

Yes and no. Some of the young composers seem to be a little daunted by how hard it is to get performed. If they don't get a concert right away and get a good fee, they don't want to do it. I had a loft here on Baker Street where in 1972 and 1973 we had a concert every Sunday at around three o'clock. We did it for years, for whatever people gave us. People are not so willing to do that now. I'm reluctant to say, 'Oh, in our day we didn't have this and we didn't have that' but I think there is an element of careerism in young composers. And you have to remember that when we were young we didn't *expect* to do well. It never occurred to me that I would be at the Metropolitan Opera House, certainly not by 1979 – and not again by 1992! I mean, I'm in Grove's Dictionary of Music, I have records all over, I do concerts all over the world – I didn't expect that. At the age of thirty I was willing to hold on for ever. I was willing to play in that loft for ever.

*Maybe it's because young people see that it can be done now, that those battles have been fought and won.*

That's very true. Perhaps they're smarter than us, and think that maybe there is a way around that. But models of success are unreliable. How our younger generation is going to manage I couldn't venture to say.

*What is the essence of Philip Glass's music?*

I don't think it's a style or technique. Obviously it's not, because hundreds of other people do it. Once, years ago, I was giving a talk at the New School for Social Research, and someone had done a computer printout of a piece of mine showing all the possibilities. It was endlessly long, and he asked me if I wanted to hear it, but I said No. What it contained was all the things I didn't do. I hadn't thought about it until then, but I said that the thing that makes the music is the choices you make. It's not the technique but the choices you make within the technique; I make certain choices. I mean, someone once asked Morton Feldman what his system was and he said, 'The system is me. I'm the system.' He was a very funny guy. He was very nasty about other composers, and would routinely condemn everyone in the field, but at the same time he was very charming. His answer was very much to the point: what you like about Bartók or Debussy isn't the style of music, what you like is *them*. It's the artist in the work that we are finally drawn to, whether it's Tolstoy or Picasso or John Cage. What you like in John Cage is John Cage.

*Wouldn't he have shuddered at that thought?*

I think he would have pretended to, but he had a very shrewd idea of who he was. But what's the difference between composers? Surely it's not the technique or the intelligence, or even the talent. There were people more talented than I was in music school who are judged to have done less well.

*Is there a certain way to listen to your music? Perhaps a non-Western way?*

No, I don't think so. There are different ways of listening depending on when I was writing, because I was thinking about different things at different times. I was thinking about rhythmic structure in the early 1970s, about harmonic structure in the mid to late 1970s, about polytonality in the early 1980s – and in the late 1980s I was starting to think about tonal relationships in a much more general way. Yet I don't really leave any of those things behind. The rhythmic structures I used twenty years ago are still there. You hang on to some things and other things you just abandon. My aim has also been to change, and it's hard to do that. I sometimes say that, for a composer, the first thing to do is to find your voice and the second is to get rid of it. Mostly I try to get rid of it.

# LOU HARRISON

*b. Oregon 1917*

After studying composition with Cowell in San Francisco and Schoenberg in Los Angeles in the 1930s, Lou Harrison worked as a music copyist, florist, record clerk, poet, dancer and dance critic in the 1940s, moving to New York in 1943. Here he became a music critic for *The Herald Tribune*, edited Cowell's *New Music Edition* and conducted the first performance of Ives's Third Symphony. Returning to California, he taught on the music faculty of Black Mountain College from 1951–3, and has since held posts at several American universities.

Harrison's music, such as *La Koro Sutro* for chorus and gamelan, embraces the huge variety of musical cultures bordering the Pacific. Inspired by the work of Harry Partch and his interest in non-Western tuning systems, he has, with his companion William Colvig, constructed a range of instruments including several gamelans, wind and string instruments. Essentially a melodist, Lou Harrison is often regarded as the father of West Coast new music.

*I'd like to start by asking you about living and composing on the West Coast of America as opposed to the East. What are the differences between the two, and why have you chosen the West?*

Well, why would anyone choose the East? The division in the United States is no longer between North and South, it's the Rockies. As I like to point out, starlings and Lyme Disease (a very dangerous disease first found in East Lyme, Connecticut) have both made it to California from the East. The Rockies are the great divide. California is a very different part of the United States – it's a very special civilization. In between the East and California is, from my point of view, the real America, that is to say the four states of Utah, Colorado, Arizona and New Mexico. That to me is America, the rest is peripheral – shore stuff.

*How would you describe 'West Coast' music? What would you say is its essence?*

Well, there's no one 'is' about it. I have defined it as being freer. We're not bound up with industrial 'twelve-tone-ism' quite so much as the East seaboard is, and also we're not afraid out here if something sounds pretty. I don't see that increased complexity is any solution at all. We also have a very strong connection with Asia. People in New York commute to Europe all the time, and that feels strange to me. I habitually go to Asia. This is Pacifica, that's Atlantica. They're different orientations. I don't think that there is a composer in the West who is not aware of that. We're all aware, from Seattle and Vancouver down to San Diego, that we're part of Pacifica. For some of us it feels more natural than for others. I came to my legal maturity (I've never really grown up) in San Francisco, where every week I went to the Cantonese Opera. I constantly heard Asian music. I heard my first gamelan in the middle of San Francisco Bay, and half of my friends go back and forth to Indonesia and Japan all the time. I mean, gee whizz, yesterday morning I finished one of my boxes of Kellogg's

Ken Mai flakes. You can't get them in this country – my Japanese friends send them to me. So we have a regular transit across the Pacific.

*Going back to West versus East, how is your relationship with European tradition changed? Was it always so clear to you that you were looking East?*

Well, I lived in Manhattan for ten years and had a breakdown at the end of it, which revealed to me that I was not a true New Yorker. So I moved back here, with an intermission of a couple of years at Black Mountain College in North Carolina, which was very pleasant. After I got back, my parents wanted to give me a little place to work in. Just a couple of doors from here was a place they had looked at. I looked at it, and it was just like my studio at Black Mountain College, so I said, 'That's it.' That was 1954, and that's why I'm here. Also, Harry Partch was in San Francisco at that time, and we stayed friends till he died in San Diego. John [Cage] was here for a long time too, but that was early on, in the late 1930s. But there's a tradition in California. For example, Mills College, the Centre for Contemporary Music has been going for a long time – Pauline Oliveros, Morton Subotnik, Ramon Sender, Terry Riley. Cal Arts has been a lively place, as has La Jolla in San Diego. There's a centre in Portland, Oregon, and Seattle is a hotbed. But it also goes along the whole coast and includes Mexico and Vancouver too.

*What is it about living in the country that appeals to you?*

Well, as I said, I 'did' ten years in Manhattan and finally had a breakdown. Three days in a city now and I'm quite flipped. There's too much noise. I just can't do with it. But these days a fax can come in from anywhere in the world, books and records can be ordered from anywhere. When I first moved here, to Aptos, there was very little: no real bookstores, the university was not here, neither was Cabrillo College. It was really rural. Then it gradually piled up, and now it's a classy metropolitan area. I used to go to San Francisco almost monthly, not only for sex but for books and galleries. Now there are lots of bookstores, galleries, craftsmen and intellectuals. There's a Shakespeare festival and the Cabrillo music festival every year. I see no reason why anybody has to live in depraved surroundings, in deteriorated air etc. Be yourself. If you want a calmer life then take it, for heaven's sake. The mind doesn't stop.

*You studied with Cowell first, then Schoenberg. What did they give you?*

Lots. Cowell gave me an enormous amount of 'how to' knowledge, including how to write a serial piece before I went to Schoenberg. Also an immense stimulation about world music. He was an absolutely fascinating man, because of his knowledge not only of world music but also of how to do different things. His book *New Musical Resources* continues to be very stimulating, as does the symposium that he put out years ago, *American Composers on American Music*. From Schoenberg, oddly enough, I learned simplicity. I got myself into a corner one day, so I took the problem to him. He extricated me by saying, 'Only the salient. Only the important. Don't go any further. Just do what is going ahead and in its most salient form.' In short, no complications – strip it. I've sometimes wondered whether, when I write a Balungan for a Javanese gamelan for only five or seven notes, it might have something to do with Schoenberg's admonition. When I left he said that I was not to study with anybody, that I didn't need that. He said, 'Study only Mozart.' That was his admonition – simplicity. He was a wonderful man, incidentally, quite unlike the image a lot of people seem to have of him as some sort of German militarist. I mean, he was Viennese! His liquor bills were very high and he smoked too much. His fingers were iodine-coloured. But he also had a good sense of his own virtues and faults.

*Could you tell us something about the American gamelan, and how it differs from the Indonesian gamelan?*

Firstly, the shapes and forms are different, because for the most part we do not do bronze, which is a very difficult metal to deal with. We use aluminium and/or iron. On the West Coast, Bill Colvig pioneered the use of aluminium (he's built two very large gamelans) and on the East Coast, Dennis Murphy and his pupil Barbara Benary used iron in a more or less traditional way. This country is flooded with gamelans – about one hundred and fifty or so – and a fair proportion of them are American-built. Bill's first gamelan was pipes and slabs, and it was his discovery that an aluminium slab resonated with cans soldered together that first stirred the enthusiasm for building, both in Berkeley and San Jose.

*So the main difference is in the material they're made of?*

Also the tunings and the range. Some gamelans in the United States have wider ranges than the Balungan instruments; instead of six or seven tones, they have maybe two octaves. All Bill's gamelans have two octaves. They run from five to five in both pelog and slendro. Predictably, there are melodies that will not work unless you have those extra tones. That's why they're there and, sure enough, some of my best music requires them. So it's range and tuning – some of us use just intonation of various sorts. In fact, the slendro part of the gamelan C Betty (which is one of the gamelans that Bill made, dedicated to Betty Freeman) is, to our great surprise, tuned to a schema attributed to Claudius Ptolemy in the 2nd century AD in Alexandria. I thought I'd invented it, but it's hard to invent anything these days.

*Was there a point in your career or a particular piece where you felt you'd found your own voice?*

Well, some day I probably will!

*Is your music performed in Indonesia?*

Yes. As a matter of fact, I'm astonished to find that there may be a retrospective of my work in Jakarta. Well, what Western composer would have a retrospective in Jakarta?! So yes, I'm well-known. In fact, I am told that my *Double Concerto for Violin, Cello and Javanese Gamelan* is required listening in the state conservatories.

*How did Partch inspire you?*

When the first printing of Harry's book came out, Virgil Thomson was sent a review copy because he was writing for the *New York Herald Tribune*. He gave it to me the following day and said, 'See what you can make of this.' Of course I was utterly fascinated and within the week I'd bought a tuning wrench for the piano, and I've been doing it ever since. The piano in here, which used to be a favourite of Percy Grainger's and was given to me by the Cowells, is tuned in Kirnberger Number Two, as is my *Piano Concerto*, and I keep it that way. Harry and I had a very close relationship which went on for years. Betty Freeman was his patron. She set him up in houses, underwrote his work, and gave him money if he wanted to do a big thing, which he often did. There was a movement to make copies of Harry's work and put the original instruments in the Smithsonian Institute. That's been going on for ever. When I last saw Danlee Mitchell, a few years ago, he and some friends had reconstructed some of the dilapidated instruments but with new and more durable materials. They sounded better, as a matter of fact. Harry wasn't a *luthière*, you know. He was, as he said, a musician seduced into carpentry. So some of them could profitably be rebuilt in more resonant and more durable materials. He accepted a large psaltery I had built – it's part of that instrumental collection – and he gave me a set of instruments too, bamboo things. So yes, we exchanged instruments, ideas, and pleasantries – and he made wonderful mint juleps too!

*You've written some of your texts recently in Esperanto.*

Yes, a few. It's a language I like. And I'm having the astonishing discovery that when I practise sign language now, occasionally in my head I slip into the Esperanto version. This morning I had an insight from reading this month's *Scientific American*, which is devoted to the brain and the linguistic centres. I suddenly realized that my recent interest in sign language is not only because Bill and George (a close friend) are getting deaf, but also because I had heart surgery three or four years ago and the first thing I noticed afterwards was that my linguistic centres were screwed up. I'd been doing spoonerisms like 'I don't want to work and work and die in my salad' instead of 'saddle'. Clearly, my interest in sign language is partly in getting into my linguistic centres again to try to remedy that.

*Do you use European models for the structures of your pieces?*

I'm mad for one European form, the medieval *estampie*. I've written too many of them, in fact; my latest symphony is the last one, and I'm not going to go any further. I like ABAs and rondos too. I'm particularly fond of the French rondo with no variation – not the Viennese rondo with its transposition of the subject, as in Mozart and Haydn. I also like some of the contrapuntal forms – passacaglias and things like that – though I use them less. I have quite a good historical background in European music.

*Did your studies of Indonesian forms throw up whole new ways of working?*

Indonesian forms are different from European forms. It knocks you numb when you first realize what the formal range is in Indonesian music. ABA would be simple-minded in Indonesia. There are forms whose first line lasts, say, eight counts and there are forms whose first line lasts, say, 385 counts. Then they go through a process known as *irama*, which is tempo layers. If you take a form of ten lines of 385 counts, for example, take one ten times that, and then shift it to the fifth *irama* – which means that it would expand by five geometric times – you get some idea where you're going. There's also the practice of using certain instruments to mark off where you are. It's a little bit like the chords: you know that you're not at the tonic when you're on V or IV – those are subsidiary cadences. Similarly, you know when you come to the great song, which is the equivalent of the tonic. So the shape, tonally, is very controlled, and it's instrumentally indicated. Its size, its interconnections and what you can do are breath-taking, that's all I can say. I will never, for the rest of my life, be bored as long as there are gamelans and players around. And writing too. If I write now, just out of my head, there are only two things I really like to do. One of them is harps and other tuned instruments playing modes, usually from the antique world but sometimes made up. And the other is gamelan compositions. I instinctively write Balungans now, which is the skeleton line for a gamelan piece. Up on Mount Hamilton, we just premiered my *Gending in honour of Max Beckmann*. It eliminates the pitch two in pelog, which makes a fascinating mode. The next one is in honour of Munakata Shiko – the other great artist of the century, I think.

*Do you have any specific way of working, like so many hours per day or certain times?*

They don't let me. The phone or the fax or visitors or whatever are happening all the time, and I do well if I get a half an hour in during the day. I have a load of work that I can never really accomplish. I've also been designing my own type fonts – I made four last year and my book of poems uses two of them. I now have a subsidiary career as a poet! I'm also sending slides of my paintings and drawings to the Los Angeles County Museum of Contemporary Art, which is originating an exhibition that's perhaps going around the world.

# ALISON KNOWLES

*b. New York 1933*

With a background in the visual arts, Alison Knowles is one of a number of downtown Manhattan artists whose work goes beyond disciplinary boundaries, mixing sound, images and text to produce rich, multi-layered environments. The only female member of the original Fluxus group that toured Europe in the 1960s, her works from that period include *Piece for Any Number of Vocalists* (1962) which comprises the sentence, 'Each thinks beforehand of a song, and, on a signal from the conductor, sings it through.'

Associate Professor of Art at the California Institute of the Arts from 1970–3, she has often collaborated with other composers and artists, including Malcolm Goldstein, Dick Higgins and John Cage.

Inspired by many of the ideas of Cage, her works seek to enrich our perception of life by re-examining our assumptions about music and art. It is a minimalist aesthetic, in that she seeks to make as profound an impression as possible through the slenderest of means. Again like Cage, she is interested in sound for its own sake and not as a conveyor of emotion or metaphor.

*Your work has covered a very wide area, from music compo-
sition to silk-screen printing and books on beans. How would
you describe yourself?*

Well, the traditional art forms don't seem to house my work well.
I'm a conceptual artist, working with sounds and images. I'm as
concerned with how things look as I am with how things sound. I
make my own instruments from found objects that I am
sometimes given or find on the street or construct from an old
instrument – such as this tambourine which has some silk-screen
fabric stretched over it and has, somehow, the quality of being a
tool.

I have very little musical background. I went through a music
appreciation course at Middlebury College before I left there,
then in the 1950s I worked in painting at Pratt Institute. I then
went with the Fluxus group to Europe and from the early 1960s
developed a particular point of view which pervades the art that I
do: that is, it's always minimal, and expressive of an environment
that's close to home – the sounds are ones that we all know but
have not necessarily put into a musical framework. I use the
sound of paper, the sound of toys, and a feeling that's generated
in the performance is that we're all looking at these things
together and discovering what they're about. It's more like a
'show and tell', to find these mysteries with the audience.

*Do you think it was significant that you didn't have a traditional,
classical training in music?*

I don't think it matters either way at this point. It's probably more
useful that I studied painting when I did, at a time when
Modernism was very fresh in the late 1950s. We were no longer
using painting that looked through at an illusory world, through a
window, as it were, to the artist's imaginative presentation of
saints. In other words, we were now not looking 'through' but
looking 'at'. Painting at that time had made the dramatic step into

being an object in its own right, with no illusion. The surface, the paint itself, was what we were faced with. So in music my point of view is the same as it was in painting, that I consider sounds for what they are and organize them in a minimal way so that they can be examined, very much in the way that painting used paint and the painting as an object in its own right.

This 'no-illusion world' is the one that I think allows the self not to resist outside influences, because they're just what they are. In a performance, what pervades the whole room is a kind of reverence for the space itself and for the things we use and for the sounds we make. So I like to make an environment in which everyone has a part. With my tools and my images I'm opening the field of music to the field of art. I'm opening music to art, to the beauty of a kind of material world of cloths and light and projections.

Often people have spoken of this descriptive quality of an object that goes on in the act of performing, that we're looking at something all together. So given that point of view, if I were to use a violin, I would use it as an object. Many Fluxus pieces take classical instruments and turn them into interesting objects for perusal – the George Brecht piece, for example, where the violin is cleaned with various oils. The other thing about the nature of the performing act is that not only is the instrument shown, not only is the toy or the tool given to the audience to see, but it's also given a gesture and seems in a way to come alive in an almost Shinto sense – it is awakened, finds itself exposed, and gives over its life, its sound to us.

*You seem to be really extending Cage's observation that musicians have eyes as well as ears.*

That's true.

*Can you tell us about your own perception of Fluxus and your involvement with it?*

With the Fluxus touring that we did in the 1960s, most concerts were a collection of 'event' pieces like La Monte Young's *Draw a straight line and follow it,* for instance, or my own *Child Art Piece*, which puts a two-year-old on the stage and gives him things to play with – the piece is over when the child leaves the stage. There's also my *To make a salad* piece, where huge quantities of lettuce are stirred up in a pickle barrel, miking the performers chopping. I am most comfortable with ordinary tools and ordinary means. The pieces that I do are refreshing in traditional music concerts. *To make a salad* was once done in a bass drum that was turned over and became a mixing barrel. These pieces refresh one's perception of life. If I can empty soya beans into a tray, it opens the possibility for anyone to make their own array of sounds. It's not necessary to organize them into a symphony. So, to make music, it's not necessary to be dependent on a musical background.

There's a very nice incident I remember seeing on film, of John Cage caught in a traffic jam. A videotape was made of the people in the back seat of the car, himself among them. The delay of the cars and the agony of the sounds of the horns made everyone very nervous but, within a very short time, through the influence of John's attitude, the people in the car began to listen to the horns as a piece of music and they settled down to enjoy the experience. Again, it's the attitude of being on your toes at all times, of being aware of the moment in order to find things in it.

*To be alert so that we can make use of all these things?*

Yes. I think that the most important of the arts right now is philosophy. We have an idea for making a work, and we find one or other of the disciplines to express it – painting or music or dance – and our philosophy allows us to move freely from one discipline to another. What this questions is the place of extreme skill in the production of music. I think this often works negatively right now. There's too much emphasis on polish and perfection.

*Many experimental composers seem averse to self-repetition and feel that it's important to keep changing, even though it can be dangerous to do that . . .*

Yes. Since everything is always changing, that seems the most realistic procedure. There are so many things to do.

*Can you tell us more about your work with John Cage? You wrote the book* Notations *with him.*

We actually worked on a number of books together. The last help
I could give him was to suggest that the images for his book X
would be better in black and white than full colour. In the
performance works, such as the reading of *Finnegan's Wake* or
the Gertrude Stein, I think we launched a kind of marathon
technique into performance art. *The Making of Americans* takes
many hours to read, through the day into the night, through the
day and into the next night. It's the same with the Joyce, but not
quite so long. That's what I mean about seeing something
through completely from the idea to the actual reading. With Jim
Tenney, we did the *Vexations* of Satie with the complete number
of repetitions.

What John and I did with *Finnegan's Wake* was to take the
punctuation out of each page, scramble it, and place it back in
different parts of the page by chance operations – all the commas,
exclamations, and periods – so they would sometimes interfere,
and sometimes not, with the actual words on the page.

*Can you tell us about your apparent fascination with beans?*

Well, I can tell you how it started. One day, George Maciunas,
the initiator and director of Fluxus, called and proposed we make
some publications. He suggested I did a book about beans, since I
have a reputation of being a good cook. I said, 'Sure' – and then
he called me back a few days later and asked me to bring the book
over. I rushed off to the library and began to compile the scraps
of information, songs, myths, stories, and transcriptions from
science that eventually ended up as the *Bean Rolls*. I find it
significant that in this first book I put four or five lima beans that
you could shake in the can and make a sound. So, in a way, it was
my first home-made instrument as well as my first bean work.

To study beans suggests again the importance of philosophy as
a base for art, of studying life and nature – in fact, of studying
*around* art in some depth rather than studying art itself. From
this first little book, the *Bean Rolls*, I proceeded to extract
information for the many small editions I've made over the years.
I use these beans in many ways, and it seems proper to me to use
them in my art. I'm always discovering new information. I've
done similar studies of shoes. I don't mind developing skills, you
understand, but they should be new skills. Not playing the violin

or doing charcoal drawings, but personal and individual skills, toward a new kind of art. I'm really advocating a self-perusal for artists that's based in philosophy, especially Eastern philosophy, and develops the right attitude for art-making.

The other thing about beans is that they're excellent in terms of communication with other people. Everyone has some information on the topic. This discovery of the sound of soya beans is a nice echo of the way soya beans are usually used, as a food. Now, what that does to the soya beans we're going to eat tonight is to make them a kind of materialization of the instrument. They're just soya beans again, but at the same time not quite. They have this echo in a musical instrument, so they can never be quite the same again for me.

*Can we talk about some of your more recent work, such as* Northwater Song?

I wrote this piece for John Cage, and it is appropriate to his position because the sounds are found from my daily experience, and at the same time they're sounds that everybody knows. There's tearing of silk, a small mechanical sound that could be from a piece of kitchen equipment or some electrical device, numerous paper sounds, and soya beans in the drum, as well as a text.

*How did you generate the text?*

I developed a text based on water, most of which comes from the diaries of Thoreau, plus up-state walk books and the *Oxford English Dictionary*. I also use newspapers, some things about beans, some things about letters. Suddenly the deadline arrives and everything collides, the objects and the texts. With *Northwater Song*, it took me the summer to make the texts, then very suddenly it all came together under the pressure of necessity.

*There's an* I Ching *hexagram on the score. Is that a means of structuring?*

Yes. The hexagram in *Northwater Song* turned out to mean 'The Family'. This is appropriate, because I have a strong sense of the art community and I collaborate constantly. I have a large number of chance-generated hexagrams from Carbondale and sometimes I use them rather than the *I Ching* itself. This piece for John, *Northwater Song*, tries to honour his great gift, to say that perhaps it's better to use an abstract source for the fundamental structure of a work than one's personal sense of structure; that we, in fact, should set ourselves aside, accepting the sounds and the sights as they come to us and organizing them from a list of numbers, some way outside of our own choice, trying to be fresh, vigilant and personal (by that I mean expressive of who we are and, if you will, the nature of the things and the nature of ourselves coming together). So John has made a great philosophical addition to the structuring of music. It is Eastern in nature, and readily available.

# DANIEL LENTZ

*b. Pennsylvania 1942*

After studies at St Vincent's College, then Ohio and Brandeis universities, Daniel Lentz won a Fulbright Scholarship to travel to Sweden and work at the Stockholm Electronic Music Studio. After a short spell of teaching at the University of California at Santa Barbara (he was dismissed for consistently awarding all students grade As), he turned his full attention to *The California Time Machine*, a live electronics performance ensemble he formed in 1968.

In 1971, tired of 'aggressive, negative and ugly' music, he wrote *Canon and Fugue*, his first overtly pretty piece. Much of his subsequent work has retained this sense of surface prettiness, often combined with the electronic wizardry of his 'live, multi-track recording system'. After the demise of *The California Time Machine* and its successor *The San Andreas Fault*, he formed the ensemble *LENTZ* in the early 1980s as the primary outlet for his work. Recent commissions include the orchestral work *An American in Paris* (1991) and *OrgasMass* (1992).

*Can you tell us something about your early studies and how you think they shaped your work?*

Well, I went to a Catholic college, where my principal teacher was Rembert Weakland, now Archbishop of Milwaukee. He was an expert on Ambrosian chant and a very good organist. So my early music-theory lessons were infused with his 'chant consciousness' (I don't know what else to call it), and that still comes out in my present work. I also learnt to sing plainchant, and it all gets in there. Not everybody would notice it, but I do.

*What were your first encounters with new music?*

On the Old Time record series, really handsomely-packaged LPs. I heard *Differences* by Berio, and work by Maderna, John Cage, Earle Brown and others. Because I lived in the country, those records were my first exposure.

*What was your first reaction?*

I loved it. The most modern thing I'd heard up to then was probably Bartók, and I was the only one of my classmates listening to that. It was a very traditional place.

*At what point did you feel you wanted to spend your life composing?*

Early in high school I got a Bell & Howell tape recorder on which I learned how to cut tape, change speeds and play the tape backwards. I really thought I'd invented electronic music, but at that point I hadn't yet heard anything like it. I didn't know about Cage, Pierre Henri or anyone. So I was fairly disappointed when I found out I'd been preceded by ten or fifteen years!

I was also a trumpet player until I got a lip infection, but I kept on playing and destroyed my embouchure. All my dreams of being a great jazz trumpeter went down the tubes. So, at eighteen, I thought the next best thing to playing was to write.

*Looking back, who would you say were your major musical influences?*

Early on it was Stockhausen and Cage. I was doing electronic music, then live electronic music, then I got into so-called 'conceptual' music, though I wasn't particularly aware of the Fluxus people. It was just in the air in the 1960s. I did a master's thesis on the 'multidirectionality of sound', the serial element or some such thing. It was the history of 'space music' from Gabrieli to the present day (1965), and it ended with an extensive analysis of Stockhausen's *Gruppen* for three orchestras. The second part of the thesis was a piece of mine where I spaced the players around in twelve places – a heavy Stockhausen influence. Soon I was abandoning that kind of thing and moving towards conceptual, live electronic theatre music. I then went to Sweden on a Fulbright Scholarship, sat there looking at my hands for a year, then came back and started to make 'pretty music'.

*To what extent was that prettiness a reaction to the European avant-garde?*

Initially, one hundred per cent. I got tired of going to concerts where the only people in the audience were other composers. When I wrote the first pretty piece, most of my composer friends felt I'd abandoned them.

*Was it at that point that you feel you began to shape your own musical voice?*

Well, I would say that really happened about 1970.

*How do you feel you relate, if at all, to the Western classical tradition? Do you think you're continuing it?*

Yes, I guess I do. Unlike some of my contemporaries, I don't have much touch with African or Indonesian music. I think there's so much material in a simple rock song that I could spend the rest of my life working on those three chords. So I'm one hundred per cent Western in that sense.

*That attitude distinguishes you from several of your West Coast colleagues, but I wondered if you shared, for example, Terry Riley's interest in native American ethnicity?*

Not really. I am part American Indian, so possibly I don't have to 'pursue' it. I have tremendous respect for Terry Riley – I let *him* do it. The heaviest influence on me is really Western European medieval music. Pop and rock influences also find their way into my music, if not literally then at least in spirit – for example, the 'drive' of rock or jazz.

*Is that sense of drive the only element you take from rock music?*

There may be some other rhythmic elements, tempi and so on. Sometimes, as in *On the Leopard Altar* or *Adieu*, I've made musical fun of pop music.

*And what does your music owe to medievalism?*

Definitely structural ideas, the use of canons, rounds and cantus firmus. There's also the very open 'harmony', if you can call it that – open sixths and fifths are everywhere in my music. I like the space or transparency that allows. I often use an overlaying echo process, so I have to make the individual elements fairly transparent.

*There is also your use of religious texts . . .*

Yes. I've used the Ordinary of the Mass twice, in *Missa Umbrarum* and the *WolfMASS*. My new piece *OrgasMass* is not a mass as such, it's just playing with the words 'orgasm', 'ass' and 'mass'. I used the Ordinary because I love Latin, and I love the fact that nobody understands it literally any more. So you can make word-plays without interrupting the flow of the music.

*So your use is in no sense devotional?*

I don't believe so. If it gets in there, it's on a subconscious level. I did go to Catholic school, of course, and I love the ritual elements of the High Mass (in Latin).

*Would you agree that minimalism is an indigenous American music?*

No. Most of the forms are just canons of different lengths – it's just another form of repetition, which you hear everywhere, in African music, Indian music. Composers go out of their way to find methods of repeating themselves. When I think of minimal-ism, I think of repetitious structures, not the minimalism of La Monte Young's long, sustained fifths (to me, his is a conceptual-based music). When I hear Gavin Bryars or Michael Nyman, for example, I think they have little to do with American music. I can usually tell where music comes from, and if I can't I don't normally care for the music. If a piece is made in New York and sounds like it comes from Prague, I hear a warning bell. That's one of the reasons the so-called 'international style' was such a disaster. I'm often criticized because my music sounds like it comes from Los Angeles, but I think that's the highest compli-ment I could get.

*How influenced were you by some of the structural ideas of minimalism? Your* Song of the Siren(s) *seems to me a classic process piece.*

Yes. That uses my cascading tape-delay process, but the import-ant thing in the piece, besides the echo system, is the phonetic structuring. Words are very important in my music. I can count on the fingers of one hand the number of purely instrumental works I've done, because I just love the human voice. Maybe 'process' was in the air – there is a relationship, but a non-intentional one. The really heavy influences for me in that area are still Debussy and Machaut. If you put some of Debussy's harmonies with some of Machaut's forms, throw in some American-like rhythms, you might get one of my pieces.

*You often talk of 'spiral forms', and say that your music reflects a state of 'becoming' rather than 'being'. Could you explain that?*

I can try! Much music, whether it be Beethoven or Maxwell Davies, goes from musical moment to musical moment, each one completed in turn. They might relate to each other in an intellectual way, as in a sonata structure, but within those large periods of time, every musical idea is always complete. But my music is always in a state of becoming something else. You hear a particle here, then the next particle added to that. In some of my pieces, you don't hear the whole thing until the very end. It's like walking through an orchestra spread out over a football field. You would go by the clarinets, past the violins . . . That's how you'd hear one of my pieces. When you finally step back, as if from a Seurat painting, only then do you get the whole image.

*Tell us something about your use of electronics. You seem to use technology as a structuring element rather than simply a means of sound enhancement . . .*

To me, that's always been the promise of electronics, the way it can change the time experience. There's no electronic sound more interesting than, say, a solo oboe note, let alone a human voice. So I was never interested in playing with that phonic element. When I look back at that music in the 1960s that was *about* sound, I think I'm right not to be concerned with it. The only interesting thing now about electronics in the phonic sense is sampling, which is nothing more than a recording machine. When I use it, I mostly sample the human voice – words. Then, when I play these on my Electronic Wind Instrument I become my own voice, playing myself, but in tune.

*Can you explain why you're so interested in writing pieces with words?*

It probably has a basis in sex. Female singers have been a weakness of mine throughout my life. The human voice is a beautiful instrument and the one thing that, until recently, electronics couldn't begin to simulate, especially the word element. But music without words is a pretty recent phenomenon in the West – really just an eighteenth- and nineteenth-century thing – and that's the music that interests me least. But if I got commissioned to write a string quartet or an orchestral piece, I'd do it. No hard feelings.

*Do you prefer writing for your own group to outside commissions?*

Yes, definitely. My group started out with eight keyboard players, six voices and one percussionist. There probably weren't any other groups in the world like that. I wrote for it, we were the only ones that did it, and that's still the case with those pieces. But when I write a piece for my present ensemble – which has just a couple of keyboards, a few acoustic instruments and a couple of voices – that is an ensemble that can be put together anywhere. I'm basically a low-tech guy, so there's nothing prohibitive.

*Could you say something about the ways you use texts?*

Well, I have an early piece called *You can't see the forest . . . Music* (1971) for three wine-glass drinkers/speakers. The text is made up of English language clichés such as 'There's a pot of gold at the end of every rainbow', 'Better late than never' and so on. There are six clichés and they all relate to the disassembling of the text and the reassembling of it via the cascading echo system. There are seven or eight tape delays, each forty seconds long (it takes about forty seconds to articulate all six clichés in a normal way) and notated rhythmically. Each performer enunciates a syllable or phoneme while at the same time hitting a wine glass (occasionally they take a drink, so of course the pitch goes up). It's all done with red wine so that it can be seen by the audience, and when a performer finishes one glass, he picks up another glass. Take, for example, the phrase 'Better late than never'. You might first hear the 'la(y)' of 'late' accompanied by a strike of a wine glass. After the next couple of cycles, you'll hear the phrase 'Better la(y) than ever' until eventually you hear the whole thing. But on the way you have all these little word-plays. In *Missa Umbrarum* I do this with Latin, taking the phonemes out of Latin and creating English words.

*How do you usually start a new piece?*

Well, it depends on what it's for and whether or not it includes the human voice. If it does, I'll either create or find a text. Then I decide if it's going to go straight from left to right or if there's going to be a 'process' of some type. If that's the case, then what kind? Live digital multitracking or just shorter digital delays? There are any number of possible ways to proceed. Then I'll determine the length and so on.

*So after the practical questions, your first musical question relates to how you structure the piece?*

Basically, I have the whole piece in mind before I get started. I'm not saying that is inspiration, but I can hear it all pretty well. So it's just a matter of writing it out, though that can take months.

But I don't want to start until I know how it ends. I'm not an improvisatory kind of person.

*Can you hear a piece in an instant because your language is now, at least for you, a given?*

Yes, I think so. That's a very interesting question. I don't know if you've asked everybody that, but out of the list of people you've interviewed, I think most of them have their own musical language. I mean, style is really just learning how to repeat yourself, sometimes endlessly. If you keep changing your language and what you do, which is a very noble thing to do, nobody will know who you are. And it's a dilemma: I like to change, but my language is now so tied to me that it becomes a habit, which isn't necessarily good. I've often thought of writing a twelve-tone piece just to surprise my friends and all these academic types who jumped on the band-wagon about twenty-five years after the fact and now make 'triadic' music. I've been thinking of jumping off for years and writing some magnum opus for full orchestra, such as a twelve-tone concerto. I'd love to do that. But I would really be interested to make a twelve-tone piece for my group and see how it would invade what one might call my personal language – if it would still sound like a Lentz piece, even though the harmonic structure would be totally different. But I don't quite have the will or circumstance to do it.

*How would you characterize what has become your language?*

Well, we've used the word 'process', but I prefer 'procedure'. It's a hard question: a lot of seconds, fifths, the general energy, that LA freeway sound. Now, the heat of the Sonoran Desert.

*One of the fascinating things I find about listening to your music is that often, for all the surface prettiness, there's a sort of dark irony or black humour . . .*

From about 1974 with *O-KE-WA* to 1983 and *Wolf is Dead*, there was a lightness about my music, a 'happiness', using chords almost always in major modes. The reason for that was very simple: I didn't like diminished or augmented intervals, especially tritones, whereas I'm happily in love with them now. My most recent piece, *OrgasMass*, is absolutely full of them, as well as minor ninths and all those dissonances that weren't in my music then. It's very dark; even when it's driving at about 500 beats per minute, there's an incredible darkness in there. And it has to do, I'm sure, with this cold, unconscious feeling where it seems like the older you get, the more friends you start losing, you know? Believe it or not, that element gets in there somehow, though I have no idea how. But when I have an opportunity to look back, even on a little, five-year span, I can identify these changes, although I never thought of them. Also, I was getting bored with that happy, major sound. I love to be happy but there's something very boring about it. It's like that story of John Cage and his mother: he wanted to take her out somewhere and said, 'You'll have a good time', and she said, 'Son, you know how I never enjoyed having a good time'.

*Do you think that where you live has affected the music you write?*

Oh man, does it ever! Though you can't determine it. You can't say that you're going to go out and write a desert-influenced piece or a piece influenced by North London.

*You don't think you'd write what you do if you lived in Manhattan?*

No way. Nobody realizes what the desert's like until they get here. It's not a calm, serene place at all. It's a violent, dark, foreboding place sometimes. And when it's not that, it's hotter than hell. There's actually nothing comfortable about it. It's like living on the North Pole. So naturally, at some point, that's going to get into the work. But I think it's too early to tell right now.

*What connects the changes between the different periods of your work?*

Probably this rebellion that I have in me. I'm a renegade by nature. I've never been able to join the mainstream because my background and personality won't allow it. The most influential advice I've ever gotten was from my mother. It concerned an assignment in high school. I had to take a position on a specific project. Perhaps I had to write a paper defending my position. Anyway, she questioned me about the teacher's preferred position, then advised me to take the opposite position. 'This way', she said, 'she will notice you'. Now, some thirty-odd years later, I am at a point in my musical life where only one thing matters. And that is 'beauty'. Like others before me, presently and no doubt after me, I've wasted a lot of musical energy pursuing the political and social issues of the time. I see now the futility of those efforts. Music can only be *about* itself. That self is beauty. Whatever the hell that means.

# ALVIN LUCIER

### b. New Hampshire 1931

Alvin Lucier is another experimental composer whose early works forced a redefinition of the term 'music'. In the late 1960s he astonished an audience by attaching electrodes to his scalp, shutting his eyes in meditation, and slowly generating alpha waves which, hugely amplified, caused sympathetic resonances from an array of percussion instruments surrounding him. This *Music for Solo Performer* is only one in an ongoing series of works exploring natural acoustic phenomena in which Lucier's primary aim is not to express himself creatively but to help us catch a glimpse of the essence of life. As he once said, he's 'trying to help people hold shells up to their ears and hear the ocean again'.

His fascination with acoustic space is explored in his 1968 work *Chambers*, in which found objects such as a thimble and teapot are used to house ambient recordings from often bizarrely disproportionate spaces (if one listens closely to the thimble, for example, one can hear Cologne railway station).

*What do you think is the difference between a demonstration of acoustics in a physics class and a piece of music?*

I guess part of it is the intent. If the intent is an artistic one, then how you execute it will probably show that. For example, the piece that's on show here [*Chambers*], where the sounds of larger environments are put in smaller environments, could be thought of as an acoustic demonstration of the filtering effects of different-sized enclosures, but the chances are that a scientist would never do it that way. He would think it isn't the clearest way to show the phenomenon. But *Chambers* brings other things in, non-scientific things. For example, the idea of recording the Köln Bahnhof and putting it in a thimble is a whimsical part of that. I enjoyed doing that because so many composers who've gotten into this idea of recording environments have used such complexity, many microphones and many channels, to record that same railroad station and they've taken it very seriously. I did too, but then I put it in a thimble so that most of the acoustics are lost. *Chambers* is an old piece actually, from 1968, and if I wanted to get any credit for things, it was one of the first pieces that used the idea of environments and their sound characteristics. The idea was that you'd move various-sized sound environments into other environments, that is, carry sounds from one place to another, thereby changing them.

*Do you see any connection with Marcel Duchamp in your use of commonplace objects in this piece?*

I do now, but I didn't then. I have a student who is very interested in Duchamp, so I've started reading Octavio Paz's book on him; but I can't say that I was influenced by Duchamp when I did this piece. Maybe I shouldn't find out about him. Perhaps it would stop me from doing things that I should do. When I chose the objects for this show, I think I did the right thing by not using much taste. Paz says that the imitators use what they think is taste when they choose objects, and then their works become 'cute'.

*Was it difficult to choose objects without using taste?*

Well, it wasn't so much that I *chose* them without taste, it's just that the best ones were afterthoughts. I was in Amsterdam and I thought of buying a fancy cigar box, but I couldn't bring myself to do it. It just didn't seem right. However, I did pick a German music-stand box I had, but that was an afterthought. Yet, taking a look at it, it's one of the nicest things. Actually, the piece isn't supposed to be focused on interesting objects, but on objects that can impose their sonic characteristics on those other sounds. I decided I should have some plastic and metal and so forth, and that's really more important than the imagery of the object.

*Do you think perhaps that the piece also demonstrates the theatrical potential of inanimate objects?*

Sure. As much as I say that I'm interested in the acoustic aspect of it, I must admit that there's something wonderful about the big railway station in Köln coming out of a thimble. I mean, a thimble is about the smallest thing you could possibly use and still be able to get a sound out of it. So there's a practical aspect too. I used the funnel because 'funnel' rhymed with 'tunnel' and in my score I started to get rhymes when I was writing the list of things.

*Have you ever been interested in working on tape and processing sounds?*

I don't process sound all that much, it doesn't really interest me. The *I am Sitting in a Room* piece does it, but it processes speech by putting it back into an acoustical space. I like acoustical spaces. I mean, if you use a band-pass filter, you'll have to decide where you're going to set the centre frequency and I have no way of making decisions of that kind.

*When talking to Cage we likened your ideas to his, in that you both draw attention to life, although Cage admits a multiplicity that you don't. You focus attention on a single natural phenomenon, revealing an inner life of which we are generally unaware. Do you see this similarity?*

Yes. I may have gotten that idea from some of his works, but I have taken it in a very different direction.

*You both also present sound for itself rather than using it as some kind of metaphor.*

Yes, I think so. That wonderful artist Robert Irwin keeps talking about reducing the metaphor to get at the presence he wants. I have to do that all the time, and it's hard. It's the process of composition I have to go through, and it just doesn't occur to me immediately what I have to do.

*In your essay* The Tools of my Trade, *you say that sometimes, when you first conceive of a piece, you begin with the principal idea followed by a temptation towards greater complexity but finally reduce it to its minimum. For example, wasn't there a temptation to use many wires in* Music on a Long Thin Wire?

Yes. People often say, 'Why don't you use two wires?', or they want one to interact with the other. That's a whole separate aesthetic.

*But do you feel you consciously have to resist this temptation?*

Yes. Sometimes I start with that, but then I bring it down to only one thing.

*How does it feel to be 'in the hands', so to speak, of the sounds? The works of most composers are in the hands of the performers. Have you ever had any bad 'performances' or outright disasters where the phenomenon simply hasn't worked?*

Oh, I have lots of disasters. Then everybody looks at me like I'm the emperor without any clothes. Sometimes I will do a piece that doesn't work all that well, but part of it does and I know it does. I have a piano piece called *Shapes of the Sounds from the Board*. When you strike a note on the piano, you can hear it moving in space.

*Does it worry you that other people might not hear that?*

Yes. Most notes on the piano are sounded by three strings and they're a little bit out of tune, so there are phase shifts going on. I can hear those shifts as movement of sounds in space. If you play the same note again, you can hear it move the same way, and if you play a different note, it has a different shape. I can hear that but very few other people can. So if you play that piece, it escapes ninety-nine percent of the people. They just don't think it's happening, or if you say it's 'moving', they think of movement in a poetic way. They don't think that you really mean the sound waves are moving.

*Can you tell us something about your more recent projects?*

Yes. I've made some pieces for musical instruments: a trio for viola, cello and piano; a septet; a piece for small orchestra; one for solo clarinet; and a kettle-drum piece. Most of them have to do with interference patterns and audible beats. I've also written a triangle piece for the percussionist Brian Johnson in memory of Morton Feldman. I happened to glance at the score of Feldman's piece for flute and orchestra and saw that he was using six triangles of various sizes. Now, I'm not one for writing pieces for someone who dies, but I thought I'd like to write a piece for solo triangle. I recently came upon a Buñuel phrase which is quite beautiful. The Surrealists hated music, you know, and he has a glossary of instruments of the orchestra, describing them in terrible ways, but he calls the triangle the 'Silver Streetcar of the Orchestra'. I liked that, and I'm tempted to use it as the title.

*You once said something about presenting phenomena in beautiful ways. Is this still important to you?*

Oh yes, sure. Robert Irwin lived in Los Angeles and at the age of sixteen he had a 'hotrod' which he maintained very beautifully. He used to lacquer parts of the car that you couldn't see, so that even those parts were beautiful. That's an important idea, that you're very honest about every part of your piece.

# INGRAM MARSHALL

*b. New York 1942*

Ingram Marshall began shaping his intensely personal approach to music-making in the mid-1960s as a graduate student working at the Columbia-Princeton Electronic Music Center. He later became a graduate assistant to Morton Subotnik at the California Institute of the Arts, where he continued to teach for several years.

It was while at Cal Arts that Marshall first became seduced by the sounds and forms of Indonesian music. As well as making occasional use of the Balinese flute (gambuh) alongside synthesizers and live electronics, his works seem to share an Indonesian-inspired sense of time and spiritual evocativeness. From the bleak expansiveness of *Fog Tropes* (1982) for brass sextet and tape to the elegaic live electronic sound world of *Gradual Requiem* (1984), Marshall's relatively small output comprises what John Adams called 'a music of almost painful intimacy'.

*What did you get from studying with Ussachevsky at Columbia University?*

As the years went by, I felt like I had less and less to do with that whole scene. But in the last few years I've felt that I got more out of it than I realized. I've been thinking a lot of Ussachevsky lately. He died a few years ago. In a way, he was responsible for my deciding to become a composer, by virtue of giving me encouragement – or almost permission – for me to do what I was interested in. He didn't have any influence on me stylistically, although his music went very much against the grain of the current serial or post-Webernesque style. He was much more interested in transforming sound, rather than creating electronic sound and manipulating it in a technical way.

*What sort of things were you producing at that time?*

Well, I was just starting as a composer. I did one or two fully-fledged pieces when I was studying with him, but then I left that scene and didn't really do much for a few years. I got involved again with electronic music when Morton Subotnik was doing a free-for-all composers' workshop at NYU. That was an electronic music studio of very different orientation from Columbia.

*One that you felt more at home with?*

Well, it was a composers' collective. The people involved in it ran it, and it wasn't situated in a strict academic scene.

*What sort of things were you making at that stage?*

I did some pieces using a Bucla synthesizer, and I did a few live electronic things. That's also when I started getting interested in manipulating voices on tape and working with concrete sounds. Very shortly after that I went out to California.

*Was that following Subotnik?*

Basically, yes. He took me and a few other people out to Cal Arts.

*What did you get from him as a teacher?*

Again, very little stylistic influence. More just encouragement in professional savvy. He was a very savvy person. He knew how to get things done.

*Did you ever feel any dichotomy between technology and expressiveness, or did you always use technology in the expressive way that you use it now?*

That's always been a hallmark of my work, attempting to humanize the technology, even unconsciously perhaps; this has been said by several critics, and I would agree with them. My way of looking at all that technology is in a way to try and subvert it, so it doesn't dominate.

*Do you think that you were able to do that because you were principally using* musique concrète *techniques? I mean, whether digital or analogue, you're generally manipulating real sound.*

I think there's a great built-in irony to electronic music. The first electronic music I ever heard, and probably one of the most impressive pieces there is, was Varese's *Poème Electronique.* I remember hearing it on the radio when I was in college and getting all geared up for it, thinking it was going to be great. I remember being amazed because it was so unlike what I expected. It didn't have a kind of high-tech gloss to it. It had a gritty, down-to-earth and very musical sensibility. I was very attracted to it because of that. That's one reason why I thought I could go into electronic music, into this technical world, and rummage around to find what I needed. I wasn't really attracted to it because of the technical aspect, like a lot of composers seem to have been. I've always been a bit suspicious of all the algorithms and so forth, but I've certainly learned enough about it to do what I wanted to do.

*What about the presentation of your electronic music? These days, there's the feeling that it's not enough any more to present it on its own, with the audience sitting in a darkened room with nothing to look at. Is that behind your collaborations with the photographer Jim Bengston?*

Actually, way before that I was doing live electronic music on my own. There's an early piece called *The Fragility Cycles*; I used a Serge synthesizer – an old analogue synthesizer – and a tape-delay system in a live performance. I also used my voice a lot, and a long Balinese flute called a gambuh. I used those things to personalize or humanize the whole electronic music context. I think the good thing about live performance is that there is always a risk associated with it, an element of improvisation. The audience puts you on your toes. Maybe you're not always able to do things to perfection, but when things happen well, it's quite wonderful. Of course, when they don't happen so well, it's quite awful. One time in the late 1970s I was doing this piece from *The Fragility Cycles* at a big festival in Berlin. There were a thousand people in the audience, and I was squeezed in between Terry Riley and some Japanese composer. There wasn't much time to set up and sound check, so I was very nervous. Furthermore, some of my equipment had been lost by the airline. Then, right in the middle of my piece, in one of the most beautiful quiet sections where I'm cranking up the feedback to the highest levels, the feedback from the tape recorder suddenly got out of control. It created a huge acoustical feedback in the room that was getting really overpowering – a loud screeching noise that you might hear at a rock concert, only worse. They turned everything down, but it was still there. Finally, I pulled the master amplifier down and eventually the sound died down, but it was just awful!

*You've said that* The Fragility Cycles *was one of the most important works for you, that it was a turning point – a 'break-through piece'. Why is that?*

With that piece I was able to combine two elements I had been working on separately up to that point. One of them was the straight tape piece, either a text-sound piece or some kind of *musique concrète*, and the other was live electronic music, in which synthesizer, tape manipulation and instrumental or vocal sounds were used and mixed in real time. Sometimes the two elements might be mixed: something might be on tape and something might be performed live. In *The Fragility Cycles* I combine a number of things from both sides. For example, there was a piece in there called *Sibelius in his Radio Corner* which is basically a tape piece, but I play it through a tape-delay system so that its acoustical ambience is in the same spirit as what's been going on, so that one thing leads to another. Artistically, that work was important for me because I was able to bring together the live and the non-live and put tape pieces into a performed context.

*You mentioned Sibelius. Did his music influence you?*

Of the older composers of that era he has certainly influenced me. I got interested in his music in 1975, and it was like rediscovering a composer that I had known about but had written off as a side-track figure. The same is true to a certain extent for Bruckner. His music started appealing to me enormously at about the same time. It seemed very regressive suddenly to be in love with this arch-Romantic music, but I found it refreshingly new to my ears.

*Do you see yourself as essentially coming from that tradition?*

I guess so. I didn't at first, but now I look back and see myself as definitely steeped in that tradition, although I've gone about it in a rather meandering, oblique way.

*Some of your music, points in* Hidden Voices *for example, could almost appeal to a thoughtful alternative rock audience.*

Well, I hope it would. A lot of my music is actually quite accessible – it's not that hard to like it. A long time ago I gave up the idea that modern music has to be a bitter pill you must swallow, as if it was something that is good for you but hard to get down. I think that's one of the great corruptions of our age. It really came out of the post-war era, when the 'gang of four' – Stockhausen, Boulez, Cage and Babbitt – banished lovely things from modernism, beautiful things. Although Cage would never say it like that. He would certainly, in his philosophy, allow anything, but I know personally that he was always uncomfortable with music that was expressive. It was basically not where he was going, and he took along a lot of people on that ride, as did European serialists like Boulez and Berio – although, again, they have both written elegant and beautiful music. What happened in the early to mid 1970s is that a lot of composers started re-examining the whole aesthetic issue and wanted to recapture things that had been thrown aside, commonly known as melody, harmony and pulse, which are things that Steve Reich did so well.

*Is that the West Coaster in you? You're not afraid of melody?*

Yes, I think so. When I went out there I suddenly felt a lot less inhibited. I could follow my own instincts, and didn't have to worry about someone breathing down my neck to make sure I was doing the 'right' thing.

*How do you explain that? Is it just because it's further away from Europe, or is there a different spirit?*

There is a sense of being further away from control centres which is part of the tradition of the West Coast. It's one of the things I try to address in the paper I wrote called *California – the Great Permission Giver* (to be published eventually by the Institute for Studies in American Music) – the whole idea of permissibles, of how there's always been a feeling in California that you can go ahead and do what you want to do and no one's going to care. It has a down-side too, because the institutions and structures of support sometimes are a little flaccid. But I strongly agree that there is a California or West Coast sensibility that allows creative people to open up in ways that they might not have done in the more academic environments on the East Coast.

*What about the influence of Indonesian music on your music?*

That was very profound. I went to Cal Arts in 1970 to do electronic music, but I got really side-tracked in the first year by the Indonesian music that they did – there was a Javanese gamelan and two Indonesian teachers. Then, in the summer of 1971, I was very fortunate to be able to go to Indonesia and continue with my studies. That one year really consumed me. When I went back and started working again on my compo-sition, I had a very different take on things. I think it had to do with time more than anything else, how to use time. Not to fight it so much, but simply to ignore it. In other words, to try to deal with time on a more glacial, long-term basis. My music's been longer ever since then. My pieces aren't always long, but there's a sense of time slowing down that comes from the Javanese music influence.

*There also seems, for want of a better word, a sense of grimness in your music.*

Well, Edward Strickland said it was gloomy. I think 'gloomy' or 'grim' conjure up horror-movie images and I can't really accept that. On the other hand, I think there is definitely a dark side to my music. It deals with minor chords a lot, it's very foreboding and apprehensive, so your adjectives are getting close. There's a certain sense of *tristesse* and a pervasive lugubriousness in a lot of my music, I can't deny it.

*How do you actually go about composing your music? Do you have a routine?*

Once I really begin a piece, I'm into it and I set up a routine. But if I'm not in that process, I don't have a routine. Last year I went to a talk by some composer who was really bragging about the way he wrote, which was a daily routine – he'd get up every morning, have his orange juice and coffee, do some exercises and then he'd hit the desk and compose for two hours, from 7.45 to 9.45. Then he'd put down his pen and go down to the school where he was teaching for a couple of hours. That was the secret of why he was able to compose so much music. And I thought, 'Well, this is why the guy is such a bad composer!' I can't do that – and I don't think I'd be able to do the kind of music I do if I did work like that. Once I'm involved in a piece and have a deadline, I try to get into as much of a routine as I can. But I may leave a piece in the middle and do something else for a couple of weeks and it doesn't bother me.

*You wrote* Fog Tropes *as a tape piece, then you arranged it for tape and brass for John Adams. Did that inspire you to work more with live instruments?*

I had done that before with a couple of pieces. There's a piece in *The Fragility Cycles* called *Gambuh* which I arranged for strings, flute and clarinet. Since then, I've done a few more pieces where I've basically taken the instruments and put them on top of material on tape. There's a fairly recent piece called *The Peaceable Kingdom* which I did with the LA Philharmonic New Music Group. I made the tape in my studio, and it contained a lot of material from recordings I made in Yugoslavia of a village funeral procession, where you hear people walking, priests singing, the village band playing and babies crying. That became the sonic material for the tape part. The instrumental part is a line on top of that, sometimes standing out and sometimes blending in with it.

*Tell us about some of the ideas behind* Hidden Voices.

The idea came from Bob Hurwitz, who was the producer at Nonesuch. He knew I was interested in Eastern European music and suggested I did something using that as a basis. I spent the spring of 1987 listening to a lot of music, from Estonia down to Georgia, and one of the things that really struck me were these women singing laments. They came principally from Romania and Hungary, with a few from Russia, and I took them as the basis of the piece. I started manipulating the recordings, using tape techniques and a sampler, and got the idea of *Hidden Voices*, with all these different voices blending and then going back again. It went through all kinds of transformations. At one point, I wanted to include something very different from the Eastern European lament, and somehow the idea of the English choirboy came to me. I was haunted by *Once in Royal David's City*, the hymn you always hear at Christmas at King's College, Cambridge. I was thinking about having a boy soprano sing it, but I had to give up on that and just used a regular female soprano. The idea was of that pure and colourless Anglican voice opposed to the very dark feeling of the lament. It's a very complicated piece, with lots of different elements, but again I basically worked on the tape parts and then wrote the live vocal parts.

*One thing we haven't mentioned yet is the word 'minimalism'.*

The M-word!

*You've been described as a minimalist, yet your music seems to incorporate so many elements.*

I've never found that label very useful except to describe the most obvious minimalist composers. But having said that, I also recognize it's become widely used. The term has entered the vocabulary of music, and sometimes you don't have any control over that. I mean, Debussy never wanted to be called an Impressionist. If I was trying to describe my music to somebody who couldn't hear it, I might use the term minimalism as a suggestion of the direction it goes in. But I don't think of myself as a minimalist.

*One aspect of your work which doesn't seem too far from that tag is, for instance, the last part of* Three Penitential Visions. *Sometimes the patterns in the piano part are such as you might hear from a minimalist composer, as are some of the brass patterns in* Fog Tropes.

Well, my music uses repeating patterns and I've been influenced by Steve Reich – I would never deny that – but I just don't think of myself as a minimalist. I have a very strict definition of musical minimalism, which I see as being very similar to minimalism in the visual arts. That means a composer like La Monte Young would be included, as would the very early pieces of Steve Reich, like *Clapping Music*, *Music for Pieces of Wood* and the six pianos piece. In other words, it's music in which the principal idea is process rather than what it's about. The piece is about the process. A composer like Alvin Lucier, who basically sets up processes and lets them run, is to me a kind of minimalist. Tom Johnson sometimes does pieces like that. But everyone seems to think that minimalism is the big style of our times – that every composer who writes music that's slightly repetitious, or uses melody, or has some nice sunny quality to it, or has been influenced by Glass or Reich, is a minimalist. I was really astonished when John Cage's obituary in the *New York Times* referred to him as a minimalist. I mean, when *Cage* is described as a minimalist, the word has completely lost its meaning!

# MEREDITH MONK

*b. Lima, Peru 1943*

Composer, vocalist, film-maker and choreographer, Meredith Monk has created more than sixty music, theatre, dance and film works since 1964. She has also recorded eight albums of her music and, since 1978, has toured extensively as Meredith Monk and Vocal Ensemble. Her output ranges from solo vocal compositions (*Songs from the Hill*, 1976–7), through small ensemble pieces (*Dolmen Music*, 1980–1), to a full-scale opera, *Atlas*, which was premiered in 1991.

Her compositions have been described as 'folk music for a culture that doesn't exist'. Her primary interest lies in exploring the trans-cultural beginnings of human utterance in an attempt to reaffirm what she calls our sense of 'ground'. Using only her voice and intuition as her basic compositional tools, Monk's music is a direct, emotional call to rediscover the sensation of life that seems at once ancient and modern, radically new yet always known.

*Who were your formative influences as a composer, dancer, choreographer?*

Well, I don't usually separate them. My background was a very big influence on me. My mother and her father were singers, and her mother was a concert pianist. My whole childhood had so much music in it, and I sang and read music at a very young age. I was not very physically coordinated because I had an eye problem, but my mother sensed that I was very rhythmical and so I went to Dalcroix Eurythmics. That was basically my first musical training, but it was also my first movement training. I think that working with music in that way, spatially and kinetically, or working with movement through rhythm, has very much influenced the way I've thought of music through my whole life. That's why I don't separate music and movement. But I would say that, in music, the composers I always felt very close to were medieval – such as Perotinus – Satie (who I played on the piano as a child), Bartók and Stravinsky, especially the children's piano pieces. So I like up to Bach, and then twentieth century.

*Has any one of those separate elements ever been more important to you, or have you continually fused them together?*

I would say that I have. I think the heart of my work is the vocal music, but I don't think the voice is separate from the body. I mean, there wouldn't necessarily be gesture in every piece, but there's definitely a sense of the voice as a kinetic impulse or a kinetic energy. With a music concert, I'm very aware of what it would look like visually, and I still try to make as full a perceptual experience for an audience as possible.

*Which aspect of your work comes first? Is it generally the music?*

It depends. There are some pieces where the music does come first. There are others where it was really like making a mosaic. *Quarry* was a piece where the music, the concepts, some of the characters and images were pretty much formed around the same time. Whereas with *Atlas*, a lot of the music was written before I went into rehearsal and dealt with the other elements.

*How do you actually compose?*

Different ways. Sometimes I'll be walking down the street and start singing something that has just come to me. Things often come to me at odd times. But sometimes I will sit at the piano, which I try to do every day. What I really try to do is start from zero. It's a bit like automatic drawing – I try just to let my hands go on the keys and see where they go. It's the same with singing. I'm trying to start as much as I can from a neutral point, to see what the first impulse is and work from that. That's a daily discipline, but sometimes nothing comes up. Sometimes I'll start with a technical idea, as in *Dolmen Music*, where we were working with different speeds of vibrato. Once I'd started on this, it was really a matter of finding the notes. Sometimes an image will come up of what the whole of the piece will be, and then it's a matter of finding the components and structuring it. Generally, the process begins intuitively and I try to stay out of the way of the material as much as I can. Then as it goes along, the intellectual aspect comes in, which is trying to find the correct form for that material. So far, I have not been the kind of person that says, 'My structure is going to be AABCD' – I don't set the bottle up and then pour the liquid in. Most of the time I have the liquid first and then I find the structure that works.

One of the disciplines I've worked on over the years is to try to let the materials stay for a while in that intuitive state and not try to structure them too quickly. It's like making soup and letting the vegetables just be themselves for quite a long time. They simmer for a while, then finally boil down to what the essential soup will be. I work at that discipline a lot because I do tend to try to put things together too quickly.

*A lot of people comment on the formal balance of your work and how beautifully structured it is. When do you go about that second stage?*

Well, again, because I'm trying to work with what's at hand, it's a matter of doing a lot of work on figuring out what the best form would be for that material. So I don't have a particular model. I admire people who work that way – it's a very different way of working, more like working on forms that have already existed. With me, every piece is a new form, and that's the hard part of what I do. But if it was *totally* intuitive, then it wouldn't have that other edge which has to do with precision and what I would call discriminating intelligence – you know, 'Why is this work better than that?'

I can be quite specific about how the process works with individual pieces. This will depend on whether it's basically a music piece, or one of the larger musical theatre pieces which involve a lot of different elements and therefore need a longer preparation period. Before *Atlas* I worked for about three years on the musical elements, on some of the movement and narrative ideas (though *Atlas* is not exactly narrative, it has strands of it) and on some of the visual ideas. Really, I was collecting these different aspects. I also remember that in pieces like *Quarry*, *Vessel* and *Specimen Days*, after I had collected a certain amount of material, I would make a chart that put those elements in layers, so that I could see all the musical elements, movement ideas and visual images on a piece of paper. I could see what the tiles of the mosaic were, not trying to weave them together at all at that point, but basically seeing what the different layers could possibly be. In the large musical theatre pieces, it's a matter of the overall composition: how these things counterpoint, how they resonate so that each element makes the other elements resonate and yet remains itself. It's not like one element illustrating another, because that's not very interesting to me. My interest is in keeping these elements independent, yet weaving them so that there's an inevitable totality about them.

*That seems very subjective – how one thing might help another resonate.*

Yes, it is.

*So if it works for you, do you just hope it works for others?*

I guess so. I'm sure John Cage and I could have had a long conversation about this, because he was someone who would try to keep the elements independent and make sure there was no subjective point of view about how they worked together. As for me, because I'm always trying to boil down to this essential simplicity of what has to be there and nothing more (that kind of simplicity has a lot of complexity and tension within it) I'm very particular about what each thing is, so I guess that is subjective.

*That was the definition that Terry Riley gave us of minimalism: 'not doing anything that you don't have to'.*

I've always had a hard time with the idea of minimalism because I feel that what I do with the emotional aspect is as 'maximal' as you can get. My sensibility has always been one of inclusion rather than exclusion. On one level it's boiling things down, but basically my method is one of expansion, of including a lot of different perceptual layers so that a human being in an audience or the human beings that are performing are utilizing as much of themselves as possible. That's why minimalism has always been hard for me.

*Do you have complete control over all aspects of your work, or do you allow input from other people you're working with?*

I always do a lot of preparation, either sitting at the piano or sometimes laying down tracks myself. I've been doing that for about ten years – laying down tracks of my own voice, trying some of the ensemble work or counterpoint, and then going into rehearsal. Particularly with the older members of my ensemble who I have been working with for a long time, there's a give and take in the rehearsals where we try variations and different configurations of who's singing what. There are some sections where the structural element is very precise, but there are always others where a singer can play with it – that comes from having sung together for a long time. If you heard two performances of *Dolmen Music*, the overall structure would be the same but phrase by phrase there would always be a place for a singer either to compress or expand a little bit.

*In that case, how do you notate?*

I never notated a piece until *Atlas*. I use notation as a memory device after I'm happy with the overall structure of a piece. The point about doing music and live performances is that things grow in a very organic way. People who come to an opening night of mine, expecting to see some kind of European concept of perfection, will get a surprise if they come back two weeks later – they will see how the form has grown through the act of performing it. With me, there's a certain point where I feel that the piece has grown into a form that feels stable, where the overall form feels very satisfying. It's at that point I would notate it.

*What form does that notation take?*

Notation is something I'm struggling with right now. I've always been very sceptical of it, and now that I'm getting older, I'm having to cope with the problem of how much I'm leaving to other people. How much can you really get from looking at a piece of paper? It's so sketchy in relation to what we're doing, especially the vocal work. For *Atlas*, the orchestral score is very clear, though instrumentalists did some wonderful things with different performances of it. But basically, what you see on the page is what you get. I don't know how you would notate some of the vocal work, and I don't know if I want to or not. I'm struggling with that right now because I do want to pass my work on. It's not that I don't want to have other people do it, but I think that the way it's made comes from a primal, oral tradition that is much more about music for the ears. In Western culture, paper has sometimes taken over the function of what music always was. I feel that my music is between the barlines: what is really happening is underneath the page, and I don't know how to deal with that.

*Let's talk about your actual use of voice. Most singers would say that the voice is a particularly interesting instrument because it can use words and therefore be even more expressive. You've said that you use the voice as an instrument without words because you want to express the emotions that we have no words for.*

The voice itself is a very eloquent language, and I've always felt that singing English on top of it is like singing two languages at the same time. There's nothing wrong with that, but basically I think that the voice itself speaks so much more directly. Also, because our world is shrinking, it's important to work with a means that speaks to people in a direct, open-hearted way. It's a direct connection to a visceral, primordial sense of human history and human existence. I guess that's why I've stayed away from text, though I have explored it from time to time. *The Tale* has these little folk refrains: 'I still have my hands, I still have my mind', and at some levels, I've felt that a lot of my music is like folk music. It often has a kind of song form. But my main thrust is what the voice itself can do.

*So by not having words, you're creating a universal language?*

That's what I'm trying to do.

*As well as using primal sounds, your music often seems to deal with primordial themes. Is that a way of getting back to basics and helping people get back in touch with their basic feelings?*

Yes, it's about exploring the beginnings of things. I'm very interested in the beginnings of human utterance, in utterance that transcends culture. I do think we've lost a sense of our 'ground' as human beings, and that it's important to affirm that 'life energy'. In a sense, it's trying to counterbalance where I think culture is going, which is rather fragmented and, certainly in this country, rather violent, very detached and very non-connected.

*Do you take elements from other cultures or do you invent your own materials?*

I start with my own voice, and always have. I know some people thought that my process had to do with studying other cultures, taking a little bit here and a little bit there, but I've always thought of this as a culturally imperialist view. I have not studied ethnomusicology, though I have a lot of respect for people who have. But basically I start with my own instrument and explore the parameters of that world. This is how I began as a soloist. But when you work with all the different possibilities of your own instrument, you do come upon things that exist in a lot of different cultures, that are transcultural. In a sense, you become part of the world vocal family. There's something very comforting about that, because it is being part of something that has always existed and always will exist. Of course, each of our voices is totally unique. You might have a set of vocal sound possibilities that I might not be able to do or which wouldn't be comfortable for me, and I would have different ones that might not be comfortable for you. Our vocal mechanisms are totally unique. Also, in all cultures there are what I would call archetypal songs – the lullaby form, work song, love song, march, funeral song. It's interesting to hook into these song categories that exist all over.

*A lot of classical singers are reluctant to attempt new techniques for fear of damaging their voices.*

There's a lot of fear in that world, and I think it perpetuates itself through the teaching. It's a very neurotic atmosphere, but I think the really good teachers would acknowledge that the voice can do almost anything. It has its own built-in healing mechanisms. But you have to have common sense about it.

*You've never really explored the use of electronics with the voice. Does that not interest you?*

So far, I'm still very interested in what the voice itself can do. I mean, I use microphones and have made records where I've laid down tracks – that's a certain kind of electronics. I love my four-track tape recorder, which allows me to work on things myself. But so far, the sound of the voice itself is something I'm still exploring. I'm still fascinated, not only by the sound of my own voice, but also by voices in general. I believe the voice can do anything electronics can. In fact, a lot of instrumentalist and electronic musician friends of mine say that what they keep trying to do is sing with their instruments! In *Atlas* I did use samplers because of the way it was set up visually; we had to have a small orchestra pit and there were only ten instruments. Two of them were samplers because we couldn't fit two pianos in the pit. There were also some spirit or ghost sections in *Atlas*, so I wanted to create a non-instrumental sound, something that you couldn't recognize. So we sampled a wineglass and played it in chords two octaves lower. You just didn't know what it was at all. That's about as far as I've gone with electronics.

*There are composers in Europe who explore this thing called 'extended vocal technique'. There seems to be a difference between what they do and what you do – perhaps in the spirit in which you approach it?*

What *is* the spirit in which they approach it?

*Perhaps finding new things for the sake of it, with the aim of 'advancing' musical language. I get the impression though that you only do things if you 'feel' them.*

Yes. I would say theirs is a more laboratory kind of approach – it has a lot to do with systematizing or codifying things. I'm much more interested in speaking in one way or another, so finding new techniques just for the sake of it would not be interesting to me as a *modus operandi*. I'm always trying to find something new myself, but I don't think my approach would be to see how many different vocal techniques I could find. If it's more appropriate for something I'm doing to sing a straight melody, then I would do that. I try to stay as flexible as I can. I'm very happy when something new comes up, though, something I haven't heard myself do before.

*Does it get more difficult to come up with things?*

Yes. After working for so many years there's a lot of baggage. So to find a new voice is really exciting. I feel very close to John Cage, in that the process of discovery is what keeps me interested. That's why every time I like to start from zero as much as I can.

*How do you feel you relate to the Western musical tradition?*

I know there are people very concerned about where they fit into music history. But I would say that's a very male point of view, and it's not one of my big concerns. It's really more an appreciation of something that has gone before me.

*Is that because men wrote that history and gave themselves the 'best parts', or because you're not really interested in the concept of history?*

I'm very interested in the concept of history, but I think that history as it's presented to us at this point is relative. And it is *his*-story! It doesn't have too much about what women have done over the years, so I don't think it's complete. It is organized in a very linear fashion, so I haven't been able to identify with it that strongly.

*An element of timelessness seems to run through your work. You manage to incorporate the past, present and future all at once. Your work has also been described as being at once 'familiar yet foreign, primitive yet contemporary, serene yet alarming' – it's interesting how you manage to evoke all those feelings at the same time.*

Well, I always think of time in a circular way, so that the 'now' also includes the past and the future. I try to make it so that the experience you have is of being as aware as possible of being here at this moment. But the moment must always include the past and the future for us to appreciate it fully. So I don't cut off roots or eliminate the forward motion of the future. We all have to think very seriously about what we're doing in society. I always think, 'Is this useful?' – and I think it *is* very useful to remind people of alertness, of aliveness, of seeing things anew, because that is something we lose so quickly. Being awake is difficult, but it is useful to human beings. That's what I've been trying to do. There was a time in the musical theatre pieces when I thought the most useful thing was to present the 'problem' – you know, what is 'wrong'. So I did pieces with very apocalyptic aspects, like *Recent Ruins*, *Specimen Days* and *Turtle Dreams*. But for the last few years I've found it much more interesting to offer a behavioural alternative, as a kind of prototype, paradigm or template of what human behaviour could be. That includes not only the way people are operating but also the energy exchange that can happen in that situation. I think that's really important because the exchange doesn't exist so much any more. The impulse now comes very much from secondary information, sitting at home and listening to a CD or watching movies. There's nothing wrong with that (I make films myself), but it's very important to fight for the 'live' situation, for the exchange that happens and the individuality of each person in the audience.

*Do you think that's a natural human inclination – to take the easy option and not be aware?*

Yes. I'd be interested to know what you say about Britain, because I always think of that inclination as an American phenomenon, a result of the television culture here. The difference between a European audience and an American one is that, in Europe, I get the sense that the 'live' situation is still very important to people. Whereas people in America will tend just not to go. It's not something they feel compelled to do, whereas in Europe it seems to be still a very vital communication.

*Is it getting more difficult to survive as an artist in New York?*

Well, we're struggling to stay alive after doing *Atlas*, which was very extreme. But we're hanging in there. A lot of organizations have gone down during this period because of the state of the economy. It's a general depression. One thing which has been good for me is the fact that I am very flexible. I can work alone and do solos, or I can work with large groups. I can just do a piece in my loft and be perfectly happy about it – the first performance of *Facing North* was right here in this loft, and it gave me a wonderful feeling of independence. I love to work and it doesn't matter to me if I'm performing in Carnegie Hall or 228 West Broadway! If I could only perform here for a while, or even for ever, that would be fine.

# ROBERT MORAN

*b. Colorado 1937*

Robert Moran studied composition with Hans Erich Apostel in Vienna, completed his master's degree at Mills College with Berio and Milhaud, and was co-founder and director of the San Francisco New Music Ensemble in the early 1960s. The breadth of his compositional output is astonishing, including *39 Minutes for 39 Autos* (1969) for thirty-nine amplified auto horns, auto lights, synthesizer, thirty skyscrapers, two radio stations, one television station, aeroplanes, dancers et cetera; and *Hallelujah* (1971) for twenty marching bands, forty church choirs, organs and carillons, rock 'n' roll groups, gospel groups and the entire city of Bethlehem, Pennsylvania.

In 1985 he co-composed an opera, *The Juniper Tree*, with Philip Glass, and has since written two commissioned operas, *Desert of Roses* (1991) for Houston Grand Opera, and *From the Towers of the Moon* (1992) for Minnesota Opera. Through his recent recordings on Decca, Moran is most often associated with the melodic minimalism of works like *Ten Miles High Over Albania* (1983) for eight harps, and *Open Veins* (1989) for violin and ensemble.

*What did you get from your studies with Milhaud and Berio?*

With Berio I learned how not to treat people. What I got from Milhaud was quite wonderful. He must have been in his seventies then and he was very open. He would bring out a score from the 1920s calling for orchestras divided into groups and choruses speaking fragments of sounds, and you'd feel (I must have been twenty-two at the time) like a dinosaur! He even brought out a piece he wrote that was a free canon based on chance operations and 'how to mix a Martini' texts!

*You came to a point in your career where you had to choose between Bombay or Vienna?*

I'd always been fascinated with Indian music. I met Ravi Shankar in San Francisco in 1961 and he said, 'Come and study with me in Bombay when you've finished your master's degree'. By the time I finished my master's I'd received the *I Ching* from John Cage and was consulting it at every step I made. I had enough money to get to India but not enough to get back. Also, Shankar was not at that point in India, but out touring – little did I know that he was really the 'Liberace of the Sitar'. I'd already been to Vienna twice and I didn't know why I should go back. But then Berio, who was working on his new opera *Passagio* in Milan, said that if I wanted to go there I could assist him. I got to Milan, but it was so expensive that I stayed around for a few months, went to the opera all the time, and then decided to go to Vienna, because there was a Polish composer, Roman Haubenstock-Ramati, that I wanted to visit. I wanted to ask how he arrived at these mobile scores that were obviously influenced by Alexander Calder. So I went back to Vienna, where I knew I could live very cheaply. That's when I started doing completely graphic scores, the summer of 1963.

*It could have been a completely different story if you'd gone to India.*

Yes, I could be playing tablas in some cheap restaurant in Madras! Or hating India forever. I finally got to India by doing a concert lecture tour in 1981. During that trip I spoke to an Indian journalist who said I should meet the film-maker Satyajit Ray – and that he would be interested in my city pieces. So I got to visit him, which was extraordinary. That, along with my love of classical Indian dance and puppets, was the Indian influence.

*What about the Cage influence?*

That was probably the *I Ching*. It's fascinating to me that, despite John's incredible influence, no-one today writes like him. That aspect didn't really catch on. There are certain things that composers use – I throw coins to determine the parameters, or Phil Corner will tear up the score, throw it on the floor and play the arrangement – but as far as writing music that sounds like Cage, there isn't anybody. We had at that time far too many people sounding like Stockhausen and Boulez, but luckily we passed through that migraine. What Cage did in music, besides throwing the windows open and letting the sunlight come in upon academia and the 'concert-hall situation', was to allow the sense of humour to come back into music. I know that having musicians bark like dogs is really off the wall, but why not? That was allowed – it was just as valid as any other sound, and it was so refreshing. Not since Mozart had we had anything that was so wonderful and goofy and elegant at the same time.

*Does that explain the thinking behind your* Pop Corn *piece?*

No! That deals with my fixation with dogs. I had one dog, Charlotte Benson, who I found in a pet-store window. She was ferociously bright and went with me everywhere. She went to Berlin, lived on both coasts, she won the Texaco opera quiz on the Metropolitan Opera broadcasts, she won the Black Woman Artist Award at the museum in Portland, Oregon, and had her picture on the front page of the newspaper. So Charlotte covered territory. And she loved popcorn. So I left the lid off one time to see what would happen, and it was wonderful. Popcorn flew all over the kitchen and the floor, and here was Charlotte leaping in the air like a ballerina. I thought, 'Well, if I got a whole stage of jumping dogs it would just be amazing'. So that's how I wrote the popcorn piece. Then I thought, 'How could I interpret this for traditional musicians?' Well, I found these goofy, gigantic sunglasses. I realized you could paint five white lines like staves on them which could be seen by the audience. As the popcorn flies out of the pan, you read it as the notes. But if you hear a recording, it sounds like something from Darmstadt, except that the audience is shrieking and falling on the floor! I've seen it done by very elegant musicians, who've finished up doing Schubert or something. And it smells good. As one critic said, 'If you don't like it, at least you can eat it!'

*What made you leave twelve-tone writing and return to tonality?*

I think it was just a natural progression. By the time I started studying with Berio, I was doing completely organized scores and I couldn't find people to play them. In all honesty, not too many people wanted to hear them.

*How do you look back on serialism now?*

I think it was a wonderful self-discipline. When I studied with Hans Erich Apostel, the last member of the twelve-tone school, he would not let me go near the piano. I had to hear everything I wrote.

*You must be the most difficult person to pin down that we've spoken to. Your music has gone through so many changes. Wouldn't you be much more 'marketable' if you stuck to one thing?!*

That's the problem. When I left Vienna in 1963 I went to London, heard the Beatles and then went back to San Francisco. I had just been handed a contract from Universal Edition and was one of the first Americans to be published by the publishers of Stockhausen, Boulez, Busotti and Berio. They let a few 'barbarians' in! Well, from that contract I couldn't have afforded a cigarette habit – if I had ever smoked in my life. That's how much you make out of publishers, at least the 'fancy' ones – zero!! Then Cage said I should show my scores to C. F. Peters. I sent them a few scores, they sent me contracts. It became like a little addiction – who could I get next? Then Schott & Sons in Mainz zeroed in on me. So I had these big publishers, but if you added up the sum total I got from the three, I still couldn't afford to walk across the street. They hardly do anything for you. As the years marched by, I would hear myself say, 'Oh, I would sell it all for one LP because that reaches everyone'. They would all publish me now, but I don't want to give them anything because I can go through BMI in New York and for $25 establish my own publishing house. And all the royalties come to me. To hell with them. At least now I have enough money to feed my dog.

*Do you think you'll make sense in 200 years' time?*

I don't think I make any sense now. Besides, I can't think about that. You get stuck in the masterpiece syndrome, where each piece becomes something more than just the piece you're writing.

*Your language is now a kind of luscious minimalism . . .*

. . . but the critics, particularly in this country (I don't know about Europe now), have trouble dealing with melody. It's almost questionable. They've finally reached a point where they can go to *Moses und Aron* and say 'Wow,' but I was saying 'Wow' over *that* score thirty years ago when I was in my first year in college. Now they don't know how to deal with people who write melody. But why waste time talking about critics anyway? They're quite useless.

*How do you actually compose? You finished your operas months ahead of schedule, which must be quite unusual.*

Well, when I get a libretto I'm already hearing things and seeing what the characters look like. With *Desert of Roses* I started at the beginning and went straight through.

*Is it an intuitive process all the way?*

I don't even think about it. I do some sketches, but I never know. The interesting thing about music theatre is that you just don't know how you'll affect people. During *Desert of Roses* many people were crying. I thought, 'What have I done?' But maybe the next person is sitting there saying, 'Oh God, what junk – I can't deal with it'. If they hate it and throw programmes, fine – or throw money, I don't care. Just react.

*Is opera the real Robert Moran? Is this where you can be completely yourself?*

Oh yes. When I was a little kid I was taken to the opera, and I didn't need, or want, to know what the words meant. Operas were my fairy-tales.

*What do you think has brought about this revival of opera recently?*

I think people are realizing that it was never originally an élitist art form. It was always popular. It's goofy and fun and passionate. Now, in the USA, we see a decent amount of opera on TV.

*What is it that really attracts you to the theatre?*

Well, when I was about seven years old there was this class activity called 'show and tell'. I had been to see *The Barber of Seville* the night before and had to tell everyone about that. So this teacher wrote to my parents and said there was a course in drama for children at Denver University, and that they should sign me up immediately. They did, and I went. It was a fantasy, another world.

*Do you think you're in theatre for good now?*

I never got out. My next opera is based upon a Gertrude Stein text. She wrote a children's book (that no one knows) called *The World is Round*. And that's where 'a rose is a rose is a rose' comes from. It's a gorgeous work, and I finally got the rights to do it.

*What about the Madonna project?*

That's on hold until I can find the money and a courageous theatre for such a commission. Preferably lots of money and lots of courage. It's about Aleister Crowley and his followers, black magic, tantric rituals and how they decide to do his favourite play, *Titus Andronicus*. Of course, it gets totally out of control. It's really all about censorship, because they did stay within their own parameters and didn't go out and offend others – although I think he probably offended the press deliberately, but that's sheer flamboyance. I thought how wonderful it would be to have this opera within a play within a play. The characters that would have to be part of this ensemble would include a beautiful German silent-screen star, plus the wealthy eccentrics and the bored. Then Mussolini and the storm-troopers move in (which is historically correct), close the place down and throw the whole gang out of Italy. Anyone such as Crowley who can be kicked out of Sicily for decadence by fascists is my type of man! When I proposed that to David Gockley at Houston Grand Opera, he asked me who I would use for the screen star. The answer is Madonna! You see, I had thought this way: all this German screen star wanted was a contract to do a big Bible film with De Mille in Hollywood. There she is in this villa in Italy where they're doing *everything* – the orgies – waiting for a telegram from Hollywood to see if she's got the role of the Virgin Mary. The idea of Madonna playing the silent-screen star waiting for the role of the Virgin Mary in Hollywood has possibilities. And of course it arrives, and she doesn't get the role. So that probably sends her down the toilet on Martinis and God knows what she's been smoking. All this is going on, and she says, 'I won't do the role of Titus's daughter unless I can play her as the Virgin Mary'. So you have the silent-screen star playing her in the costume she's brought with her thinking she was going to go off to Hollywood as the Virgin Mary – playing the daughter who gets gang-raped, her hands cut off, her tongue ripped out, etc. Imagine Madonna, minus her tongue, singing an aria . . . it boggles the mind. All of this comes to a halt when we bring in the contemporary camera-crew stopping the whole thing, saying that the funders have pulled out on the film because they say this is not acceptable. Madonna would jump at this.

*Let's talk about the 'Waltz Project'. Your own contribution is very attractive . . .*

Thank you. It just happened. The one thing I can't stand about composers is when they say, 'It just came to me'. I think, 'Oh sure!' But this waltz just came to me. I hadn't written anything like that before. I called up my friend Bob Helps, who's a concert pianist and composer, and I said, 'I'm really slipping. I've just written a waltz. I think I've lost my mind.' He said, 'Don't worry about it, I've lost mine too. I'm just working on a waltz here.' His was *Waltz Mirage* and it's quite wonderful. We invited his Bernstein and Copland friends to contribute a waltz. We also invited Frank Zappa, and I even wrote a letter to Boulez saying, 'We're doing this waltz project and we'd love to have you write a waltz. My friend has a $5 bet with me that you can't write a waltz'. I had a very charming letter back saying, 'Thank you very much for the invitation, but unfortunately I can't write the waltz because I'm very busy'. We received twenty-five new waltzes and not one was a commission. The rules were, it's a waltz if you call it a waltz! It could be easy or extremely difficult, five minutes in length or open, like Cage. That's how it happened.

*You've been described as a minimalist. Do you fit comfortably in that role?*

I don't even know what it means. It's very limiting. We can thank journalists for words like 'minimalism' and 'avant-garde'. When was the last time you heard someone say 'I'm an avant-garde artist'? They don't. They wouldn't. So where did it come from? It has to be from journalists.

*Do you have any more colourful projects in mind for the future?*

Yes, there are a number of things I want to do. There's a Nancy Reagan opera called *Just Say 'No'*. That's what she said, and she couldn't have cared less about the ghetto kids taking drugs. Michael John La Chiusa, who wrote my last two libretti and is a specialist on presidents' wives (any trash, he knows all about them) suggested I read the Kitty Kelly book. It's just unbeliev- able. It's not as good as Mrs Reagan's book about herself, *My Turn*, which is the ultimate in trash. I read it and it was just heaven – all the people I hate, all the politicians. As I read these books, I kept thinking, 'Good God, and these jerks were manipulating the world!' Here are these people who were running the world, and they're just despicable. She was wonder- ing where she was going to get her next $5000 dress to go to an Aids benefit while she and her goofy husband were doing nothing for Aids research. I mean, what the hell's going on? I thought, 'This is perfect for an opera'. You've got her affair with Frank Sinatra, who's climbing in and out of windows. Shouldn't

Margaret Thatcher drop in on the opera too? It offers lots of possibilities. It's the perfect contemporary *singspiel*. It's all real . . . and no one in their right mind will believe it.

# PAULINE OLIVEROS

*b. Texas 1932*

Pauline Oliveros is considered by many to be the founder of today's meditative music. In the early 1960s she founded the highly influential San Francisco Tape Music Center and began exploring the musical applications of combination tones and supersonic frequencies. She later joined the faculty of the University of California at San Diego and began to study the relationships between meditation techniques and improvisation. This work led to an ongoing series of compositions entitled *Sonic Meditations*.

Many of her works are inspired by studies of myth and ritual, and are often notated in a mandalic form. The sustained, almost ceremonial, tones of her accordion, expanded into multiple layers by live electronics, seek to cultivate an intense sonic awareness in the listener.

*Your work has spanned many areas, from improvisation to theatre, from electronics to meditation. Did you consciously decide to keep moving on to new challenges, or were these natural progressions?*

It was a natural progression. Meeting change is the most challenging task. Some people think keeping things the same is a challenge too.

*And what effected these changes?*

Well, the core practice for me is deep listening. Listening leads one to change.

*And presumably the theatre grew out of your need to start looking more as well?*

Yes. Composition is a matter of dealing with various elements, and I didn't want to limit myself to one particular thing. It seemed important to be able to compose with whatever elements seemed appropriate for what I needed to express. Theatre's exciting to me, and I continue to go in that direction.

*At San Diego you formed an all-women music theatre group. Could you explain your reasons for that?*

What was important to me was encouraging women to express themselves creatively, because they are not generally supported by the culture to do this.

*Have these different stages in your work led you from a selective perception to a more complete awareness?*

Well, I think it's a lifetime practice, an evolution of perception, with the possibility of increasingly fine-tuning one's perception by training oneself to perceive smaller and smaller differences, and conversely to attend to more and more of the field – which is infinite!

*You also suggest we should strike a balance between linearity and multiplicity, the left hemisphere of the brain and the right, whereas a lot of experimental composers negate the concept of line. Could you expand on that?*

To go right to the essence, I believe we need to use everything that we have in order to cope with the world, with our reality, and with our need to express ourselves. If we limit ourselves too narrowly, we're in denial of our capacities. So the interaction of those two processes can give rise to increased awareness and perception.

*You've done a lot of detailed research in many areas which appear unrelated to music, such as Jungian psychology, dreams, the unconscious, the hemispheres of the brain, even karate. How have these affected your work?*

Well, for one thing I don't feel these areas are unrelated. It's simply that I have a number of interests. I'm interested in the relationships of these various activities and those relationships in music, in performing and composing. They're all interrelated, interdependent. I don't see a difference. It's a different focus of interest, but in discovering relationships and interactions you can bring that information to another discipline.

*Is your music a therapy?*

It is when people report to me that they originally began their listening feeling one way, and afterwards felt another way — meaning that they've gone from something painful to something releasing. In that sense, yes it's therapeutic. But actually you could say that of any music.

*I was thinking specifically of pieces like* Teach Yourself to Fly *as suggesting a means of self-discovery.*

Yes, that piece is an entry level and an experience for, say, people who have not had any music training. Or it could be therapeutic for someone who has a fear of using their voice to sing because they've been abused in any number of ways or made to feel inferior about their vocal abilities. So it's a way of working with the voice which is a little bit different, based on breathing and exploring what the voice can do if you aren't trying to force it into a particular performance context.

*Do you see any connection with the work of La Monte Young and his use of concentration and focus?*

I think there's a relationship. La Monte's work has perhaps a different focus because it's centring around what he's doing. He's training himself, perhaps setting an example, but he's not sharing the process of it so much.

*How do you respond to the criticism that your music advocates a preoccupation with the self to the exclusion of political issues?*

I think there's a real misunderstanding on the part of that critic, because I consider a work like, say, *Sonic Meditations* to be deeply political in that it challenges certain premises in the musical establishment, that it opens the way for people to participate who aren't musicians. That's pretty political, pretty subversive!

*The majority of the composers we've spoken to on the East Coast seem to have a great affection for New York – one which you don't appear to share.*

Yes, I live upstate in Kingston. I prefer a more quiet atmosphere. New York is certainly an exciting and stimulating environment but I don't feel at ease there. It's very difficult to do things – there's a constant pressure, a very competitive, thrusting kind of energy.

*You've also left academia now?*

Well, I was hired at the University of California in the 1960s because of my experience (I only had a Bachelor of Arts, so I doubt if I could be hired now). But when I resigned, it was as a full professor, third rank. I didn't have the training others had in terms of academic background, but I had trained myself in my work. That's a very difficult path, which requires real persistence, devotion and confidence. But if you have to build confidence through identifying with an establishment or an institutional idea of training, well, that's what you have to do. If you're going to be nagged all your life with the thought, 'I'm not a real musician because I didn't do X', you have to deal with that. But if you feel you are expressing yourself fully as a human being, and music is the vehicle, then get the training that you need. It may not necessarily be what the establishment says you need, but there are mentors, and you can find the relationships that really nurture what you wish to express and bring into being as a contributing member of society.

I resigned in 1981 because I felt there was a very conservative wave in the university and I didn't feel comfortable there any more. The students were becoming more conservative, but I wanted to challenge myself, move out and see what I could do.

*How do you think people can be encouraged to be more open in their views about music? How can that situation of growing conservatism be changed?*

Well, I think the most important thing is to listen and to express what you think you need to express. But in order to change things, you first need to change yourself – that's the first target. And if you change yourself, you change your relationship to others, and that spreads. If you refuse to participate in anything that perpetuates a situation which is not interesting, not productive, not contributory to an evolution in society, then you're doing something.

*Could you explain your interest in just intonation?*

I like the resonance and colour of the sounds made possible.

*Would you return to equal temperament after working with just intonation?*

Sure, I am not committed to any one intonation. Just the ones that work for the music to be expressed.

*Who or what would you say have been the most significant influences on your music and your ideology?*

The influence of just listening is the deepest for me.

# STEVE REICH

*b. New York 1936*

After graduating in philosophy from Cornell University in 1957, Steve Reich went on to study composition at the Juilliard School of Music. In 1963 he received his MA from Mills College, where he studied with Milhaud and Berio. During the 1970s he studied African drumming at the University of Ghana, Balinese gamelan at the American Society for Eastern Arts in Seattle and Berkeley, and traditional forms of the cantillation of Hebrew scriptures in New York and Jerusalem.

In 1966 he founded his own ensemble, Steve Reich and Musicians, which has since completed more than twenty tours throughout the world. His music has come to enjoy an ever-widening popularity. *The Desert Music*, for example, immediately entered the US Billboard charts, *Different Trains* won a 1990 Grammy Award, and his 1993 documentary music-video-theatre piece, *The Cave*, achieved both popular and critical acclaim.

Reich's earliest works, such as *Come Out* (1966) or *Piano Phase* (1967), reflected his interest in perceptible compositional processes that determined both the local and global parameters of a work. After 1968, however, his aesthetic began to accommodate a greater element of personal choice and intuition, leading to works of greater colouristic, harmonic and melodic variety, such as *Music for 18 Musicians* (1976) and *The Desert Music* (1984). His formal structures also expanded in range and depth, whilst preserving the purity and integrity of an underlying process. It is this insistence on clarity and audibility of structure, combined with a radical simplification of musical means and an emotional directness, that characterize the music of Steve Reich.

*Let's start with your early musical training. You studied with Berio and Milhaud . . .*

Actually I went through some fundamentally more important studies with Hall Overton way back in the 1950s. Some people are well-known, like Berio and Milhaud, but they may or may not have a gift for teaching. In my experience, the best teachers have not been the most famous composers. When I was working with Berio, it was very good to find out about Berio, but it was only indirectly useful in finding out about myself – in that I wasn't Berio. Whereas someone like Overton could literally look at the score and say, 'This ought to be a B flat instead of a B'. That kind of information is priceless. That kind of critique, where you get down to the details, usually comes from someone who maybe doesn't have such a powerful musical personality as a composer, but who can become your *alter ego* because they have a good deal of musical technique and they're open to a lot of different styles. So I would say that my most interesting and beneficial teachers were Hall Overton and Vincent Persichetti. Certainly, working with Berio was exciting, because at that time – 1960–61 – he was a big hit. But I think it helped clarify for me that I had absolutely nothing to do with that tradition, which was basically the end of German Romanticism – through Schoenberg into Stockhausen and Boulez. Stravinsky and Bach were more my tastes. Milhaud was a very old and sick man who was not really physically in shape to do much teaching. It was more like you would spend time with Mr Milhaud and he would reminisce in your presence. He reminisced a great deal about Satie, and I think he really wanted to be Satie – which really wasn't something I would put high up in my list of learning experiences.

*So you had no skirmish with serialism?*

Oh yes, I had to. From 1961 to 1963 I wrote that way. But I had to figure out a way to deal with it for myself, so I didn't transpose,

reverse or invert the row. I just repeated it, because by repeating
it one could sneak a little weird harmony in the back door. You
could divide up the first notes into four groups of three or three
groups of four, and that kind of thinking paid off rhythmically
later – the idea of twelve as a rhythmic number rather than a
pitch number. When I did this, Berio said, 'You want to write
tonal music, write tonal music'. And I said, 'That's what I'm
trying to do'. At the time I was studying with Berio I used to
spend my evenings going to the jazz workshop and hearing John
Coltrane play. It was a wonderful counterbalance to sitting in a
class with a lot of students who were writing music that had a lot
of black ink on the page but they couldn't play it at the piano or
hear it in their head. At night I'd go and see someone pick up the
saxophone and just play. It was a kind of moral choice.
Coltrane's model seemed very persuasive, and was nearly dia-
metrically opposed. He was saying, 'Look, you can stay in one
key as a centre and that will free you to make any sound that you
want, including noise'. That was a very important and interesting
time.

*Didn't Cage pass through at that time?*

Yes, but he was really there all the time anyway, because at that
period he was the other part of the equation. A lot of people at
Mills College in the early 1960s were either very interested in
Boulez, Stockhausen and Berio, or very interested in John Cage.
To tell you the truth, I was interested in neither. I respect Cage
and I got to know him a little bit, but his most useful role for me
was as a music that I could push against, no more or less than I
pushed against twelve-tone technique.

*So those negative influences are important too?*

Well, I was in a situation where I felt there was just no place for
the likes of me. I was interested in tonality, repetition, rhythm,
non-Western music. At that time, most people were into music
that basically had no beat whatsoever, whether it was American
or European, no tonal centre whatsoever, and had no techniques
to deal with them. They treated those techniques as irrelevant –
dead and gone. Boulez said, 'It's historically necessary to write
this way'. I felt, 'Well, just count me out of history then'. I can

talk about it now in a much more free and easy way, but it was rather lonely and slightly depressing at the time because, even amongst the student body, most people went along with that.

*Looking back, was there any point where you could say that you had found your own voice?*

I finally felt that way when *It's Gonna Rain* and *Come Out* were done. I did *It's Gonna Rain* in San Francisco, but as you can tell by listening to it, it has a rather bleak outlook. It's basically a piece about the end of the world, so you can imagine the psyche of somebody who had made it. Indeed, it's quite autobiographically correct. I had found a solution, but somehow it took a while for that to sink in. What really made it sink in was instrumental music. The idea of those tape pieces really seemed very persuasive, very solid, very real. I saw then that it was some kind of canonic technique, but it also seemed crystal clear that no human being could do anything like that. After several months of deliberation I put on the tape recorder, sat down and did *Piano Phase*. Then it was a big rush of energy going from there right through to *Drumming*.

*A lot of people think that your style emerged after you had been to Ghana and studied African drumming, but that's not quite true is it?*

No, that sounds good on paper, but doesn't fit if you look at the dates: 1965 was *It's Gonna Rain*, 1966 was *Come Out*, and by 1967 I had finished *Piano Phase* – the first section of it is in 12/8. I went to Ghana because it completed a circle. I'd been a drummer since I was fourteen, but I'd never really written any percussion music. There'd been tape music and piano music, there was *Reed Phase* for John Gibson, *Violin Phase*, *Four Organs*, *Phase Patterns*. I had been listening to African music, and had also discovered Jones's book on African music. I read the book, I looked at the notation, and I thought, 'Well, I'm a drummer, so where does percussion play the dominant role in the orchestra?' The answer was two places, Africa and Indonesia. Africa seemed more interesting to me. So I went to London in 1970 to get cheap airline tickets and ended up flying on Nigerian Airlines as a 'flight engineer'! I met Michael Nyman for the first time, we hung out and that led to a long-lasting friendship. Going to Ghana was really a kind of pat on the back – I knew the experience would do something. What it did was to say that the sound of acoustically-produced percussion music is richer than anything electronically-produced, and it can swing and be a classical music at the same time.

*That distinguishes you from a lot of other people around at that time.*

Yes, I was the one who went to Africa. Everyone else went to India, either physically or in the head. It's not that I dislike Indian music, but I was a drummer so I had to go where it was good for me. I was an American kid who grew up interested in jazz, and who knew that jazz was primarily a black music. Part of it was undoubtedly about going back to the roots of why I had been interested in jazz in the first place. For me that really made sense.

*And yet you didn't come back using Ghanaian instruments, for example, like many other composers might have done.*

When I went to Ghana I almost drowned while I was swimming off the coast. Africa is full of pitfalls for white folks, and in fact I almost killed myself in a number of ways – malaria, a motor-cycle accident, and swimming into a rip-tide. For me, that was a kind of metaphor for what an individual composer faced, from Perotin on down, from a total cultural phenomenon which is nothing to do with individuals. I'm sure there are important individuals in the history of African music, but not in the way we have them, because the tradition is accepted – it's modified by the living musicians, passed on to the next generation, and so on and so forth. That's all over now, but it was still intact when I was there. But what I'm trying to say is that a lot of American, British and European musicians, when encountering Indian music in particular, are in a situation where they can drown. And some, without mentioning names, can get into states of asphyxiation that have long-lasting negative effects. When faced with that, you really have to ask yourself, 'What am I doing here?' I felt, 'Well, I'm a music student. Specially, I'm an ethnological music student, and I want to be able to apply this in some way to my own music'.

The first thing that felt instinctively wrong was using Ghanaian instruments.

When I opened the book by Jones, what excited me in the first place was the way the music was put together: repeating patterns in 12/8 of various rational divisions – 3, 4, 6 – superimposed so the downbeats didn't coincide. I thought, 'Aha! I never saw that before. It looks like a bunch of tape loops spinning around, all landing in different places'. And when all is said and done, that's really what I got out of it. I consciously tried not to pretend I was an African drummer. Maybe it was easier because of the racial difference, or maybe it's just because I am who I am. Maybe in India, because Indians aren't culturally as far away from us as Africans were, it was easier to glide into an imitation of that culture, but it seems to me that some people can end up being neither great Indian musicians nor working successfully in a Western tradition. They end up stuck in a kind of no man's land. That's unfortunate, because ultimately it doesn't help either Indian or Western music to move ahead. In a sense, I take a rather conservative view of non-Western music. I'm all for the original forms. It's very understandable that African music will be very involved with rock 'n' roll, and everyone from Paul Simon to Laurie Anderson and Phil Glass is now involved with musicians who are getting recorded in multitrack studios and so on. But the price you pay for that is the end of classical African music. And that is a high price. Understandable and human, but nevertheless worth a tear or two.

*How important would you say that the concept of ethnicity is in your music? Later on you came back to Judaism – is that part of it?*

Yes, it's all of a piece. I began to get interested in who I was shortly after coming back from Africa. It's such a contrast. You can either just submerge and merge – or say, 'Wait a minute. Who am I? Do *I* have any ancient tradition? And if so, what is it?' And I didn't even know. So I began to reclaim my own background. The trip to Africa definitely played a role in that.

*Do you think that 'minimalism' is an indigenous American music?*

Yes, I do.

*What spirit do you think motivated the start of that?*

A lot of the things I've been talking about. I was growing up in
the 1960s, a period memorable for many positive and negative
reasons. It was musically noted for such well-known figures as
Junior Walker and Martha and the Vandellas – who did rock 'n'
roll where you have repeating basslines that don't change for the
whole tune – and going up to such powerful figures as John
Coltrane, as we've already discussed. You also have Ravi
Shankar and Ali Akbar Khan visiting universities in America,
and Balinese ensembles and Gagaku appearing here for the first
time – musics where, basically, the harmony doesn't move as
rapidly as it does in the West. All this was bubbling up
spontaneously; harmonic stasis was in the air, the product of
various non-Western and indigenous black musics, together with
the leftovers of French Impressionism. Later I began to realize
how Debussy and Ravel fitted into all of this. French Impressionism was very definitely French, German Romanticism was
definitely German, and a number of composers at different
periods in history, from Dunstable to Elgar, are noticeably
British. I think those things are real, and I admire them. So, yes, I
think minimalism started off that way, and that has made it
difficult for Europeans to deal with, just as German Romanticism
and its modern components were for American composers,
starting with Charles Ives and more recently Milton Babbitt and
Charles Wuorinen – who are basically Americans imitating
Europe, which has been the norm in this country up until about
John Cage.

*Going back to this complex issue of ethnicity and cultures. If a*
*European uses simple, repeating patterns in tonality, is that*
*aping someone else's culture?*

It all depends. Some people do it out of their own inner necessity,
but with others you get the sense that they don't. I'd like to stay
positive, so I'm going to talk about Arvo Pärt. I met him when he
came to New York a few years ago and he told me he'd heard my
music in Russia. For me, it's so wonderful to have helped him in
any way to get where he was going to go, because clearly it's his

own voice. That's finally what I prize above all else in composers – that they have their own voice. I like Glenn Branca, for instance, because he's for real. I think that in Pärt's case, because of whatever inner necessity in the psychology of the man – maybe his religious commitments – it's for real. The techniques that may have influenced him from the outside have become totally his own. Other people I could talk about show varying degrees of that. Louis Andriessen has, I think, in some of his pieces made a very positive coming-together with myself and *Les Noces*. Because *Les Noces* always seems to be with Louis in one way or another – but who could criticize that? I certainly couldn't. Of course, I make no claims, but there's a family resemblance between the kind of music I do and much of Stravinsky's music. But ultimately, 'influenced by' means nothing, because what really matters is 'how is the music?'. In Pärt's case the answer is 'great', and in Louis's case the answer is 'very often very good'.

*The influence of baroque music also seems to figure in your work.*

Oh, sure. But that isn't mysterious. Bach and jazz have a fixed beat. In fact, baroque music and jazz share most forms – there are repeating cycles of chords both in jazz and in the various passacaglias, chaconnes and so forth of baroque music. They also share an improvisatory spirit – baroque music gives numbers for the harmonies, and jazz indicates the chord-changes. There's also a kind of expression that didn't depend on dynamics but more on phrasing and keeping within the beat, within a certain discipline – a certain reserve, if you will (which includes Stravinsky too for that matter). That's an aesthetic I still feel totally a product of.

*How have your aims as a composer changed over the years?*

They keep changing. I value the intuitive process, which is really, finally, the only thing anybody's got. And you don't want to mess with it. It will lead in different directions in different people. Take, for example, a 'minimal' artist like Donald Judd, who in the 1960s built a lot of boxes, and in the 1970s built slightly different boxes, in the 1980s built more colourful boxes, and in the 1990s will, I think, produce slightly different kinds of boxes. Then, for contrast, look at Frank Stella, who in the 1960s made black and white striped paintings, in the 1970s made Degor-striped paintings, in the 1980s did punk, spray-paint reliefs coming off the wall, and I don't know, and neither do you, what his next show will be. I think that's great. I see the continuity, I see the honesty, but he goes in an unforeseen way. Now I happen to be the latter type of artist. I don't think things are so consciously decided. *I* certainly didn't consciously decide them. I did *It's Gonna Rain* and *Drumming*, then I just got fed up with the idea of phasing. I had to start going somewhere else, but I went very slowly – *Clapping Music*, for instance, is the same kind of piece except that you 'click' ahead. You don't move ahead gradually. That's the way it's been, though sometimes there's been a big jump.

*Would you say* Different Trains *was an important piece for you?*

Oh, *Different Trains* is a line in the sand.

*What does the line demarcate?*

Well, *Different Trains* is not only going forwards but backwards too. That's the nice thing about the piece; it says, 'What about *It's Gonna Rain*? It's been all these years. All these people have gotten so much out of that piece – what do *I* get out of that piece?' I have always been very drawn to documentaries and the use of documentary material in art – Rauschenberg's paintings in the 1960s, for example. *Different Trains* was a way of bringing documentary material back in, only this time it could fit hand in glove and actually be the determining factor. I knew that speech has musical content, so I decided to let that be the content for a series of string quartets. *Different Trains* was really done as a kind of study, and the piece I've been working on ever since [*The Cave*] has been a gigantic extension of that.

*How did the idea for* The Cave *come about?*

Well, I've been collaborating with my wife, the video artist Beryl Korot. Her work involves multi-channel video where the timings between the channels are very highly worked out – four channels where the first and third and the second and fourth would be interlocked. These are very musical-type structures, so it was a natural collaboration. But the question was, what's it all about?

Within a few minutes we decided it would be the Cave of Machpela. Beryl and I had both become interested in our Judaic backgrounds, and had both begun studying the Torah. We discovered that there's a town, Hebron, in a very politically sensitive area of the world – thirty miles south of Jerusalem on the West Bank – where Jews, Muslims and Christians all accept that Abraham is buried. Whether he's there or not is really immaterial. I think part of the decision to choose the Cave of Machpela was because, on a political level and as a human being living in the world today, you cannot understand what's going on in the Middle East unless you understand the biblical and Koranic level of the conflict – otherwise you miss the base on which it all stands.

So the piece, on one level, is about three different cultures: the Judaic culture in Israel today, the Arab culture in the West Bank, and the American culture in New York City and Dallas and Austin, Texas. We decided to ask the following questions of people from each of these cultures: 'Who for you is Abraham? Who for you is Sarah? Who for you is Hagar? Who for you is Ishmael? Who for you is Isaac?' The answers ranged widely. We found that in Israel, people basically knew and cared; even if they were secular and were intent on denying any religious overtones to all of this, they nevertheless had an historical view of who Abraham was. In the Arab section we again found that everybody, regardless of the extent of their religiosity, knew these people because they were cultural figures. We in America know Abraham Lincoln and George Washington. It's just part of the money, it's part of the imagery of the civilization.

Now if you're going to do good music theatre you need a good dramatic story. So you have a man (Abraham), a wife (Sarah) who's rather elderly and can't give birth, and a young Egyptian handmaid (Hagar). As was the custom in those days when they couldn't have a child, Sarah says to Abraham, 'Go into my handmaid and perhaps I shall be builded up through her'. Abraham does this, and Hagar has a child called Ishmael. Then, miraculously, Sarah is able to give birth, and she has a son called Isaac. There's always tension in that kind of situation. The two mothers are also from different cultures, so it's an inherently dramatic situation which makes good musical theatre. But every time Beryl and I would think, 'Maybe we should ask the Arabs what they think about having a Jewish state' or 'What about the Holocaust?', we just said, 'No, stop! Abraham, Sarah, Hagar, Ishmael, Isaac. That's it'. And that has kept us in very good shape because all that comes into the answers anyway – only it comes indirectly, in innuendo (and sometimes less than innuendo). It comes in around the edges, which makes for good theatre. So basically it's about how people project themselves and their compatriots on to the biblical story, and that's why we did it.

*Is this the first time you've worked with your wife?*

Yes, it's the first time I've really worked with anybody. It's a collaboration in which I get my melodic material from the interview material, then give it back to Beryl and she works on the talking heads. She's got five channels – the talking heads appear on 1 and 2, and the others are entirely of her own devising. What Beryl did was to take a videograph from a computer and zero in on bits of clothing, hair and background, then make those full screen. So when you see the people, they're in a set which you don't always immediately recognize but you know is right because all the colours are right and it all fits together – but it takes a few seconds for you to realize it. As the piece progresses these get more abstract, and she begins to build structures out of these realities by taking little bits of them and superimposing them. But everything – and this is the ethos of the piece – comes out of the documentary material, musically and visually.

*So you share a common source.*

Yes. That's the material. There's nothing else except text.

*When you say that the musical material is taken from the interviews, is that the same way as you use the interviews in* Different Trains?

Yes, I've jotted down selections of what people say and written down the notes that most closely approximate to that. On a musical level the piece is about having to interface, as *Different Trains* was, only here it's a much larger situation and one has to think in terms of unifying the piece tonally as well. The first two

acts, for instance – the Jewish and Arab sections – are both in A
minor. They go all over the place in between, but they frequently
rest there.

*Is there a particular reason for using A minor?*

Yes. When we finally got down to the Cave of Machpela, after
incredible political machinations between the Muslims and the
Israeli military, I heard a sound which turned out to be an A
minor hum. It was due to the voices and the structure of the
room, so I took it as a given that was going to go at the end of
both acts. In fact, at the opening, the first two pitches that you
hear are A and C natural.

*How are you feeling as the première approaches?*

Nervous.

*Nervous that it might be sensationalized? It's quite a difficult
subject.*

Well, for everybody's well-being we're going to try to make sure
that we minimize that. But really it's a question of the attitude
with which the piece was done. For instance, we were keenly
aware of the Muslim community and we've gone to great lengths
to have several Muslim advisers tell us how to deal with the
material – what could be done and what couldn't be done.
Basically, we tried to conform to Muslim and Jewish law in all
respects, which imposed limitations – but then life imposes
limitations. But I think people will feel very well-presented in the
piece.

*The* Cave *has often been described as an opera, but is it true that
you don't see it as such?*

Yes, and that's a very large and very worthwhile topic. I have no
interest or affection for the opera from Mozart through to
Wagner, or even Mozart through to Berg. I do like parts of *The
Rake's Progress* because I can take almost anything of
Stravinsky's. But the operatic, *bel canto* voice just irritates my
ear, similar to the way that scratching on the blackboard might
irritate yours. When I hear somebody singing that way I feel a
little bit like Groucho Marx in *A Night at the Opera* – someone

should swing from the chandelier or do something zany, because it all seems so stilted and such a period piece. I mean, it's fine to recreate *Rigoletto* or *Don Giovanni*, but to assume that one will write for that type of voice in our time seems to me absurd.

*What are your particular objections to it?*

Well, for a start the microphone was invented. That's a fact of musical life which had a profound effect on vocal style. I mean, the operatic voice was created for a reason. It was created in the early days when it had to be heard over the orchestra. Along comes Wagner with a big brass section and, baby, we're talking *big* voices, because it was an acoustical necessity. I may not like the Wagnerian voice, but I understand the necessity for it. It's part of the whole musical fabric. But to recreate even the Mozartian opera voice now we have microphones, or to amplify that voice, seems to me absurd, a musical mistake in very bad taste. This is why I have really come to appreciate Kurt Weill. He was working at the same time as Berg, who was basically looking to German Romanticism with *Wozzek* and *Lulu*, and it's all horrible and tragic. I can understand that, but it's a man looking backwards who wrote those operas. Berg was a man facing the past, but he was dealing with it in his own times. At about the same period Kurt Weill was saying, 'Yes, German Romanticism is dying, so better do something else'. He was a man who studied with Busoni, who lived in a world where it would have been quite natural to write symphonies and string quartets, but he said, 'No. Banjo, saxophone, trap drums – and I'll use this woman who can't sing, but I think it will work out'. It did work out, and it's a masterpiece of *his* time.

When I look into a music shop now, what I see in the window doesn't go with the *bel canto* voice. Things like reverb units, digital delays, samplers and all the rest of it are part of our folk music. They're not recherché things that only professors know about. That's how kids make rap. That's what's going on in the street, and I think it's very healthy when there's some sort of converse between the concert hall and the street. I always have. That's why musical theatre will always exist. People will always have ideas, they will be concerned about life in one way or another, and they will want to bring that into their music in some way. I do too. I've been asked to write operas, but I just say, 'Is there anything else I can do for you?' I'm aware that people around me have been very busy writing operas, but I just didn't think it was something I could do, because I didn't believe in it. It wasn't until *Different Trains* that the thoughts that had been bubbling and percolating since *It's Gonna Rain* found the right way to go. Now, I don't think that means everybody should go out and do pieces with documentary sources, but I do think it's one legitimate solution to a way of making music theatre nowadays. There are undoubtedly lots of others. I think, for instance, that *Einstein on the Beach* – you can take it or leave it – is a genuine statement for our time. Operas that followed it just seemed to me to be a step backwards.

*So opera for you 'means' the operatic voice?*

Well, there are people like Laurie Anderson who say that what they do is opera. And I say, 'Well, if you want to call it opera, I understand'. I mean, 'opera' means 'work'. Everything's an opera. But I don't think that way in general. I'm into making distinctions. There are people who say to me, 'How's your opera?' and I don't correct them, that's just insulting. I say, 'Fine. How's yours?' But it's not an opera in the sense in which the word conjures up Pavarotti. Opera does *mean* something: it's sort of Italian, sort of European – black tie. It also has very specific musical connotations: – orchestra in the pit, *bel canto* on stage. That's opera with a capital O, and since at least two very well-known composers who are frequently lumped together with me are very busy writing opera with a capital O, I am forced to be clear about what I'm doing.

*How do you feel about the symphony orchestra? Do you feel that's a living medium?*

Frankly, things change. In the 1980s I became increasingly interested in the orchestra, but by the time I did *The Four Sections* (which I'm very fond of) I felt that was enough. When I was doing *The Four Sections* I felt very much as if I was writing with one hand tied behind my back, partly because it had to be done in two or three rehearsals and partly because of the way orchestras work. I don't want to deal with that – I don't want to work in a situation where most of the musicians can't wait to get back to Brahms. I mean, I don't blame them. That's what they've devoted their lives to, but I just don't want to be a part of it. It's not me. I don't want to hold them back, to have them be polite for my première and then forget about it. I want to go to the London Sinfonietta, the Ensemble Intercontemporain or the Ensemble Modern, where people are pulling at your sleeve to see what's coming next, because that's *their* life. That's the way they make a living. That's what they do when they get up in the morning, like you and me. So I'm casting my lot with those people because I'm interested in very well-done, serious, intense, musical performance. Without that, why bother?

# TERRY RILEY

*b. California 1935*

Terry Riley, alongside La Monte Young, is widely regarded as a founding father of minimalism. Indeed, his 1964 work *In C* is often credited as launching the movement single-handedly. Certainly, its radical simplicity and hypnotic patterns captured the spirit of an age that sought a return to the spiritual essence of life through social and political liberation.

During the 1960s and 1970s Riley wrote a series of solo works for electronic keyboards and soprano saxophone (such as *A Rainbow in Curved Air* and *The Persian Surgery Dervishes*) which pioneered the use of tape delays in live performance and set the stage for the New Age movement that developed a decade or so later.

In 1970 he travelled to India to study raga with the vocal master Pandit Pran Nath, with whom he has frequently appeared in concert as vocal and tamboura accompanist. Later, whilst teaching composition and raga at Mills College, Riley met David Harrington, the founder and leader of the Kronos Quartet, beginning the long association which has produced nine string quartets (including *Cadenza on the Night Plain* and the large-scale cycle *Salome Dances for Peace*). More recent works have included *The Jade Palace Orchestral Dances*, commissioned by Carnegie Hall in 1990, and *June Buddhas* (1991) for chorus and orchestra.

*How do you work as a composer?*

I have a definite routine. I rise very early – usually around five-thirty or six – and start out with a cup of good Indian *chai*, this jet fuel which gets the cobwebs out and gets me thinking about what I want to do. I always practise North Indian raga in the morning. It's a very good way to tune up for any kind of work, so I always do it first thing for at least an hour. That's one reason why I moved up here into the country – I liked the quiet for practising raga. You can actually hear your own internal sounds which, if you've been in the city, are racing. I work pretty much throughout the day – I usually take an exercise period to ride my bike, take a long walk or work in the yard. The rest of the day I'm usually either writing or practising music, or taking care of business.

*Can you tell us about the use of just intonation in your music?*

Well, it has a particular colouring in the intervals that you can't get in equal temperament. Once you've worked with it, it's very alluring. Just intonation is a very beautiful system, though not all musics work equally well in it.

*Is there more to it than just the sound of it – do the resonances create sympathetic resonances and moods within the body?*

There are a lot of theories like that, and I think my experience would bear them out. Listening to those resonances slows everything down, because they're very much in focus. If you threw up a bunch of slides on the wall that were out of focus, you'd tend to go through them quickly. None of them would satisfy you. But if you could get one that's really sharply focused you'd want to look at it longer, just because it's peaceful, it's happening, you don't need to go on right away. That's the way these intervals are – they make you want to hear them more. So just intonation is very good for modal music, or for music that it is not modulating and moving all over the place but is making this very static, but deep, statement.

*How does your use of just intonation differ from that of La Monte Young?*

Well, La Monte works exclusively in just intonation and I don't. I do use equal temperament occasionally. I consider it another kind of tuning. What it does, it does best. But there are many variations in tuning. It's a very big field that's often overlooked by musicians – they'll usually just take whatever tuning is given to them and work with it without questioning it. After three or four hundred years of playing in equal temperament, our ears are used to it and we're a bit lazy about it. You didn't see even the synthesizer manufacturers creating possibilities for just intonation until recently. Now they're starting to produce synthesizers that are tunable. But of course the keyboard with just twelve keys has laid down a lot of limitations to tuning. I think the voice, not the keyboard, is the best way to express just intonation because of its emotional quality and the possibility of singing any frequency within its range.

The problem, of course, is that you can't take just intonation and play music designed for equal temperament. You suddenly find that these sounds require something else compositionally. So most people, when they get a keyboard that's tunable in just intonation, say, 'Well, I've got it, but I don't know what to do with it'. You have to be tuned into a kind of music that works. I was lucky because I worked with La Monte in the 1960s, when he was already working in just intonation, and I then got involved in Indian classical music, which is also in just intonation. So at least half my practice has always been in just intonation because of the kinds of music I play. Indian classical music only really works in just intonation if you want to get the real colours of the raga, the shapes and shadings.

*David Harrington of the Kronos Quartet suggested that working with you had brought them back to understanding the essence of sound and what it is to play music in a group. This remark seemed to touch on a principle of minimalism, and I wondered if you could help us define it?*

The word itself doesn't inspire me to come up with a definition because it sounds too scientific and dry and cold. It isn't romantic enough for my nature – there's not enough intuition in it, and it doesn't allow for the real freedom of the human spirit. When you say, 'I'm a minimalist', that nails you down to doing something in a certain way. What I feel they're trying to say with minimalism is that they're stripping music down to its essential factors – what moves us in music. Minimalism is 'not playing anything that you don't have to'. You can still get to the nerves and bones and fibres of what music is without great decoration. To me, that's part of what it is.

*John Adams regards minimalism as a technique: small, repeated cells, rhythmic propulsion, and tonality. Yet this seems to rule out La Monte Young.*

Well, again, that's a technical explanation and I don't think that'll satisfy on its own. The repetition is certainly part of it, but repetition is a part of all sacred music, all gospel, rock music, north African music. Repetition is a very basic element. But if you're talking about minimalism as being a definable field, at the time when people like La Monte and I were starting to work it was more of a climate. People didn't necessarily adhere to those technical principles – they were doing it in different ways. It had more to do with the climate of the time – just like impressionism, it made people feel aesthetically something they hadn't felt in previous musics.

*How did that climate arise?*

Well, I think it was a new era of hope. The musics of Webern and Schoenberg were created during a time of very great distress on the planet – World War One, the discovery of psychotherapy and the dark sides of the mind. The influence of that very gnarled, anguished music continued on through most of the first half of the century in some form or another. Some composers were outside of it, but most were touched by it – even Aaron Copland and people like that who were essentially bright-sounding composers. After World War Two there was a change in the climate, just before the 1960s – in my view the high point of the twentieth century in terms of really wanting to be free, to tear off the bonds of society which said you had to live a certain way or do certain things to be a valid individual – and that was when minimalism happened. The climate was one of hope, of deepening spirituality, as was the whole of the 1960s. That changed in the 1970s. As far as I was concerned, by the time the public caught up with minimalism, the real heart of the movement had gone. Now you have minimalism taught in colleges, which means it's dead. Something else has to come now to be a real powerful element for young composers.

*Much of your own recent music is very large-scale. Is it in any sense minimalist?*

Even though the way it's presented is not like minimalism, the way I think still is. I still usually start from small kernels. The way I compose hasn't basically changed since I started. It's probably all I'm capable of – each person has their own limited way of looking at things. Even though I try to increase my scope, and things do change, essentially I tend to look at music in a certain way.

*You, La Monte Young, Reich and Glass are often lumped together with younger composers like Adams and Torke and labelled minimalists. Are you comfortable in that setting?*

Well, it's like any category – Catholics, Buddhists – within it, you have all these different people. Even though they lump all those composers together, there are vast differences between them. I would like to keep my individuality. I don't reject the term as an easy handle for people to recognize a group of composers that do similar things, but it certainly doesn't acknowledge the individuality of its members. The only time I call myself a minimalist is in a joking way, or if I'm writing programme notes!

*Let's talk a little more about your work with the Kronos, which has been a big part of your music recently. You had a period when you were teaching and didn't compose very much, and then you met the Kronos. Is it true to say that they inspired you to get back to writing?*

Yes, I have them to thank for any music I have written down. You don't know what makes you start doing things again, but I had gotten to the stage in the 1970s where I didn't feel there was anything worth writing down, that it was enough just to *play* music. If people wanted to play my music, my attitude was that they could listen to the records and learn it from there. I was pretty firmly embedded in that idea, and actually I didn't feel at the time there was anything I could write. I remember trying to write on the blackboards at Mills College and just giving up. It was a period when notation was not pleasant for me to think about, it was a great deal of effort. But I liked the Kronos so much, and so respected what their goals were, that I forced myself to do it as a challenge. It was difficult to get geared up to write the first few pieces, although I felt they turned out very well. But I didn't want to commit myself to any one direction. I thought, 'I could play this a hundred different ways, so why should I write it down one way?'

*Was that because you were so steeped in a tradition that didn't set any store by notation?*

Yes, Indian classical music. But even before I studied that, I had written *In C*, which is hardly notation – it's just one page. I thought that if you can't get it down, if you can't do it with just that, it's not worth doing. Also, as I said before, I didn't want to write anything that could only be done one way. Eventually I gave in and started doing things, thinking of them as my best shot at that moment. I think most people who write music come to that conclusion and think, 'OK, maybe this isn't perfect but it's the best way I can do it right now'.

*Presumably the attraction was the Kronos themselves rather than the string quartet, which seems a very traditional medium?*

Yes, it was the Kronos, but the string quartet also had a lot to do with it – I happen to love string quartets. I remember when I was a student spending hours listening to the Bartók string quartets. To me, that was like heaven – I couldn't hear them enough. I like the modern string quartets, but don't listen much to the older ones. I think the Kronos's particular approach influenced me to want to write for them – that and the fact that they really had faith I could do it.

*You once said that writing for orchestra didn't appeal to you at all, and yet you've now also written for Kronos and orchestra.*

I distrust the organization of the orchestra, which is like the army. You've got this general sitting in his chair, then the lieutenants, and so on down to the privates on the back rows. There's a lot of that kind of politics in the orchestra, which I find pretty disagreeable as a way to make music together. Not all orchestras are guilty of this kind of hierarchy, but it exists to a degree in most. So it just didn't seem like a very healthy climate. Yet here's this form with which you can make music and which doesn't exist anywhere else – and it's probably largely due to that political structure that it succeeds. It's very strange. Philosophically, I don't agree with it at all and yet I can see how it works. If you have a very good conductor who is firm enough, yet compassionate enough to get the musicians to play the music with lots of feeling, you can get great results. The first orchestra piece I did was for Carnegie Hall's one hundredth anniversary, and I was afraid to write it because I had never done anything bigger than a string quartet. About that time I discovered computers and notational software, so that made it possible. I don't think I could have written it without the help of the sequencing software that allowed me to hear it – it would have been too complex. I hadn't been brought up around orchestras – I never went to many orchestral concerts – so I had to do it like I did my studio projects, such as *Rainbow in Curved Air*, and think of it as multi-tracking. I ended up writing a fifty-minute orchestra piece. It was huge. It took me hours! Months! Years!

*The next orchestral piece was the concerto for Kronos and orchestra,* The Sands.

Yes, I learned a lot from that. *The Sands* was written on the eve of the Gulf War, as a protest against shameless aggression. I scaled it down a bit from the *Jade Palace* written for the St Louis Symphony – it was composed for a small, almost Haydn-sized, orchestra, though I added a few more woodwind. I learned from the St Louis piece that if you want to get a good performance you have to scale down some of your more grandiose ideas! So the concerto is simpler.

*How did* Salome Dances for Peace *come about?*

It was a kind of child of the *Harp of New Albion* – that's how it got started anyway. I had been working on the *Harp* and playing it quite a bit in Europe. One of the sections wouldn't fit for some reason, but I really liked the music. Then one day I was practising and it just came into my head: 'Salome Dances for Peace' is what this music sounds like. I wasn't really thinking about titles, but it just hit me. About that time the phone rang and it was David Harrington wanting to commission a new string quartet. So I said I wanted to write a string quartet that was a ballet. I had written out this big story of Salome Dances for Peace where she's reincarnated in the twentieth century. I kept writing the story then writing the music – it was leading me on. *Salome* was a big theatre piece in my own mind. I was imagining all kinds of things happening while I was writing it. Even though it's for string quartet, it's this vast thing.

*How do you actually go about writing these large-scale pieces? Do you just start at the beginning and work right through?*

Yes. I'll usually start with one central idea – which may be just a scale – and a few patterns start developing out of that. Then often some totally unrelated theme will come to mind from that scale. That's happened so much that now I just trust it – I always write the theme down. I put it in the notebook and think 'Somewhere along the way, this is going to relate.' That's the way it was with *Salome*. The first part of the quartet, the *Peace Dance*, came first, but there are many ideas throughout the piece that came quickly. I just put them away until they found their way into it – they just said, 'Here I am. This is where I come in'!

*There's a real mixture of different sorts of material in that piece.*

Yes, but they're all very related, even though they sound so different.

*What unites them?*

Different elements. Sometimes the basic scale is the element, but other times it's a transposition of that scale which maybe I didn't even recognize at first. Sometimes it's little kernel ideas – tiny motifs that are not leitmotifs but repeating figurations which get turned around and become another movement if you change them slightly. I don't do an awful lot of analysis afterwards, but I do see relationships.

*You said* Salome *basically came out of the* Harp of New Albion. *Is that how it usually happens, the next piece being a step on from the last one?*

Not always, but there is often unfinished business in one piece which has to be taken up in the next, especially if you didn't feel like you'd really completed an idea. Sometimes ideas like that run through several pieces and you just can't quite get enough of it to satisfy yourself.

*How does* Harp of New Albion *relate to La Monte Young's* The Well-Tuned Piano?

I probably wouldn't have thought of doing it if *The Well-Tuned Piano* hadn't been there first. It's a piece I'd admired since I first heard it in 1974. I didn't have a piano until about 1982 – until then I was just playing electronic organs. The piano, of course, is so different from electronic instruments that when I got my first one I had to start re-acquainting myself with it. Then it occurred to me to write a piece, but *The Well-Tuned Piano* was standing there like a giant monument. I thought, 'Well, should I write this piece?' Then, as I kept practising and tuning, I felt it just had to be done, that it was significantly different. It definitely draws inspiration from *The Well-Tuned Piano*. In fact, a lot of my music draws inspiration from La Monte Young – I consider him a very powerful influence in my life. We're like brothers. Another of the major influences is Pandit Pran Nath, who is also a composer. His music is not as well-known to the public, but a lot of what I compose is influenced by his compositions, especially the great melodic subtleties and invention that he's brought to raga, which are distinctly his own.

*How important is ethnicity in your music?*

I have a little difficulty with the term ethnicity because of my strange and strong belief in reincarnation. I don't feel removed from ethnicity as I am ethnicity myself, I'm a part of all the things

I hear. If you mean the musics of primitive peoples, yes, I like them a lot, I feel very close to them. I like the music of India and China, Africa and South East Asia. Also the Ainu! I feel like I've already been trained many times before in these musics – I have a good understanding of them and their feelings. Basically, music is not about technique, it's about spirit. Ethnicity is a very pure, preserved spirit because the music hasn't gotten out enough to get changed much yet. As those musics come out and get assimilated into pop culture, they lose a lot of their initial impulse. When you first hear didgeridoo it's very powerful – but then you listen to an aboriginal rock 'n' roll group and you think, 'Where did it go?' I'm interested in keeping that feeling. So when people hear my music they feel that spiritual impulse underneath it.

*So all the stylistic aspects are just superficial?*

Yes, they're not important. When people first heard those musics they wanted to play sitar or ethnic sounds on the synthesizer or something, but the real value was these cultures retaining their spiritual approach to music.

*Steve Reich has said that many of the composers of his generation who went to study world musics came back trying to emulate those cultures somehow. He was almost suggesting that people on the West Coast got a bit too excited and started growing top-knots and . . .*

. . . went crazy, yes! That's the way he thinks. But I think his rhythms sound very much like a Westerner doing African music. I think out here in California there was a great feeling for the Orient, it being the gateway for oriental people immigrating here. I think we had much more contact with that feeling than they do on the East Coast, where it's much more European. They call this the Pacific Rim culture out here, and you notice it when you go across the country – it's such a different feeling between the East and the West. I think culturally that makes a big difference in the way people approach their music.

# MICHAEL TORKE

*b. Milwaukee 1961*

Michael Torke has fast become one of America's most widely-performed young composers. During his relatively conservative musical training at the Eastman and Yale Schools of Music, Torke claims to have had very little interest in popular music, though it is the punchy, exuberant, 'pop' sounds of works like *Adjustable Wrench* for which he is now best known.

Written when the composer was twenty-three, *Ecstatic Orange* received its first performance in 1985 from Lukas Foss and the Brooklyn Philharmonic, the success of which led to the acclaimed collaborations with the choreographer Peter Martins of the New York City Ballet (including an expanded, three-part version of *Ecstatic Orange* and *Slate*).

Though often large-scale, his music proceeds by dramatic changes of pattern and sequence rather than by any sense of 'symphonic development'. Indeed, whilst the balance of surface elements in Torke's unique musical fusion seems to vary from one piece to another, it is his tight, kaleidoscopic structures and seemingly limitless rhythmic energy that remain most strikingly characteristic.

*Let's start with your early development. How did you come to music?*

I started early. I got a toy drum when I was four years old, and a friend of my mother's suggested they should start me on piano. She found this woman, Audrey Wood, who had a system of writing music with numbers, and I would come to lessons and change things around. Instead of seeing that as not behaving, she encouraged my creativity to the point where she would leave some measures blank and get me to fill in the rest. Gradually, within that first year, I was writing entire pieces. It felt like a normal part of learning how to play the piano. When I was nine I started studying privately with a teacher and worked all the way through high school. So it was always a part of me. Then I went to Eastman School of Music and got a Bachelor's degree in composition. I spent one year at Yale with Jacob Druckman and Frederick Rzewski, then I came to New York.

*Who were your main influences around that time?*

When I was in high school I felt that Stravinsky offered the most direct way for my ears to get into the world of twentieth-century music. I was at the Eastman School of Music from 1980 to 1984, and around the late 1970s and early 1980s was when people outside of New York started talking about minimalism. So I'd have to say that listening to Steve Reich's music in 1980 and 1981 was a real eye-opener. Also, I grew up listening to classical music and not really liking popular music at all, so when I started listening to popular music in college it sounded really fresh to my ears. I was different from colleagues who had played in bands in high school; they came to Eastman because they wanted to be serious composers and they wanted to get this popular influence out of their ears. For me, for some strange reason, this was the first time I had really listened to this music, and I thought that this was a resource.

*How did you manage to miss popular music for such a long time?*

I was too busy practising Mozart sonatas. Also, I had a cousin who would always want to play me his rock records, and I suppose his enthusiasm had, unfortunately, the opposite effect on me. I'd just go back to the classical records that I'd borrow from the public library. This music was really lifting my spirit – I'd sing classical themes to myself as I did my paper round. It wasn't that I was snooty about the other stuff, it just didn't really register.

*What was the impact when you did discover it?*

I think popular music is designed to be disposable, and all of a sudden I thought, 'Isn't that interesting?' It's also direct communication. I suppose that because it's designed for the market, it has to affect you right away. But I thought that the way it uses tonal materials was interesting. I mean, we were taught in school that tonal music was exhausted at the end of the nineteenth and early twentieth century, but pop music didn't feel that way. It wasn't caught up in dogma. They were writing this vital and exciting music that immediately made an impression on you. There was no intellectual noise getting in the way. That appealed to me.

*Did you have to struggle through years of that intellectual noise when you went through school?*

Well, I wouldn't say I struggled, because I liked it. I happen to like and admire intellectual pursuits, but not to the exclusion of other pursuits. Human beings aren't only intellectual. There was a class given by Robert Morris called 'Current Practices' (which was really funny because it wasn't exactly 'current' – we studied music from the 1950s and 1960s and a little bit of the 1970s, all the difficult music). But I was fascinated by that. Any time there was some new theory about how to put notes together, I was all ears.

*Were these mainly European exports you were getting?*

Yes. There were a few developments in the States that he talked about – Earle Brown, Milton Babbitt, Cage – and he brought his knowledge of ethnomusicology to the class, but mostly it was post-World War Two music. I wanted to hear and learn everything. After a while, you had to sift through it and say, 'What would I find useful for what I want to say in music?' I do come out of the philosophy which says that, when a composer puts certain kinds of structures and inner relationships between notes, rhythms and harmonies into his music, this appeal to order creates value. Intellectual constructs are important to develop.

*What sort of music were you producing around this time? Was it always tonal?*

No, it wasn't always tonal. *Vanada* was composed at Eastman and one of its influences is Milton Babbitt's time-point system, which I don't really understand. I came up with a sixteenth-note riff and then used heterophony to pull out slices of sixteenth notes and accentuate them, which was something that Berio was doing in a piece like *Coro* or *Points on the Curve to Find*. So even though people might think of *Vanada* in terms of a popular influence or a kind of jazz antecedent, I was thinking about Berio and Babbitt.

*Much of your music has a tremendous energy to it. Was that something that came from pop music?*

That's one of the things I liked in pop music, but the idea of having energy in my music came before that. It was just a natural thing. You could probably say that because the influences on the music I was writing in high school were Bartók and Stravinsky, there was always this rhythmic drive, this search for something that had conviction, which I felt was conveyed by having a strong rhythmic profile.

*How were your early pieces received?*

For the most part they were received very well. There was support for the music right away. That was one of the reasons I left Yale, because work and performances were coming in and I was starting to be paid to write pieces. It didn't make sense to take these commissions and bring them in to some teacher who had his own agenda. I had a teacher at Yale who said, 'All right, it seems to me that you have strengths in these areas but you have obvious weaknesses over here'. For instance, I hadn't written any vocal music or slow music. So he said, 'Let's take all your weaknesses and try to strengthen them'. Now, academically, that makes a lot of sense, but to me it seemed that, if you had any strengths at all, you should try to capitalize on them. I mean, I was excited about writing music, getting out there and participating in it. I didn't want to sit around making the 'bar graph' level of what I had to offer as a composer. It seemed pointless. So I left school after finishing my first commission – from the Brooklyn Philharmonic to write *Ecstatic Orange*. That attracted the attention of Boosey and Hawkes and also of Peter Martins of the New York City Ballet, which was a very fruitful relationship.

*You've written a number of works for the NYC Ballet . . .*

Yes. Peter Martins said he'd like to make a ballet to *Ecstatic Orange*. That was mounted in January 1987, and soon after we decided to expand it by adding other movements. *Green*, which had just been given its première by the Milwaukee Symphony, became the first movement and I wrote a new slow movement called *Purple*. So, together with *Orange*, we had this three-movement, half-hour ballet. That was followed by *Black and White* in 1988 and *Echo* (set to the music of *Slate*) in 1989. In 1990 Lincoln Kirstein, who founded the ballet, asked me to write a mass, and when I finished that the NYC Ballet staged it. The most recent commission was for 1991, but when I finished that piece it turned out to be bigger than what they wanted, so they took another piece of mine called *Ash* and made a ballet to that. So in all we worked together for five successive springs.

*How did you come to be such a skilled orchestrator? It's quite unusual for someone so young. Does it come naturally?*

There was mutual agreement among my friends at school that Joseph Schwentner and Jacob Druckman were great orchestrators. One of the techniques they shared, which was very simple, was having instruments share responsibilities for pitches. That of course went against the idea that Schoenberg talked about, that you don't want to double things at the octave. There was a feeling in the air at academic establishments that any doubling was a very dangerous thing. But if you talk about orchestration in the traditional sense, doubling is the essential problem of orchestration. Somehow I never thought I had to obey Schoenberg's rules or be so cautious about doubling. The idea of combining more than one instrument on a given line is an algebraic kind of thing – pushing variables around. It's like doing a crossword puzzle. That is something that I personally find fun. Whether it comes naturally I don't know, but I certainly don't get bogged down with it. An established composer I know will write, say, a 45-minute piece for orchestra – he'll finish a piano version of it in one month and then take a year to orchestrate it. He finds composing very easy but orchestrating very hard. I think it's strange not to have a one-to-one correspondence between orchestrating and composing, because usually when there is an idea, it is not only about pitches but also about who is going to play it – it's about the distribution of those notes among the members of whatever ensemble I'm writing for. The orchestration is part of the conception of whatever ideas I'm working with. I feel strongly that you're going to have more cohesiveness of intent that way. If orchestration is built into the concept, you actually end up with fewer decisions to make. In fact, one of the things I like to do is to make the orchestration automatic. That may sound really uncreative, but I set up certain systems where I only have one or two choices and that actually produces a really good orchestration. A favourite orchestrator of mine is Tchaikovsky. I think he's brilliant. Yet I noticed, looking at his scores, that he would always do things in one or two different ways, which seems the antithesis of 'creative' orchestration.

*Can you explain the use of colours in your titles?*

Yes, that was something I started thinking about in school. I had always had a synaesthetic reaction to music, which I felt was a personal and maybe even dangerously indulgent thing even to talk about. It's like when a person has perfect pitch. What does that mean? OK, maybe it's a convenience, but colours is not a convenience – it's like a conceit. But I started getting these thoughts on the issue of form. Someone taught me that to create a form you have to establish a frame of reference like establishing a room, and then you move out of the room and return to it somehow. Sonata form actually works that way. Then I thought,

'If you're in a room and there's a party going on, why would you want to leave it? Couldn't you create some kind of form where you never leave?' And then the idea that, if you found a harmony that associated with a colour, you could choose never to leave that harmony; the piece would then be about that colour, or the colour would identify the building-block I decided to use. Then it wouldn't be so indulgent to call a piece a colour because I'm saying something about the form. Also, I'd always liked the cataloguing effect of 'symphony', so when those pieces came out there was a kind of 'rainbow' series that nicely organized them.

*Could you explain more about the way you structure your pieces? You've said that you go to a room and you don't leave it – but in that case how do you make such large-scale pieces? If, in the traditional sense, you don't state your theme and develop it, where do you go and how do you stay there?*

Well, if you're going to have the harmony be stationary, then the movement is going to have to come from somewhere else. For me, the movement is what I'm doing rhythmically, canonically, how I'm shifting the pitches around. In *Ecstatic Orange* for instance, there is a six-note theme where the pitches are always in the same order and it keeps reappearing but the material gets put in different contexts all the time. It's as if the theme wears different clothes. In that sense there's the constant turnover of manipulation, and that presumably gives the piece itts interest.

*For all its scale, your music sometimes finds itself with the post-minimalist tag. What do you feel are the links with that movement?*

People now think that labels are really dangerous, because the minute you slap one on to something it confines the definition of what you're trying to do. Composers get really angry saying, 'Oh, but I'm not just doing that, I'm doing all of this too'. But when you think about it, labels have been very useful. If you talk about Impressionist painting, you're not confining Monet, you know that he does other things too, his work transcends that. We use labels because they're useful. So why not use 'minimalism'? Why do even the hallmark minimalist composers like Steve Reich say, 'My music isn't minimalist'. I mean, come on! It's minimal.

So what? That's kind of a nice thing. That's addressing the idea of labels. Obviously the music is going to transcend it, as it should. Whether I belong in any tangential way to post-minimalism is I suppose more up to other people to decide. But it's dangerous for me to start thinking in terms of labels. You do things, then other people sort out what it all means.

*Do you find yourself being criticized sometimes for being too accessible?*

Yes, but I don't think about that. It's an odd criticism and it's an old-fashioned one. Of course, the standard response is that accessibility was never a problem in other areas of musical history, so why should it be a problem now? It strikes me as being such an irrelevant concern. I'm interested in music that works, that sounds good, that is engaging, that has some intellectual stimulation to it, that's moving. When you think about it, that isn't so far away from the entertainment industry. Because, even in entertainment, after you've seen a movie most people talk about it and discuss it. That's being intellectual. Having any response is intellectual activity. I mean, culture is how people use their spare time when they're not producing things and making a living. When they have leftover time, what do they do with it? That's culture. This country's biggest export is its pop culture, and maybe that's our most important contribution. As a person wanting to be involved with culture, I ought to open up my eyes and see what that means. The disposability of this pop culture is fascinating but also problematic, because it's my goal to make something that *isn't* disposable. But I think we have to be very careful not to be snooty and say that it's trash and it's only going to make money. What we do with our spare time says something about basic needs of human beings. We have a need for culture and we respond to it.

*How do you actually go about composing? Do you have any kind of routine?*

I have a synthesizer and a simple four-track machine, which enables me to try out counterpoint and see if it works. I don't use a computer and I do everything by hand. I always think of myself as a workaholic, but most people with a job go from nine to five and put in an eight-hour day. Now I know they sit on the phone and go and make coffee and have their lunch-breaks etc, but most people have a very disciplined life. So I just thought, 'Who am I to be so special and have some privileged life lying around in bed till two in the afternoon. So why don't I clock eight hours on a stop-watch?' Well, I'm a little more severe. If I use the bathroom, I'll stop the clock. If I make lunch, I stop it. I've found that when I'm under pressure, that kind of discipline really makes me maximize the productivity. If I start feeling like I'm being too severe on myself, I remind myself that most people work eight-hour days, so why should I be exempt?

*How do your pieces start? Where do the ideas come from?*

Well, with *Ash* I remember seeing the movie *The Thin Blue Line* where some guy was thrown into jail and falsely accused. It was a very weird documentary. I came back home playing F minor chords on the keyboard, thinking how weird it would be to construct a piece from materials you thought maybe weren't as useful as others, and that just turned into *Ash*. So the idea was an F minor chord, but the idea of using that was some November night in 1988. Sometimes I'll copy down a four-bar rhythm of a pop song – usually it's more dance or R & B stuff – and I'll, say, throw out all the pitches and the instrumentation and just take these rhythmic values to see what would happen if I assign them to new material I'm devising. Whenever you take something and translate it into another parameter, you lose something and you gain something. That transaction interests me. That's why this idea of appropriation is inaccurate. I don't appropriate anything. I think that's an interesting thing to do, but I don't do it.

I wrote a piece called *Rust* which was done here in New York, and I talked about the fact that I had listened to some rap music. In 1989 rap was still considered something to think about – now it's different. There was a rhythm used in the vocals against a very simple drum track that I transcribed, assigned new pitches, and did all these canons. In the programme notes I said, 'I disassembled this rap rhythm, etc.' Then, when the reviews came out, everyone was up in arms saying, 'This has nothing to do with rap music. How can he say this? The piece fails because he's trying to be of the streets and he's not.' I felt that was missing the whole point. But I realize I should have just shut up and not even mentioned it. You see, rap has this political component and my music is very apolitical, so I supposedly 'failed' because of that irresponsibility.

*A lot of people are writing operas now, and there seems to be an ever-growing audience for them. Why do you think that's come about?*

The first time I came to New York I sat in the front row of *A Chorus Line* and it changed my life. This idea of having music and theatre speaks to a passion that's innately human. It's so seductive and powerful, and I think that composers want to participate in that. There's a bigness about it – not just because people are opening their mouths and hollering out their emotions, but in the way the economics of the industry work. Things get big. Take John Adams, for example, with *Nixon in China*. That put him securely on a certain kind of map. Composers look at that and think, 'Wow!' What other form lifts you up like that? It also introduces the idea of collaboration, and that exchange of ideas is extremely stimulating.

*What music do you listen to?*

I try to keep up with some of what's going on in popular music. Lately I've listened to metal bands. They've introduced this new idea of having all-girl metal bands now. Also, I'm interested in the R & B dance side of things, where the producer makes tailor-made songs for the artist. So I've been buying albums according to who produced them rather than who was singing on them. I even like 'bubble gum pop', because the song element is so strong. So I even like Kylie Minogue. I know everyone hates her, and everyone thinks that Stock, Aitken and Waterman should be shot, but they have written some good songs.

*What about Western art music?*

Lately I've been listening to Michael Nyman on Argo. I've heard the string quartets and the music from *Prospero's Books*, and I think he's a composer who has been misunderstood. There's something really interesting going on there. When I put on his music I have creative thoughts. I'm also finding that, lately, when

I listen to Glass's music the wheels turn. I put on Messiaen the other day, but the wheels didn't turn – I was disappointed, because I've always liked Messiaen.

*What about Kylie?*

Yes, the wheels turn. She does it, creatively. I'll listen to anything!

# CHRISTIAN WOLFF

*b. Nice, France 1934*

After emigrating to the United States in 1941, Christian Wolff was educated in Classics at Harvard University, where he subsequently lectured in Greek and Latin until 1970. He then joined the music faculty at Dartmouth College and was appointed Strauss Professor of Music in 1979.

In the 1950s he became closely associated with Cage, Feldman and Earle Brown in New York, and the sparseness and non-development of his earliest works reflect Cage's influence. Around the turn of the 1960s his work (such as *Duo for Pianists II*) began to introduce elements of indeterminacy, often involving the performers in 'game' structures, passing pitches or cues to one another, according to the instructions of the score. Wolff's later work became infused with a more or less overt political message, either using texts (as in *Changing the System*, 1972–3, for unspecified instrumentation) or musical material from folk music and labour songs (as in *Bread and Roses*, 1983, for chamber orchestra).

*How did you come to be involved with Cage and Feldman in the early 1950s?*

I was taking piano lessons with Grete Sultan, and had begun to compose on my own without any guidance whatsoever. I played the piano less and less and worked more and more on my compositions. In order to apologize for not being properly prepared for my lessons I would bring compositions along, and she would say, 'Well, this is all very well but you must go to someone who can help you with the compositions.' I said, 'That's fine, but who would that be?' My work was experimental. I mean, I was determined to do something unlike anything else, and the only composer whom I knew and who might have been accessible was Varèse. He was a neighbour of ours in New York, but somehow I was a little uneasy about him as a teacher. Anyway, Grete Sultan said she knew this person called John Cage, who at that time was more or less unknown. And that's how it happened.

I think Cage had met Feldman a few months before I came to see him. I brought my work in and he looked at it, seemed interested in it and said, 'OK, I'll take you on.' Shortly after, he introduced me to Feldman. At this time I was in high school, so I would come after school and on weekends and especially in the summer. I stayed that next summer in New York, and as I had no piano at home I went down to Cage's to use his piano. Feldman moved into that same building, so basically we just hung around together for a year or so.

*Do you feel it was significant that you didn't have a conventional musical training?*

Yes, I think so. There are times when I wish I had more of the conventional skills, but that feeling did not arise until maybe ten years ago. What was available as regular music education in the 1950s was very stultified and uninteresting. I had no desire whatsoever to get involved in traditional music training.

*It seems that you were influenced by both Feldman and Cage.
How has your thinking developed in your more recent work?*

My work has roughly two phases, though one can see connections between them. The earlier work is more concerned with
indeterminacy. What I was particularly interested in, more than
either Cage or Feldman were, was the question of how performers relate to each other, not necessarily in the psychological
or social sense, but more in the sound that resulted when people
had to co-ordinate with each other in certain unpredictable ways.
That applies to much of the earlier music, but the very earliest
music was in fact fully notated. For about two or three years
from the time I started working with Cage, I wrote a few
minimalist pieces for just, say, three pitches. Only after that did I
get interested in indeterminacy. Then, in the early 1960s and
1970s, like some others – including quite close friends of mine
such as Frederic Rzewski and Cornelius Cardew – I went through
a kind of political reorganization, and felt that music should have
some relationship to that. It's perhaps simple-minded but I took
the notion literally, and tried to incorporate political texts into
my work. But after a while, I became more interested (again on
the analogy of work done by Rzewski, Cardew and others) in
using not necessarily texts but material from the traditions of
political music – which tended to be folk music of one kind or
another, songs from the labour movement in this country or even
from Civil War days, anti-fascist songs from Europe and so on –
and to use the songs as the basis for something like variation
writing, but not quite. I've never written formal sets of variations, but the songs become material in the sense that they
provide, say, interval sequences or rhythmic material. That's at a
technical level, but more importantly, the material interested me
because I wanted to connect my music to traditions of populist
music, most of which tends to have a strong social or political
orientation.

*Are these two phases of your work connected?*

Yes, there's still a connection with my earlier work, because
although the music I started writing in the second phase was fully

notated and looks much more like conventional music (my earlier music has a kind of invented notation), if you look more closely you discover that there's a great deal of information performers normally expect that is not there. For instance, there may be only the vaguest of tempo indications, no dynamics to speak of, and no articulations. In fact, I have no one specific image of how a given performance should sound. It creates great problems for me when I work with performers, because they will have worked on a piece and they come and play it for me, and they say, 'Is this the way you want it?' and I have to say, 'Well, it could be.' I have to work out a way to talk to them which encourages them to make the piece for themselves and not to make it some image of what *I* want. So that's rather similar to the way I worked originally. In other words, there's an indeterminate dimension there which is still quite strong, though it is masked.

*Do you prefer to work with people who you know are politically sympathetic to your work?*

In general yes, but not exclusively. It's interesting to work with professionals, or indeed anybody who doesn't have experience of the music, because my hope is that they would become involved in some way. It becomes a kind of educative process in which part of the function of the music is to interest people or perhaps even convert them at some level – to expose them to things they don't normally run across – and that's more likely to happen if you are not dealing with the converted to start with. That has happened: it's very nice to see musicians who have not had to deal with that kind of music, either with the freedoms at the technical level or with the type of material, suddenly discover that this is quite interesting for them and that they enjoy doing it.

*You've said that all music is propaganda music, and that even though Cage is saying nothing, 'nothing' is nevertheless what he's saying. Is it then, in your view, impossible to assume an apolitical stance?*

Pretty much, yes. But I don't think that's peculiar to music. Everything one does says something, not just about oneself, but about where one is coming from politically and socially. I could take it a step further and say that, given this fact, one might as well be explicit about it and self-aware. In other words, I think one of the most dangerous things is people who are in fact highly representative, who are in clear political positions, and who don't seem to be aware of the fact. From my experience that's very common in the academic world, where there's an assumption that something is normal because it's always been there, and everything else is attacked on the basis of being not normal or mainstream, as though what's 'normal' is in fact God-given or natural and does not in fact represent a clearly articulable position. I said that about Cage; it's a little paradoxical, because he disapproved so much of the notion of political music, yet I think he would himself agree that his music is not just music, but in fact comes out of, represents and – if you will – proselytizes for a view of the world. He even puts a name to it, 'anarchy', which is a political position with a very concrete, specific history. So I try to underscore that a little bit and get people to think about it.

*Do you think text is necessary to make a political point?*

It would depend on the circumstances. If you're making a piece based, say, on a song which your prospective audience knows, then it doesn't seem to be necessary, because the audience would react to the song and to the associations that came with that song. The music itself would carry it, so in that sense you wouldn't need a text. Otherwise yes, you need some kind of text, although you could take 'text' in a more general sense. The critical thing seems to me to be the context in which a thing is played. The context becomes the text, so to speak.

*So it's not so much what you say but how you say it that matters?*

Exactly – and also *where* it is being said. For example, there used to be an organization in New York called the Musicians' Action Collective which was made up of people with Left sympathies and political interests who happened to be musicians from various kinds of music – just about everything from people who played in the Philharmonic to street musicians, Puerto Rican folk musicians, jazz musicians, avant-garde downtown composers. You name it, they were there. They were trying to figure out how to get their politics into their music in a sensible way. What they finally came up with was the notion of doing a series of concerts, each of which would be dedicated to some kind of cause they felt was important. It could be a concert for, say, the farm-workers. The music that was programmed would come from all these different kinds of people, a completely heterogeneous collection of music, and there'd be some effort to make the music connect to the theme, although that wasn't absolutely necessary. For example, the folk singers might perform one of the traditional songs about farm-workers' struggles, but the classical musicians might play something like a Mozart woodwind quintet. Now, in my view, that Mozart woodwind quintet in that context has a political meaning. The text is, you might say, the whole 'context' in which it appears. You might say that the minimal text, simply the title *Concert for the Farm-workers*, makes the Mozart take on a political character.

*If your main aim is to raise people's political awareness, wouldn't it perhaps be more useful to work in a more popular area of music rather than one which is regarded by the general public as high-brow and esoteric?*

It's what I know best how to do. It's what I was brought up on. Maybe it's a little bit cowardly, but I'm not confident about my capabilities in the popular media. I listen to a lot of that music. I mean, like it or dislike it, much of it is of an extraordinarily high technical competence, and at this stage in my life I just don't feel up to learning those skills. So it's a practical consideration. I suppose there's also a theoretical one, which is that I have very mixed feelings about the nature of popular music at that level and its involvement with the whole commercial machine, although one can probably find ways of getting round that. What I do best, I think, is write the kind of music that I write.

*But you did at one point start to feel that your music was becoming more and more esoteric, and you made a conscious decision to do something that people would actually like . . .*

Yes. That came at about the time I underwent this whole political reorientation. It's not at all peculiar to me, though – one sees it in various forms, some of which I don't like at all. For instance, a lot of modernist composers have turned around and are now writing neo-romantic music, trying to make it with a bigger public. I find that whole business less than attractive, although at the same time one wants one's work first of all to extend to as many people as possible. From a political point of view, if the work has potentially something to say to more people – something that's not too esoteric, too specialized, too introverted and so forth – then we should make some effort to foster it.

*What difference do you see between your work and that of European political composers such as Luigi Nono?*

Yes, Nono's very interesting. There are probably others, but he's certainly the most distinguished and best-known example of a composer who was been determinedly modernist and political at the same time, whereas I don't think of myself in that way at all. He uses all the latest technical means, like electronics, and writes music which is very difficult for the ordinary person to listen to. I don't know what reception that music gets, but I do know that, for example, he's written a piece called *La Fabbrica Illuminata* which uses the sounds of a particular factory and interviews with the people that worked there, and was then performed for the people in that factory. From the accounts I've been able to gather, they seemed to have been very interested in it, but I'm not too sure whether they actually liked it – or suddenly became fans of Stockhausen and decided that new music was their thing! In my case, I've tried to make music easier to listen to, or somehow more like what people think of as music.

But we're all caught in this dilemma, that is, to what extent and how completely can you integrate your own work as a composer with some kind of larger social situation, given (and this is the crucial point, it seems to me) the kind of society in which we live, where the process by which music is mediated and gets out to people is itself full of alienating features. Obviously it's a big subject; to put it very simply, I suppose it's that whole division of music into high-brow and low-brow. As far as politics goes, on the one hand everybody can pursue the politics they think are correct, and on the other hand they do whatever else they do with their lives. You do the best you can to co-ordinate the two.

I'm much less optimistic than I used to be. When I first started this, I thought, 'Well, I'll just get these few things together and everything's going to work out beautifully', but it's obviously not that simple. In a way, what's more important is that you do what you can politically – and if you can bring your work into that as much as possible, and are always aware of the political implications of your work, that's maybe the best you can do.

# LA MONTE YOUNG

*b. Idaho 1935*

After studies at the University of California at Los Angeles and formative experiences as a saxophonist in a number of blues bands and jazz groups in the 1950s, La Monte Young enrolled as a graduate student at the University of California at Berkeley. It was here that he wrote his first extended-tone pieces such as *Trio for Strings* (1958). A leading figure in the conceptual music scene of 1960s New York, Young presented a series of legendary concerts in Yoko Ono's downtown loft, and edited *An Anthology*, which included his *Composition 1960 no. 10* ('Draw a straight line and follow it').

1964 saw the beginnings of the still-evolving epic, *The Well-Tuned Piano*, a version of which was released by Gramavision in 1987. His life-long interest in drones, tuning and Indian classical music also lie behind the ongoing works, *The Tortoise, His Dreams and Journeys* (1964–present) and *Map of 49's Dream The Two Systems of Eleven Sets of Galactic Intervals Ornamental Lightyears Tracery* (1966–present). Young continues to perform worldwide with his wife and collaborator, the lighting artist Marian Zazeela.

*I imagine it's very expensive to have custom-built glass filters made; it must be expensive to have a Bösendorfer grand piano custom-built and maintained; it also takes a great deal of time to prepare for a performance of* The Well-Tuned Piano *– so I wondered how you survive when your work is so, for want of a better word, impractical?*

Good point. Right now we're fortunate still to have some support from our main patron Heiner Friedrich, and at one point we had significant support from the Dia Art Foundation, particularly for the period between 1979 and 1985 when we were involved with the *Dream House* project at Harrison Street. That was a ten-year commission which was actually supposed to have gone on longer. It was the period during which the second of the two Bösendorfer pianos – the Imperial grand – was collected, and when we were really able to do the work with the custom glass filters. But we have, in our entire lives, put every cent that we've earned back into our work. We didn't ever take an interest in buying a better car or a better television . . .

MARIAN ZAZEELA: . . . or buying a house and paying a mortgage. We never even got a car until 1976 – that was our first car and we still have it.

. . . and I don't know when, or if, we'll ever be able to afford a new one. So how did we do it in the early days?

MZ: We don't know! I can't imagine it any more.

What I really find to be the question is this constant balancing between wanting to do pure creative work and earning a living. Because, you see, in between these extremes are questions like, 'Are you going to write something that communicates right now, or something that's really pure and might only communicate in two thousand years?' and 'What are you going to do to get money coming in so that you can continue to create?' Those are really the questions that I'm interested in, because I have ideas about things I would like to do but the only person that would support them is our patron Heiner Friedrich, and he's already giving me all he can afford to.

*When the Harrison Street Dream House ended prematurely, did that change your attitude towards what you were doing?*

Well, since we thought that was a permanent project, we took the approach that we were first going to make the building perfect. So thousands of dollars went into totally redoing the heating system and repairing the roof. We also ran wires throughout the entire building so that you could hear on any floor what was going on on any other floor. We were working from the bottom up, to make every penny count toward what we thought was going to be a permanent institution to present our work. We also spent a lot of money on archiving our work, because we thought that was really important and it's the kind of thing you cannot get funding for. All people care about is commissioning new work. I consider it a very greedy attitude. Nobody cares about what you've already done, only what's done now. Sure, I want to create new work all the time too – it's very exciting and it's a lot of fun – but I don't just want to keep on creating new work while the work I already created turns into dust because it's not being properly taken care of. Had I imagined that the project was going to be so short-lived, all that money could instead have been spent on putting out records and book editions, on more concerts, and on everything that would have had more immediate public relevance and could have given us much more gain, both as artists and personally. I mean, everything was done from the point of view of making a perfect building out of which we could gradually expand and present our work to the world.

*Have you always been such a perfectionist in your work?*

Yes, we have both always been very perfectionist. I used to have a motto at Harrison Street: 'I'm not interested in finished work, I'm interested in perfect work.' It used to drive the staff crazy, because most people are much more goal-oriented than I am. They want to see results, but I'm extremely interested in the process and having it eventually evolve into something incredible – but I don't think you can do that overnight.

*Do you think your relationship with, or your discovery of, Indian music contributed to that perfectionism?*

Possibly. I certainly did feel strong roots in Indian music. It's an enormous body of knowledge which has been very highly classified and classicized. In the beginning, I was just extremely inspired by it – I felt the roots, learned something about it by reading books, and pretty much used it as inspiration for my music. But after I worked with Pandit Pran Nath, I learned something about it I had never realized: what a highly-evolved tradition of melodic and pitch inter-relationships it had – the sense of how to go from one note of the scale to the other. This was something that had never even been hinted at in my study of Western music. So I found in Indian classical music, particularly in Pandit Pran Nath's line of the Kirana style, that this under-standing of the inter-relationship of melody and pitch was extraordinarily evolved. The other thing I learned from Pandit Pran Nath was an organically-evolving approach to improvis-ation. However, I have never tried to take an Indian raga and make one of these 'mix-and-match' situations where you get fusion music!

*So there's nothing overtly Indian in your music.*

Nothing at all, and I really want to keep things pure. But I have allowed the understanding I have attained about Indian classical music to be absorbed and then manifest itself on a higher level in my own composition. And so I guess the answer is 'yes', I think it has supported my approach toward perfectionism.

*You and Pandit Pran Nath seem to be similar souls: your own description of his 'unwillingness to change his style to meet modern tastes' could equally apply to you. You must have learnt a lot from him besides music?*

Oh, absolutely. My entire understanding of why I'm here and what I'm doing was greatly clarified through my studies with him. I was totally, completely committed to music before I met him, and very interested in spirituality. Yet meeting him and observing how he related to this ancient tradition, and how it related to spirituality, helped me have a more holistic understanding of music as life and life as music. I also had the opportunity to observe what it meant to be a really great master of something. I felt that in order to have a fully-realized life it was important to become a master of something; you then had a gauge for everything else you observed in life, because you could view it in relation to that understanding.

*What was it in particular about the Kirana style that attracted you?*

Well, if you were to set up a line which had two poles, one of which was pitch and the other was rhythm, the Kirana style would be at the extreme end of the pitch pole. I think that's what attracted me about it: the understanding of pitch, the emphasis on the delineation of raga, and these extraordinarily beautiful melodies which are so in tune. One reason I went into Eastern singing instead of Western singing was simply because it seemed that in Western singing there was no interest in this concept of intonation and a pure tone, whereas in Indian singing it was one of the central ideas.

MZ: And the technique of vibrato has really spoiled the hearing in Western musicians.

There's no way to know if you're playing in tune with vibrato, because the only way to sing perfectly in tune is to listen to acoustical beats. There's no other way. I've had a lot of experience working with musicians in just intonation, and your subjective sense of pitch is not sufficient to allow you to play perfect intervals. When you have vibrato you can never tell, you can't distinguish the vibrato from the beats. The vibrato is always colouring the situation. It's interesting, though, that so many people allow vibrato and don't even try to get rid of it, or even think about it. As long as vibrato is there, people will never even know that the pure intervals exist, because the kind of intervals that are going on today in equal-tempered music and music with vibrato are only approximations of intervals. They're like reminders of the truth. But if the reminder of the truth is always just a reminder and you never see the truth, eventually people will doubt that the truth ever existed and say, 'Well, there was nothing there in the first place', and it's lost.

*You seem to have an ambivalent relationship with Western music. How do you feel you relate to the classical tradition?*

Well, I think that Western classical music has produced some incredible works, forms and tools for the composer. One of its great contributions is of course the system of notation. Never before in any other culture has notation achieved such a degree of precision and clarity, and as a result of that never has form been so imaginative and creative. Even though I love Indian classical music and think some of its features – such as the 'alap', the opening section of a raga – are among the most profound contributions of all time to music, I would be the first to point out that the form is pretty straightforward. It's an evolving form, it's where I learned how to improvise in a way that evolves out of the first note. This form works in Indian classical raga performance pretty much in a climactic, directional way. It's somewhat goal-oriented. European music opened that up a lot, and I think that form in the way that I, Feldman or Cage practise it is really imaginative and totally expanding the concept of what form really is. So I think there's this problem with equal temperament that I've talked about many times before, and the problem that improvisation got lost as a process.

*Perhaps that's one of the prices we've paid for a more precise notation?*

Yes, that's what I think happened. As people went deep in one direction they lost the other direction. What's happening now, with people like myself and Terry Riley, is the possibility of combining both worlds. This then produces something that is capable of expanding into still-untraversed realms.

*Does your earlier work with equal temperament strike you as inharmonious now?*

Well, let me say that I like all my early work. Naturally, I'm more interested in my current work, but I have taken an interest in transcribing some of the early equal-tempered pieces into just intonation. I definitely wouldn't write anything in equal tempera-

ment again. I can't see any reason to. But I like those pieces for
what they were. I'm glad that I learned about the limitations of
equal temperament, then left it. I really want to create work that
expands the horizons of art. I know I made the statement that,
once *The Well-Tuned Piano* gets out there, it will influence
everybody to write in just intonation. Several people have said,
'Well OK, it's out there now and people are still writing in equal
temperament.' My response is that I still feel it is going to change
things. Look, Pauline Oliveros is now writing in just intonation;
Terry Riley started several years ago; Wendy Carlos, Glenn
Branca, Rhys Chatham, Ben Neill . . . you're going to find more
and more people. It's not going to happen overnight, but I still
say it's going to happen.

*How did you choose the particular version of just intonation for*
The Well-Tuned Piano?

I was extremely moved by that tuning. The sevens, threes and
twos (intervals factorable by the primes seven, three and two) are
like my most basic musical mode because they leave out the fives
(which had been out since the time of *Trio for Strings*). But it
came intuitively. I felt inspired by it.

*Do you think you'll stay with that tuning?*

I think I will always stick with that tuning and expand out of it,
go further out but refer back to it as a base, like a drone, a
constant. I think *The Well-Tuned Piano* is my greatest composition, for several reasons. Not least among those reasons is that
it's my most evolved work. It also presents most serious listeners
with the key to unlock a door that will allow them to go into the
multiplicity of levels, stairways, hallways, rivers, streams, valleys
and so forth in the world of complexity that is *The Well-Tuned
Piano* — a complexity that I think extraordinary works of art
generally need to contain. What differentiates a really extraordinary work from a good work or a nice work is that it
contains such levels of complexity that you just cannot absorb it
in the first glance or the first listening.

*It seems ironic that you've used the piano, such a symbol of
Western classical tradition.*

Pandit Pran Nath made the comment at the world première in Rome that I had taken this symbol of European culture and literally turned it into something else. The piano is a great instrument. I have a very profound relationship with pianos.

*What's behind the subtitles of the different sections of* The Well-Tuned Piano?

Well, they're all just inspired.

*They cover a range from the mystical to the comical. Are they sometimes tongue-in-cheek?*

Yes! *The Brontosaurus Boogie* and *The Dinosaurs Dance*. Sometimes you feel more humorous, other times you feel extremely profound and moved, and sometimes you feel more classical or romantic. I play them for a period of time and then suddenly I get an idea for the title.

*Does your work, like much Indian music, assume a universal perception? Can it arouse specific states of mind in the listener?*

I have defined the state that a raga creates as 'the spirit of the raga', and a great performer can call forth this essence. To call it a spirit is one way of giving it a form, something that you can latch on to. I'm not saying it's the only way to describe it, but it's a description that ties in with more traditional, spiritual philosophies such as those that Indian classical music embodies. It's almost like an incantation. When Pandit Pran Nath sings, people are transformed. I never have such a deep experience listening to music as when I hear him sing. It made me realize that's what it was all about as far as I was concerned, and that anything else was beside the point. This was the truth that should be sought and made manifest for others to experience. Each raga has very definitely its own mood or rasa, a psychological state that it creates. I really feel that these states are like universal truths. They're special structures of vibrational patterns that are perceivable and performable, that stand for us as models of vibrational structure in the abstract. The universe is, I think, more and more understood to be made up of vibration on various levels. Whereas there may be many levels, you have to walk before you can run – and the intervals of the octave, the perfect fifth, the major third and all the other simple intervals are like learning to walk.

I developed a new theory which is a reaction to the proposition by psycho-acousticians that we developed our ability with pitch-perception as a by-product of our abilities with speech-comprehension. Prompted by Marian's view that she was not satisfied with that approach, I proposed instead that human beings were capable of more than that, that we developed language for more than just day-to-day, mundane communication. I proposed that, even before speech was developed, there was a need to understand our position and relationship to universal structures and, in particular, to time; we needed to ask very simple questions such as 'Where do we come from? Why are we here and where are we going?' We can't have a concept of time without a concept of periodicity, and everything about us is structured in terms of periodicity: the sun, the moon, the planets. Even if you go into a dark cave and never come out, the body has various periodic activities, and through these we measure time, define time and have a concept of time. Only rational frequency ratios produce periodic, composite wave-forms. It is through listening to these rational frequency ratios in simpler or more complex groupings that we can have our first real experience of vibrational structure in time. These events take place in time, and by listening to more and more complex sets of these ratios, we have more and more profound experiences which are models for abstract vibrational structures. These are a type of universal truth because they're a structural truth, a vibrational truth. And I feel that if two people sing together, or if one person sings in a cave where the tones resonate, what do you get? A tone over a drone. It's the simplest two-part harmony, where you begin to listen to two tones together. I feel this was the step towards resolving the need to understand our relationship to time and universal structure, and that these higher attributes and needs were even more fundamental, if not more urgent, than the need to be able to talk. So the thing to do is to allow these frequency structures to become manifest in situations that will allow people to experience them, that will allow their thinking and creativity to evolve to higher levels of the imaginative process.

LA MONTE YOUNG 271

*Perhaps we could now talk a little about lights. How do you feel they interrelate with the music?*

MZ: I think that the lights serve the music in the way they create a specific atmosphere which probably enhances one's ability to concentrate and listen. When La Monte and I started presenting concerts together, we wanted to introduce a lot of different approaches. The introduction of environmental lighting into the concert situation provided a kind of soothing atmosphere.

I also perform much better in her light environment.

*I imagine* The Magenta Lights *really involve the audience in a way that the conventional, proscenium set-up doesn't. Was that an intention, to engage the listener?*

MZ: Yes, to a large degree. We really wanted to perform in darkness, and the light environment helped. Because of this very soft light, it made it like performing at dusk.

You know the profundity that takes place at two times of day – dawn and dusk. It's really a special time when the light is just coming or just going. That's what it's like to perform in Marian's lighting. It is extraordinarily serene, majestic and profound – it brings out the most noble aspirations in the performer and in the audience, so that you have something to focus on visually when you need to focus. This lighting seems to work extremely well for us, as there are many parallels between the concept of the lighting and the concept of sound. But the two are not tied into each other on a one-to-one response plane.

MZ: The lighting involves some kind of sculptural form – generally mobiles and coloured lights which create coloured shadows because of where they are placed. But a shadow is not real. So it's an analogy to the harmonics or the combination tones that rise in this cloud-like form out of the piano. They're not real either, and yet they're *completely* real. A very interesting parallel interplay between reality and illusion is conjured up by both the sound and the light.

*What for you is the attraction of living in New York?*

Well, you have to understand that I was born in a log cabin in a little Swiss dairy community of 149 people, where there was space, time, and a kind of purity. Then I lived on the shore of Utah Lake, where my father managed my Uncle Thornton's celery farm and I worked on the farm. When I graduated from UCLA I went to Berkeley and did two years of graduate work, then came to New York. I couldn't wait to leave Berkeley, because it was a very narrow, confining situation. In that situation, the politics are always so close – everybody's fighting for that same university position or for that one chance to be on the only concert series of new music. Although that's an extreme simplification, I think it helps demonstrate why I like the converse situation here in New York, where there are so many opportunities to present one's work. There's an enormous audience that is interested in hearing this kind of work. So although, as a place to live, New York has severe limitations – there's no sunshine, no plants, no fresh air, and it's dirty and crowded and noisy – I do feel at home. I feel I'm better liked here and that the creative, intellectual, seething volcano of activity is good for me. I feel that it's extremely important for my work to be heard in the New York area. Also, the reviews that appear in the *New York Times* and other New York papers are considered extremely relevant in international terms, so to be here and to be able to present a lot of concerts demands a certain attention from that press machinery. I feel that when you do something here, it's like when one air molecule bumps against the next one – it resonates throughout the world. I don't think you get that effect any place else.

# DISCOGRAPHY

## JOHN ADAMS

1987    *Portraits* [including Adams' *Light Over Water*]. New Albion.
*Nixon in China*. Elektra Nonesuch.
*Common Tones in Simple Time/Christian Zeal and Activity/Tromba Lontana/Short Ride in a Fast Machine/The Chairman Dances*. Elektra Nonesuch.

1989    *Fearful Symmetries/The Wound Dresser*. Elektra Nonesuch.

1991    *The Death of Klinghoffer*. Elektra Nonesuch.
*American Elegies* [including Adams' *Eros Piano*]. Elektra Nonesuch.

1993    *Hoodoo Zephyr*. Elektra Nonesuch.

## CHARLES AMIRKHANIAN

1980    *Lexical Music*. 1750 Arch Records.

1985    *Mental Radio*. Composers Recordings Inc.

1988    CD accompanying the journal, *Perspectives of New Music Vol. 26 No. 2* [includes Amirkhanian's *Pas de Voix*].

1991    *Electro-clips*. Empreintes Digitales.

## LAURIE ANDERSON

1977–9    Various releases on 110 Records, Giorno Poetry Systems, 1750 Arch St. Records, Holly Solomon Gallery.

1981    *O Superman* 7-inch EP. 110 Records/Warner Brothers Records.

1982    *Big Science*. Warner Brothers.

1984    *Mister Heartbreak*. Warner Brothers.
*United States*. Warner Brothers Records, 5-record set.

1986    *Home of the Brave*. Warner Brothers.

1989    *Strange Angels*. Warner Brothers.

## ROBERT ASHLEY

1978    *Private Parts*. Lovely Music, re-released on CD in 1990.

1985    *Atalanta (Acts of God)*. 3-record set, Lovely Music.

1990    *Yellow Man With Heart With Wings*. Lovely Music.

1991     *Perfect Lives*. 3-CD set, Lovely Music.

1992     *Improvement*. Elektra Nonesuch.

1993     *A Chance Operation* [includes Ashley's *Factory Preset*]. Koch International.

1994     *A Confederacy of Dances Vol. 2* [includes Ashley's *Love Is A Good Example*]. Einstein Records.
         *Sign of the Times* [includes Ashley's *The Producer Speaks*]. Lovely Music.
         *With and Without Memory* [includes Ashley's *Van Cao's Meditation*]. Lovely Music.
         *el/Aficionado*. Lovely Music.


## GLENN BRANCA

1982     *Music for the dance* BAD SMELLS. GPS Records, re-released on CD, 1993.

1983     *Symphony No. 3 (Gloria)*. Crepescule, re-released by Atavistic on CD, 1993.
         *Symphony No. 1 (Tonal Plexus)*. Roir, re-released by Danceteria on CD, 1992.

1987     *Music for* The Belly of an Architect. Crepescule.

1989     *Symphony No. 6 (Devil Choirs at the Gates of Heaven)*. Blast First, re-released by Atavistic on CD, 1993.

1992     *Symphony No. 2 (The Peak of the Sacred)*. Atavistic.
         *The World Upside Down*. Crepescule.

1994     *Symphony No. 8 (The Mystery)*. Atavistic.


## HAROLD BUDD

1978     *The Pavilion of Dreams*. Editions EG.

1980     *The Plateaux of Mirror* [with Brian Eno]. Editions EG.

1981     *The Serpent (in Quicksilver)*. Cantil, re-released in 1989 on Opal/Warner Bros.

1984     *Abandoned Cities*. Cantil, re-released in 1989 on Opal/Warner Bros.
         *The Pearl* [with Brian Eno]. Editions EG.

1986     *The Moon and the Melodies* [with The Cocteau Twins]. 4AD.
         *Lovely Thunder*. Editions EG.

1988     *The White Arcades*. Opal/Warner Bros.

1991     *By the Dawn's Early Light*. Opal/Warner Bros.

1992     *Music for 3 Pianos* [with Ruben Garcia and Daniel Lentz]. All Saints.

1994     *The Orange Ranch Archives (1981–3)* [with Eugene Bowen]. All Saints.
         *She is a Phantom* [with Zeitgeist]. New Albion.

## JOHN CAGE

1988 *Works for Piano & Prepared Piano.* 2 Volumes, Wergo.
*Music Of Changes.* Wergo.

1989/92 *The Complete String Quartets.* 2 Volumes, Mode.

1990 *Singing Through.* New Albion.

1991 *Etudes Boreales etc.* Etcetera.
*Works for Percussion.* Wergo.
*Music for Five.* hatArt.

1992 *Diary.* Wergo.
*Etudes Australes.* Wergo.
*Roaratorio.* 2-CD set, Mode.
*Indeterminacy.* 2-CD set, Smithsonian/Folkways.

1994 *Europera V.* Mode.

## PHILIP CORNER

1978 *Gamelan in the New World Vol. 1* [includes Corner's *Gamelan II: Number – Measure – Increase – Downward*]. Folkways.

1979 *Gamelan in the New World Vol. 2* [includes Corner's *Gamelan PC (Prelude and Conclusion)*]. Folkways.

1983 *Two Pieces for Gamelan Orchestra.* Radio Taxi.

1984 *Pictures of Pictures from Pictures of Pictures.* Edition Boch.

1985 *Playing with the Elements.* Lebeer-Hossmann.

1992 *Sounding the New Violin* [includes Corner's *The Gold Stone*]. Non Sequitur.

## GEORGE CRUMB

1985 *Haunted Landscape.* New World.

1987 *Apparition.* Bridge Records.
*Processional/A Little Suite for Christmas A.D. 1979.* Attaca Babel.
*An Idol for the Misbegotten/Vox Balanae/Madrigals I–IV.* New World.

1988 *Songs of America* [includes Crumb's *The Sleeper*]. Elektra Nonesuch.

1991 *Songs, Dances and Refrains of Death.* Bridge Records.
*Zeitgeist/Celestial Mechanics.* Mode.

1993 *Complete Works for One Piano.* 2-CD set, Attaca Babel.
*Black Angels.* Teldec Classics.

## PAUL DRESHER

1985 *Portraits* [includes Dresher's *Channels Passing*]. New Albion.

1987    *Another Coast* [includes Dresher's *Other Fire* and *Water Dreams*]. Music and Arts.

1991    *Opposites Attract* [with Ned Rothenberg]. New World Records.

1992    *Slow Fire* [with Rinde Eckert]. Minmax.

1993    *Dark Blue Circumstance*. New Albion.

1994    *From A to Z* [includes Dresher's *Underground*]. Starkland.

## JAMES FULKERSON

As a composer

1973    *New Music/New York* [includes Fulkerson's *Patterns II and VII*]. Folkways.

1979    *Music from the VCA* [includes Fulkerson's *Music for Brass Instruments*]. Move Records.

1980    *James Fulkerson*. Irida Records.

1994    *Force Fields and Spaces*. Etcetera.
        *The Ladder of Escape*. Attaca Babel.

As a performer

1985    *Phill Niblock: A Trombone Piece*. India Navigation.

1992    *The Works for Trombone by John Cage*. Etcetera.
        *The Barton Workshop plays John Cage*. 3-CD set, Etcetera.

## PHILIP GLASS

1983    *Glassworks*. Sony.

1985    *Mishima*. Elektra Nonesuch.

1986    *Songs from Liquid Days*. Sony.

1989    *1000 Airplanes on the Roof*. Virgin.
        *Songs from the Trilogy*. Sony.

1992    *Music from* The Screens. Point Music.

1993    *Low Symphony*. Point Music.
        *The Essential Philip Glass*. Sony.

1994    *Two Pages/Contrary Motion/Music in Fifths/Music in Similar Motion*. Elektra Nonesuch.
        *Hydrogen Jukebox*. Elektra Nonesuch.

## LOU HARRISON

1971    *Pacifika Rondo*. Phoenix, re-released 1992.

1981    *Suite for Percussion*. CRI, re-released 1991.

1988  *La Koro Sutro*. New Albion.
*Piano Concerto*. New World.

1989  *Ariadne*. CRI.

1990  *Music for Guitar and Percussion*. Etcetera.
*Double Concerto for Violin and Cello with Javanese Gamelan*. Music and Arts.

1991  *Third Symphony*. Music Masters.

1992  *Concerto for Violin and Percussion Orchestra*. Crystal Records.

1993  *Mass to St. Anthony*. Koch International.


## ALISON KNOWLES

1991  *Friloles Canyon*. Nonsequitur Foundation/What Next? Records.

1992  *Nivea Cream Piece for Emmett Williams*. Slowscan Editions.


## DANIEL LENTZ

1975  *Spell*. ABC Records.

1980  *After Images*. Cold Blue Records.

1983  *Anthology*. Cold Blue Records.

1984  *On the Leopard Altar*. Icon Records.
*Point Conception*. Cold Blue Records.

1985  *Missa Umbrarum*. New Albion, re-released on CD, 1992.

1986  *the crack in the bell*. Angel/EMI.

1992  *Music for 3 Pianos*. All Saints.


## ALVIN LUCIER

1965  *Music for Solo Performer*. Lovely Music.

1967  *North American Time Capsule*. CBS Odyssey.

1970  *I am sitting in a room*. Lovely Music.

1977  *Music on a Long Thin Wire*. Lovely Music.

1980  *Sferics*. Lovely Music.

1985  *Music for Pure Waves, Bass Drums and Acoustic Pendulums*. Lovely Music.

1990  *Nothing is Real*. Eastworld.


## INGRAM MARSHALL

1979  *The Fragility Cycles*. IBU Records.

1984   *Fog Tropes/Gradual Requiem/Gambuh 1*. New Albion.

1990   *Three Penitential Visions*. Elektra Nonesuch.

1991   *Alcatraz*. New Albion.


## MEREDITH MONK

1981   *Dolmen Music*. ECM/Polygram Classics.

1983   *Turtle Dreams*. ECM/Polygram Classics.

1986   *Our Lady of Late: The Vanguard Tapes*. Wergo.

1987   *Do You Be*. ECM/Polygram Classics.

1990   *Book of Days*. ECM/Polygram Classics.

1992   *Facing North*. ECM/Polygram Classics.

1994   *Atlas: an opera in three parts*. ECM/BMG.


## ROBERT MORAN

1992   *Desert of Roses*. Argo/Decca.
       *Balanescu Quartet* [includes Moran's *Music from the Towers of the Moon*].
          Argo/Decca.

1993   *Of Eternal Light* [includes Moran's *Seven Sounds Unseen*]. Catalyst/BMG
          Classics.

1993   *Piano Circus* [includes Morans' *Three Dances*]. Argo/Decca.


## PAULINE OLIVEROS

1982   *Accordian and Voice*. Lovely Music.

1984   *The Wanderer*. Lovely Music.

1985   *Sleepers*. Finnadar.
       *The Well and The Gentle*. 2-record set, HatArt.

1988   *The Roots of the Moment*. HatArt.

1989   *Deep Listening* [with Stuart Dempster]. New Albion.

1990   *Troglodyte's Delight* [with The Deep Listening Band]. What Next?
       *Crone Music* [with Panaiotis]. Lovely Music.


## STEVE REICH

1978   *Music for 18 Musicians*. ECM New Series.

1980   *Octet*. ECM New Series.

1982   *Tehillim*. ECM New Series.

1984   *Variations for Winds, Strings & Keyboards*. Philips.

1985    *The Desert Music*. Elektra Nonesuch.

1987    *Come Out/It's Gonna Rain*. Elektra Nonesuch.
        *Drumming*. Elektra Nonesuch.

1989    *Different Trains*. Elektra Nonesuch.

1990    *The Four Sections*. Elektra Nonesuch.


## TERRY RILEY

1968    *IN C*. Columbia Masterworks, re-recorded in 1991 on Celestial Harmonies.

1969    *A Rainbow in Curved Air*. Columbia Masterworks.

1972    *The Persian Surgery Dervishes*. Shandar.

1978    *Shri Camel*. Columbia Masterworks.

1983    *The Ten Voices of the Two Prophets*. Kukuck.

1985    *Cadenza on the Night Plain*. Gramavision.

1986    *The Harp of New Albion*. Celestial Harmonies.

1989    *Salome Dances for Peace*. Elektra Nonesuch.

1991    *June Buddhas*. Music Masters.

1992    *The Padova Concert*. Amiata.

1993    *Cactus Rosary*. Artifact Music.

1994    *Chanting the Light of Foresight*. New Albion.


## MICHAEL TORKE

1990    *Vanada/The Yellow Pages/Slate/Adjustable Wrench/Rust*. Argo/Decca.

1991    *Color Music*. Argo/Decca.

1992    *Balanescu Quartet* [including Torke's *Chalk*]. Argo/Decca.

1994    *Four Proverbs/Music on the Floor/Monday and Tuesday*. Argo/Decca.
        *John Harle* [including Torke's *Saxophone Concerto*]. Argo/Decca.


## CHRISTIAN WOLFF

1972    *Christian Wolff: For Piano I/For Pianist/Burdocks*. Wergo.

1973    *Music Before Revolution*. Electrola.

1976    *Christian Wolff: Lines/Accompaniments*. CRI.

1982    *Dartmouth Composers* [includes Wolff's *Hay Una Muier Desaparecida*].
        Music from Dartmouth/Philo.

1991    *Norwegian Wood – Aki Takahashi* [includes Wolff's *Eight Days a Week
        Variation*]. EMI/TOCE.

1992    *The New York School* [includes Wolff's *For prepared piano* and *For 1, 2 or 3 people*]. HatArt.

1993    *TA Chance Operation – The John Cage Tribute* [includes Wolff's *Six Melodies Variation*]. Koch International.


## LA MONTE YOUNG

1969    *31 VII 69 10:26–10:49 PM Munich* [La Monte Young and Marian Zazeela]. Edition X.

1974    *Dream House 78' 17" 13/73 5:35–6:14:03 PM NYC* [La Monte Young and Marian Zazeela]. Shandar Disques.

1987    *The Well-Tuned Piano 81 × 25*. 5 CD-set, Gramavision.

1991    *The Melodic Version* of *The Second Dream of The High-Tension Stepdown Transformer* from *The Four Dreams of China*. Gramavision.

1993    *Five Small Pieces for String Quartet, On Remembering a Naiad: a wisp/a gnarl/a leaf/a twig/a tooth*. Disques Montaigne.
        *Just Stompin'/Live at The Kitchen* [La Monte Young and the Forever Blues Band]. 2 CD-set Gramavision.
        *Just West Coast: microtonal music for guitar and harp* [including Young's *Sarabande*]. Bridge Records.